The
MINORITY
of
ONE

The
MINORITY
of
ONE

Henry Chaim Goldberg

Pentland Press, Inc.
www.pentlandpressusa.com

PUBLISHED BY PENTLAND PRESS, INC.
5122 Bur Oak Circle, Raleigh, North Carolina 27612
United States of America
919-782-0281

ISBN 1-57197-224-2
Library of Congress Control Number: 00-31651

Printed in the United States of America

FOREWORD

Henry Chaim Goldberg is a man who always had and still does, at the age of 75, a lot of love in his heart for his family and mankind. He never turns his back on anyone! Because of his goodness and trust in everyone, he has been taken advantage of so many, many times.

He gives of himself so lovingly and freely, but at the same time, he cannot be influenced. He has always been a rebel and he has always stood alone.

Many people say that Henry has a strange way about him. They either love him or they dislike him. There is no in between. He is the most unusual man that I have ever met with a heart of "gold" - AND - that is why, I married him!

Henry and I have been married now for 21 years and there isn't anything that I wouldn't do for him. Naturally, within reason.

Although I'm not Jewish, Henry's mother and father and the rest of their family have welcomed me and my family into their home and hearts.

Henry is a person full of life and love for everyone!

-Lorraine A. Goldberg

1
I AM NOT A CHILD

I was born in 1926 or 1927, the date being somewhere around the end of September or the beginning of October. Since I didn't have a birth certificate, the date is taken from my parents' memory. Mother remembers that I was born very close to the Jewish High Holiday. My parents could not afford to pay for a birth certificate. That might give you a hint that we did not belong to the well-to-do. Anyway, according to my father, a birth certificate is not very important. To prove it, he told me a little story: nobody dies according to the day he was born. People die very young, young, old, and older. To confirm his story, he told me if I ever have a chance to see a cemetery, just look around. People die according to a mysterious plan, and nobody knows how the plan works. He did not include God in it.

Warsaw, the capital of Poland, had a population of approximately 1,300,000 people. The Jewish population in Warsaw was close to 300,000.

I don't know how the school system worked in the rest of the country, but in Warsaw we had schools for Christian children and schools for Jewish children. In the Christian school, religion was a part of the curriculum as was math, geography, and so on. Religion was taught by a priest.

In the school for Jewish children we didn't have a rabbi, but a teacher who taught us "The Biblical History of the Jews." It was not considered religion, but Jewish history.

We lived at 23 Stowki Street. The only way to describe our neighborhood in a few words is ghetto slum. More than ninety percent of our neighborhood were very poor Jews and the other ten percent was made up of poor Christians. By the time I was old enough to go to school, our financial situation improved and gave us a chance to move to a better neighborhood. In Warsaw, or any other part of Poland, being surrounded by ninety percent or more Christians, was not considered a pleasant or healthy situation.

I had two older brothers: Abraham was the oldest, next came Shlomo, I, the youngest boy, and then a beautiful blonde, blue-eyed little sister - Sally. Sally was a little pain in the ass. Father spoiled her rotten. For example, she would not eat what her brothers ate. If we ate bread, she had to have rolls. If we ate rolls, she had to have challah. Sally could do no wrong. When she did not want to finish her meal, she'd ask me or my other brother to do it for her. If we refused, she started to cry and would tell Father that I hit her. That was reason enough to get a beating from Father. No questions were asked as to whether I hit her or what really happened. It was enough that my sister shed a tear. She could do it on command.

I was different from my brothers and my sister. I was a rebel even when I was about five years old. Even today, Father very often reminds me of an incident that I had with a candy store owner. I bought a candy whistle for a penny. When I tried the whistle, it didn't work. I asked the owner for another one, please. The owner, a six-foot, four-inch Christian bully with a huge moustache told me, "Listen, you little Jew Bastard, you had the whistle in your mouth, and you will not get another one. Get lost or I'll beat the shit out of you." Though I did not know what a bastard was, I knew it was not a compliment; and, being like I was, I felt that I was mistreated. Being called a "Jew bastard" on top of it, I decided not to be intimidated. I told the big bully, "If you don't give me another whistle, I will destroy everything I'm able to." Of course, he went wild and chased me out of the store. War was declared on the spot between a "five-year-old Jewish bastard" and a "six-foot, four-inch Christian bully."

I kept a close watch on the store. When he was busy, I overturned candies in the window showcase, threw rocks into the store, broke his window, and kept shouting, "I want my whistle!" On the sixth day a truce was declared, and I got my whistle on the condition that I never come into his store again. When my father found out what had happened, he was very much upset because this man really could have killed me. In our beloved "democracy," killing a Jew was not a capital crime. You might be charged with a misdemeanor like a minor traffic violation but no more.

I began my education at an all-Jewish school, the same school that my two older brothers attended. My two brothers would take care of me. In the mornings they took me to school, and when school ended, they escorted me back home again. The winters in Warsaw can be very harsh. Two years later an all-Christian public school opened up across the street from where we lived. I told my father, "I don't want to walk nearly two miles to school anymore, to the school where my brothers used to go, when I can go to school right across the street." Of course, Father tried to talk me out of it, explaining, "Being the only Jew in an all-Christian school is not too healthy, to say the least."

You guessed it right! I attended the school across the street beginning with the third grade, the only Jewish child there. Name-calling was a normal daily routine. I fought every day. Although my teacher told me to report any harassment to her or the principal rather than fight, I never believed in asking anyone for help. I stood up for myself.

Once a month, sometimes more, Father was called to the principal's office because of my so called "misbehavior." The principal explained to my father that the only reason I was still in school was I was one of the best pupils in school. Also in my favor was the fortunate fact that my teacher, Mrs. Bublewicz, liked me very much. She would call me "Zydowskie kepele" (Little Jewish head). When no one knew the answer to a question, she would call on me. I always came up with the correct answer. At least most of the time. The only person that wanted to see me expelled from school was the priest, who was our religion teacher.

My conflict with the priest was that I kept asking too many questions. When he could not answer, he would say, "You do not question the deeds of the Lord." After awhile I used to answer him, "The deeds of the Lord don't bother me. It's the deeds of the people that bother me very much."

As we all know, until recently, the Catholic Church always told its parishioners that the Jews killed Jesus Christ. Most grown-ups have been conditioned not to question what the Church tells them. Being a rebel, I cannot help but question things that do not make sense to me. I was that way as a child, and am still that way today. I never outgrew the rebel in me.

After the priest's lecture, I asked him a question about the Jews killing Jesus. "Father, I would like to know — did the Lord send his son to die for our sins, or didn't he?"

"Yes," the priest said.

"In that case, the Jews' killing of Jesus was fulfilling the wishes of the Lord. Why then blame the Jews for fulfilling the Lord's wishes? If it was not the wishes of the Lord to sacrifice his son for our sins and the Jews killed him anyway, then, Father, the Church creates doubt in our mind that God could not protect his own son. If God cannot protect his own son, then how much faith do you expect us to have that the Lord can protect us?"

I was thrown out of class and suspended for a week. But I was not about to give up the history of Christianity that easily. After awhile, the Priest did allow me to come back to class, providing I did not interrupt the class with what he called stupid questions. Naturally, I could not keep that promise for very long.

Several weeks passed when I started to ask questions again. I asked the Priest, "Father, when you speak of Jesus, you always tell us how he loved his fellow men. Love and more love always follows Jesus's name. Why, then, Father, do you teach your pupils to *hate* Jews? Is this not something Jesus never did?"

The priest replied, "You want to know? You want to know, you little Jew?"

As I looked up at the priest I once again felt like the little five-year-old "Jewish bastard" that went to war with the six-foot, four-inch Christian bully, who lost the whistle war.

"Yes, Father, I would."

He said, "Because the Jews turned away from Jesus, they are being punished for it."

"Oh, I see. You teach love and hatred at the same time! The Church amazes me. You are the judges and the executioners."

Christianity and I were no strangers. When I was four years old and lived in the ghetto in poverty, nuns came to take poor Jewish children to summer camp, the purpose being, of course, to convert Jews to Christianity. For two years my brothers and I had been taken to summer camp. The camp was run by the Catholic Church and all the teachers were nuns. When I came to realize their true motive, it seemed strange to me that they would let poor Christian children starve in their quest to convert the Jews. This was the only time as a small child that I can remember having enough to eat. At summer camp we were taught the New Testament. We also had to kneel and pray before every meal and at bedtime, too. It might seem strange, but I still remember most of the prayers.

The nuns did not come for us the third year since my parents did not attend the meetings given by the Church specifically for the purpose of attempting to convert Jews to Catholicism. It is easy to convert religious people from one denomination to another; however, my father was not religious and our house was not considered a kosher home.

Father was a yeshiva graduate and very knowledgeable about the Talmud, a collection of ancient rabbinic writings and commentary on the Torah. In spite of an Orthodox upbringing, my Father felt that religion was for the ignorant. We observed Jewish holidays as a tradition not as a religious service. All the children in the family had a Hebrew teacher who came to the house to teach us Hebrew and Jewish tradition so that we would know something about Judaism and know why we were hated.

The only time I was defended by my Christian classmates was when, as a teammate, we had arguments with the other schools we played soccer against. What the heck, a teammate is a teammate! That was the only time they called me by my real name, Cheniek. The rest of the time they called me Zydek (little Jew).

I finally managed to make a few friends. Though my friends were few, I had three very close Catholic friends with whom I used to go to museums, movies, and even church. Church was always an experience that I could predict. After the services, the priest would always remind us that it was the Jews who killed Jesus. Every time that I would hear this — and believe me, I heard it every time — I would be amazed at the stupidity of the idea that people could kill a god. How could grownup people listen to this and believe something that did not make sense to a child? Of course, the Church has many answers.

As a child, and even today, I look at religion as a dictatorship. People are manipulated by fear of punishment and the promise of heaven or hell. You're promised heaven only after you die. I don't want to wait to enjoy death. I believe that religion does give too much power to God. My wish as a child, and even now, is that God would have the power that we attribute to him. This world would be a much better place. All good things are credited to God, and all bad things are blamed on someone else.

My father was very strict. All of us except my sister used to get a beating almost weekly and sometimes daily. Of course, we were mischievous. The most important thing to my father was, no matter what happens, you never talk back to a grownup. Respect for your elder was absolute law in our house. One Saturday, Father's friend Mr. Hashendorf came over to play chess. At the age of ten or eleven, I played chess better than my two older brothers and sometimes I even beat my father. Mr. Hashendorf had beaten my father in two close games of chess. With the excuse that he was going to make tea, my father asked Mr. Hashendorf if he would like to play with his little son. Mr. Hashendorf made a remark that he didn't like to play with children. Being called a child, my feelings were hurt very badly. I thought to myself, if he plays me after that remark, I will beat him if it kills me. I had to win to show him who he called a child.

Father finally convinced him that if he would play me just one game, it would give him time to make tea and serve it. When Father came back, we were playing the second game. Father asked, "What happened?

You're playing the second game already." I did not answer, but Mr. Hashendorf said, "I lost the first game because I took him too lightly." The second game he took me seriously, but he lost that game also. I won the third game, too. By the fourth game he loosened his tie, took off his jacket, and with perspiration running from his forehead and no trace of a smile, he settled into full concentration. Mr. Hashendorf lost this game, too. He turned to my father and said, "One more game. I know where I made my mistake. I will not lose this time."

Father stood behind Mr. Hashendorf and, using sign language that only I could see, was signaling that I should lose the game for the sake of Mr. Hashendorf's dignity. In spite of my father's signals, I could not respond and fake a loss because Mr. Hashendorf had insulted me by calling me a child.

After Mr. Hashendorf lost his fifth game, Father called me out of the room into the kitchen. The minute I came through the door, I was met with a fist squarely in my face. I didn't cry. I had my day with Mr. Hashendorf, and it was worth the throbbing punishment to satisfy my ego. I felt like a grownup. I was not a child. Quietly Father said to me, "A four to one score is a winning score. You shouldn't have to win all five games."

Father then went out to try to continue his role as a gracious host for Mr. Hashendorf. He gave him his tea, but Mr. Hashendorf did not drink it. Father tried to converse with him, but Mr. Hashendorf was silent and sulky. I thought my pride had been hurt, but his had been shattered. He left after only ten or fifteen minutes.

2
MY POLITICAL EDUCATION BEGINS

On Friday nights our house was like a political forum. Relatives and friends would gather, play cards, and the evening would always end up in a political discussion. The group would always consist of some Liberals, a Social Democrat, a Socialist, a Communist, and not to be left out, a Conservative. As the players would sip tea, eat homemade cake and cookies and drink a little wine, they would carry on discussions until 3 or 4 o'clock in the morning. Mother would go to bed around midnight.

I would sit in my room with my ear pressed against the door and listen to the philosophies of each participant until I fell asleep on the floor. This event would take place, like clockwork, every Friday night without fail. After months of listening to each person's personal philosophy, I decided that from what I had heard that the Marxist philosophy was the most just.

When I was a child, Marxism had this appeal because it seemed to offer justice and equality for all, fulltime employment, education, and health care for the people. The slogan was "Produce according to your ability and receive according to your necessity." No fewer words can describe justice more eloquently.

I used to take the knowledge that I learned from these wonderful evenings of eavesdropping, which I considered "political science lectures," to the courtyards which were filled with the youth. To those young people, some a little younger and some a little older, I became the "advocate of political news." I became their politician. No matter what question they had, I always had an answer, even if I had to make up one. I loved this. I think they liked it, too!

I read the newspaper daily and knew what was going on, not only in our country, but throughout the rest of the world. At night when I was alone, I would listen to "Radio Berlin" on our shortwave radio. I used to imitate Hitler's speeches. I learned quite a bit of the German language by listening to the radio. I did not realize at that time that I had the ability to pick up a foreign language with very little effort.

I knew, even as a child, that Poland was on the verge of collapse. I knew what kind of a country Poland was, and I could see what was going to happen. I was able to observe and realize things that some grownups were totally oblivious.

The Communist Party was illegal in Poland. If the government had any suspicion (no evidence was necessary) that a Pole or Jew was a member of the Party, they would be sent to a concentration camp called Kartuz Bereza, the most inhumane place in Europe at that time. After you were released, if you were lucky, it would take months and years of rehabilitation for a person to get over the physical and mental strain. Some people never recovered. But if a government agent infiltrated the Communist Party as an informer and was found out, he was executed. The Communist Party used this as a deterrent against any infiltration and spying on them.

I once witnessed an execution in the middle of the day. I was walking with my father when we saw a horse-driven carriage with three occupants. They opened fire on a man who was standing on the corner of the street. After the slaughter, all three men disappeared within seconds. I was very scared and clung to my father like any frightened child would. In a matter of minutes, the police arrived and formed a cordon on the street. Father grasped me up into his arms and retreated into a building until this terrible event was over.

In Poland, Labor Day is May 1, as it is throughout the world. Only in the United States does Labor Day fall in September. On Labor Day, unions would march in parades. Slogans of "Chleb Praca" (Work and Bread), "Rownosc Sprawiedliwosc" (Equality and Justice) would be held high, proclaiming the parade's purpose. Inevitably during the course of the parade, the red flag of communism would appear. The appearance of this flag was just like waving a red flag in front of a bull. Mounted police and government agents in civilian clothes would attack the crowd, shooting indiscriminately.

In the early 1930s many Nazi and Fascist parties began to spring up. The headquarters of one of the Fascist parties was only half a block from where we lived, Dzika 29 Street. We lived on Dzika 35 Street. After each meeting of NARA, the "Union of National Nationalists," the members would go out and look for Jews. My father was attacked and beaten many times. It was so bad that my older brothers had to escort my father to the streetcar, then on a predetermined schedule, they would wait for his return so that they could provide him with some protection.

We never would have survived without our equalizers, better known as brass knuckles. My brothers were always getting into fights. The Poles would never take them on one-to-one. They had to have four or five to one before they would fight my notorious brothers.

I still carry a three-inch scar under my chin where one of the Poles tried to slit my throat. I had my brass knuckles with me, and when he caught me in the throat with his knife, I landed a vicious blow to his jaw, then kicked him with all my might in the groin. He fell to the ground screaming "Jezus, Kochany" (I love you, Jesus). For as you know, the Poles are good Christians, even when they tried to kill you they would call to Jesus for help. They follow church teachings faithfully. We were both taken to the hospital. I was grateful to be alive.

Poland has excellent police. When the Poles were attacking the Jews, the police would stand by and not interrupt a "friendly little youth squabble," but when the Jewish boys got the upper hand, the police would step forward and stop the terrible street fighting and send all the delinquents home or have them arrested.

Poland was the only country in the 1930s that had pogroms. Police and Poles attacked Jews in small towns and took what they wanted and destroyed the rest. Once they tried to do the same in Warsaw, but the Jews were strong and had the support of the PPS (Polish Socialist Party and Communist Party). The PPS combined their forces with the Jewish people and there was blood all over the streets. After the beating the progromers experienced in this encounter, they never tried to harass or attack the Jews in Warsaw again; but, individual attacks never stopped.

In late 1938, we moved to a predominantly Jewish neighborhood. We had to leave the old neighborhood because it became impossible to survive as Jews. We moved to Dzielna 42. This was a much nicer area within Warsaw. The apartment was bigger and better. We had a five-room apartment, and for the first time in my life we had a full bath in the house. Once again, my parents had improved their economic condition. We were even able to go away in the summer to a rented home. Also, by now our shirt business had grown into a small shirt factory. We employed about twenty girls. They worked in our living room. My brothers seemed to know more about the girls than I did, as I was about twelve years old.

My oldest brother, Abraham, was a cutter. Shlomo, my next oldest brother, was a mechanic. We were the only small, independent factory that employed such few employees, and we treated them like they were union employees. They only worked eight hours a day, five-and-a-half days a week.

Father practiced what he preached. I remember listening through the door to the political discussions with Father, proclaiming the Socialist point of view, that of treating workers with dignity.

Mother's sister and youngest brother were very poor. They used to come to our house a few times each week with the children to eat. When Mother and Father decided to buy a truck, they gave the job of hiring it out to my mother's younger brother—Yosel. They did this in order to help Yosel out by providing him with an income. After school I used to love to go with Yosel. I guess most children like the excitement of riding.

One day our truck was hired to transport the posters that were to be put up for the elections. It was an all Christian Liberal Party—ZZZ (Union of Professional Professionals). This was the Polish intellectuals. We were supposed to drive from midnight to 4:00 A.M. with party faithfuls to hang posters. These posters had pictures of their candidates and were to be hung up all over the city. After we had worked for a little over an hour, four trucks pulled up. Police in civilian clothes jumped out with guns in their hands. They started shooting indiscriminately. Many of the workers were killed or wounded. Bodies were lying all over the street. There was utter confusion. I hid under the truck. My uncle sat in the driver's seat, trembling. The attack was a nightmare!

One of the attackers looked at my uncle and said, "Oh, you are a Jew." One quality that the Poles have is the ability to recognize a Jew. I don't think that any other nation in the whole world has the keen ability to recognize a Jew on sight as well as a Pole.

The attackers confiscated the posters from the truck and put them in their own vehicles. They told us to get lost. In terror, I jumped back into the truck, fearing for my life. My uncle took off so fast that on the first corner he nearly overturned the truck. Had anyone seen my uncle that night, they would have thought that a ghost was driving the truck. It was fortunate that it was the middle of the night when there was no traffic. My uncle needed the whole road that night.

The ZZZ behaved like gentlemen. One week later, we received a check for twenty zloty ($4.00) for one day's work. They didn't hold my uncle responsible for what happened. We weren't involved in politics. We had just hired out the truck.

The conservative-fascist government, who were right extremists, did not want the posters of the liberal candidates exhibited. They did not want them elected. I have learned by now that no government will willingly surrender the power they hold. They will use any means, legal or illegal, to make sure they maintain the power they have.

In 1938-1939 Hitler started to make his move: Austria was taken. Sudetenland was taken from Czechoslovakia and Hitler made an offer for Poland to take a part of Czechoslovakia called Zaolzie, and Germany would take Danzig. Stalin asked France, England, Poland, and Czechoslovakia to join a defense alliance against Hitler. The proposal was that should Hitler attack any country in the alliance, all parties would declare war against Germany. Except for Czechoslovakia, none of the other countries wanted to have Stalin as an ally. Everyone was just waiting for Hitler to make his move against the Soviet Union.

The German slogan, "Drang nach osten" (surge to the east and destroy communism) laid heavy on the Western countries' mind. Poland's answer to this was splashed all over the newspapers: "No Bolshevik foot would ever step on our Polish soil."

After the death of Marshal Pilsudski, Poland moved more to the right and formed a much closer relationship with Germany. Antisemitism became a good vehicle to ride on, and Germany worked hard to keep it that way.

Poland had a population of approximately thirty-two million people. Over ten million of them were German, and the majority supported Adolf. The German army, after taking Czechoslovakia and Danzig from Poland, was now preparing to take the rest of Poland.

The Polish foreign minister, Mr. Beck, was of German descent and occupied Parliament with very important issues. I say this sarcastically. For months, the Parliament discussed a very "humanitarian" subject: "Should the Jewish people have the right to slaughter cows, goats, sheep and chickens according to their religious ritual, or is it better to shoot them?" It was not easy coming to a decision concerning a matter of such importance. Mrs. Pristerowa, a member of Parliament, kept up her argument in favor of all anti-ritual laws.

Then on September 1, 1939, before our Parliament came to vote on the issue of ritual or no ritual slaughter, Hitler's army invaded Poland from all sides. The German air force was very busy. Warsaw, being the capital, received plenty of bombings. It only took the German army a few weeks to destroy the Polish army, and now they stood at the gates of Warsaw.

France and England declared war on Germany. Warsaw was jumping for joy, and everyone was confident that in a few weeks they would destroy Germany. All we had to do is hold out and not surrender our city. Little did the Polish people know that the declaration of war against Germany was lip service and was only meant to create a border between Germany and Russia. The Western world, a civilization as we call it today, was pleased with Hitler's move. He was getting closer to Russia. "Drang nach osten" was coming soon, a direct road to Russia and the destruction of communism.

After weeks of bombs falling on Warsaw, the Germans sent an ultimatum to our heroic mayor, Mr. Starzynski. Being misled by France and England's declaration of war against Germany, the mayor decided to mobilize the city and fight. The city became an armed fortress. Everyone capable of carrying arms was called on. My two older brothers went too! I was only thirteen years old, so I remained at home with my parents.

After forty-eight hours passed and the Germans received the answer of no surrender, all hell broke loose. Air force artillery started pounding away at our city without a stop. One air squadron left, the next came. The planes flew so low that they were shooting into the windows of our homes. The night was like HELL. The city was in flames, and there wasn't too much the fire department could do.

It is amazing how fast children learn to survive. Standing in the middle of the street, you'd watch the planes and run towards them so the bombs would fall behind you. The shelters were death traps. After the building above the shelter collapsed, there was no way to get out of them. Most people suffocated. The screams and cries could be heard for miles. For seventy-two hours, without a stop, Warsaw was hit by air and heavy artillery. After about a week, we got used to it.

We used to go to get food wherever we could find some. Naturally, there wasn't too much. If a horse got hit, his carcass would disappear within minutes. You would never know that a horse had once been there except for the traces of blood left behind. We used to go to bombed factories or produce markets in search of food. I remember my brother Abraham and me going to a pickle factory where we found two large cans of pickles to bring home. Thousands of people were there climbing over the dead and wounded. Who cared? There were so many, that after awhile it seemed a normal occurrence.

After two weeks of fighting and suffering, Mayor Starzynski realized that France and England were not heartbroken over what was happening in Poland and decided to surrender the city to the Germans. The only condition was that all the Polish defenders would be allowed to leave the city. Mr. Starzynski was still hoping that our allies, France and England, would soon come. Little did he know. The release of the Polish soldiers would enable them to join ranks with the French and English armies, so Mr. Starzynski thought, not realizing that Poland was completely occupied already by the Germans on the west and the Russians on the east.

Silently, I stood with my father when the mighty German army entered our city with loaded and pointed guns ready for action. Behind them came the infantry, goose-stepping and singing the song "Erika." It certainly was a beautiful parade. I was happy and sad at the same time—glad to get rid of the Polish government that was rotten, antisemitic, Fascist, and ruled by the Catholic Church, and sad that Hitler's Germany had to do it. The next day a proclamation came from the German High Command. "All stores and businesses must open and return to normal." No one dared disobey a German order.

3
ESCAPE

In 1939 Maxim Litvinov, the Soviet foreign minister, was replaced by Vyacheslav Molotov. It seems that Stalin and Molotov pulled a dirty trick on the West. The Soviet Union signed a friendship and non-aggression treaty with Hitler's Germany. This left the Western powers holding the bag. This also made Hitler move towards the West and, by his taking all of Europe, left England praying that the German army would not land on their island. Russia and Germany also agreed that the occupation of Poland would exclude western Ukraine and the western part of Byelorussia, which had been under Polish rule since 1921. The Russian army entered Poland at almost the same time the German army attacked, leaving Poland divided between "friends."

After a few weeks of German occupation, the townspeople were getting upset with the German soldiers doing whatever pleased them. They went into homes and stores, taking anything they wanted. Naturally, the townspeople didn't utter a sound. They knew that if they did, they surely would not be around to object a second time.

I'll never forget when I went with my father to Nalewki Street, which was a Jewish center of commerce. A high-ranking German officer stopped his car, stood up in his convertible DKW, and shouted, "Alle Jude werden erschosen! Alle Jude werden erschosen!" (All Jews are going to be shot!) He had never seen so many Jews all in one place. There were some Orthodox Jews in their attire.

We had a family meeting. It was decided that my two older brothers, Abraham, about eighteen years old, and Shlomo, seventeen, would go and see where the Russian army was and what the situation was like there. They would come back as soon as possible and give us a report. Two days later, away they went with maps and routes. What my two brothers saw was enough to scare the devil. People, mostly Jews, were being shot and buried in mass graves or being hung in the middle of the village or town for whatever reason. Justice was carried out.

We did not hear from my brothers for almost two weeks. Every night Father, Mother, and friends sat trying to decide whether to go over to the Russian side or to stay. I decided to go now and not wait for my parents. My parents had the shirt factory, and it was not easy to give up something that you worked for all your life. You have to remember, too, that in the late 1920s we had been very poor and now, we were at least able to make a living.

When I decided to leave, I stole four shirts and sold them to some German soldiers. In the early morning, I took my bicycle and, without saying good-bye to anyone, left. Remembering the route my two brothers took, I followed. Before reaching the city of Minsk Mazowieck, my bike was taken by a German soldier and I had to walk the rest of the way. I arrived about midnight in a very small village.

It was late October or the beginning of November. Winter had set in, and temperatures often went below freezing. Not knowing where to go or what to do, with nobody around to ask and afraid to knock at a door, I decided to wait until morning to go on. I entered a shed or stable and laid down between some cows and a horse. The horse was frightened by my presence and started to make very loud noises. The owner, grabbing a pitchfork, ran into the stable screaming, "Get out before I kill you. Trying to steal my cows, eh?" With my childish voice I answered, "I just want to stay here overnight. I have no place to sleep." Hearing a childish voice he said, "Come out. I won't hurt you. Come. Come."

When he saw me he realized that I was not a thief. He took me into the house, fed me, and made up a straw mattress for me to sleep on the floor. In the morning his wife served me a good breakfast. The man then explained to me in Yiddish how to get over to the Russian side.

I only had to walk a few miles to get across the border without being detected by the German border guards. Once crossing the border, I was stopped by the Russian border guard, the first Russian soldier I ever saw. I was shocked, after seeing the Polish army and the German army so organized — clean shaven, boots shining, uniforms looking like they just came from the cleaners — and now here was a Russian. I couldn't believe my eyes as I looked up at the Russian soldier's unshaven face. He wore a hat with a pointed tip on top, old boots, and a uniform that looked like he slept in it for a month. It had a red star/hammer-and-sickle emblem on it. As I looked him over, he stood there smiling at me. At least there was something good about him. He spoke Russian to me, but I did not understand a word. He then took my hand and led me into a large house where many, many people were, all from the German side.

The border between Russia's newly acquired territory and the German-occupied territory was opened for four weeks, allowing people to go back and forth so families could be reunited after the war. We were held for about six hours and then taken by military trucks to the city of Brest Litovsk on the river Bug. We arrived at the city in the evening and were let loose. I did not know where to go or what to do. I asked a militia man where I could sleep just for the night. He took me to an orphanage. From nowhere, my brother Shlomo called my name with excitement. Seeing him, I was filled with relief and thankfulness. Once our emotions calmed down, we sat and spoke for awhile. He told me that our oldest brother, Abraham, had gone back to Warsaw to speak to our parents and to tell them to come. He told me what he had seen on his way here, and that was enough for him. Under no conditions would he go back to Warsaw.

The next morning after breakfast, Shlomo told me that the Soviet government was offering to take them all deep into the Soviet Union and give them work. All the children could get schooling and live in foster homes. He wanted me to go with him so we would at least be together. We had one week to make up our minds. We were each given pocket money and taught some Russian. I decided to go with my brother instead of staying there all alone.

When the time came, we were loaded onto a Pullman car. There were about ten cars in the echelon, each Pullman car having about fifty people in it. We moved out of the city near midnight. After stopping and waiting for hours, we crossed the old Russian-Polish border, the border that existed before the war started. This border was never removed and was still being very heavily guarded like two different countries. We entered the real Soviet Union about 10 A.M. What I saw was an unbelievable sight. Most of the farm houses had Red stars on the roof. Some even had large pictures of Stalin or Lenin and red flags with the hammer-and-sickle emblem. All the lawns were manicured, clean, plain, and picturesque.

After stopping and going and making room for military trains, we arrived in a little town in Byelorussia called Petrikov. Here one car was removed from the train. A few miles down the track, in a different place called Kapcevitch, our car was released from the others. We were told that this was the place we would have to settle in now. It was a big village.

We were lead into a large hall. The hall was decorated with pictures of Stalin, Lenin, Engels, Marx and the red flag. Six people sat at a long table on the stage. They introduced themselves: one was the secretary of the local chapter of the Communist Party; one was a director of a plywood factory located in the same town; another the director of education, a judge, an undersecretary of the Communist Party, and a member from the Communist Party of the Soviet Union.

In the group that was left here in Kapcevitch there were some families with children, some couples, some single people and me, who was the youngest (twelve or thirteen years old). Each family received five hundred rubles, about one month's wages for an average worker. All single persons received two hundred rubles. Living quarters were distributed accordingly; singles were assigned rooms and families were given homes. My brother and I were housed in a large barracks having one room to ourselves.

I was told that I would be contacted tomorrow by the undersecretary of the Communist Party in order to discuss my future. My brother got a job about seven kilometers away in a collective farm as a mechanic for farm equipment. He was a mechanic back home, so it was to his liking.

The next day when the undersecretary of the Communist Party came to visit me, I was told that I should go to school, study, learn Russian better, and if I was a good student, I could go all the way to the highest university in Moscow. I listened very carefully. When he was finished with his advice, I asked him, "Who is going to pay for all of this? My brother cannot pay for all this schooling." He looked at me and smiled. He said, "Don't worry. You are a minor. The government must pay for you. You saw the director of the plywood factory?" Yes, sir. "Well, this factory is adopting you. All the bills for your food, clothing, and whatever else you may need will be sent to the factory, and they will pay them. Don't worry about a thing."

I didn't know what to say. I was taken by surprise. All I could say was, "You're not joking, are you?"

"No!" he replied.

I managed to say, "thank you" in Russian. "Next Monday you will be taken to school and then you will go by yourself."

"Thank you again," I answered.

Now that my brother was working at the collective farm, he didn't come home until midday on Saturday. This only left us half a day on Saturdays and all of Sunday, to be together. I started to get homesick. I couldn't sleep well anymore.

The teacher, Anna Andrevna, was very kind. After a week or two had passed, she noticed that I was not myself. I was very quiet. She notified the undersecretary of the Communist Party, and he came to see me in order to find out what was bothering me. He spoke to me like a father. He suggested that I move in with a Russian family. He thought that would make things easier for me, and I wouldn't be all alone for most of the week. I agreed to do it, but after a few days I was homesick all over again. I started to wet my bed and that made me very embarrassed in front of the family. They had a son of eighteen years and a girl of fifteen years. Imagine how I felt wetting my bed at the age of thirteen, but I had no control over it.

We lived in a private house. The streets were mostly unpaved, and the sidewalks were wooden. The church was made into a club, "Krasny ugolok" (The Red Corner). We played chess, checkers, ping pong, soccer, and sometimes went skiing and skating. All the villages had such a club. At least that's what I was told. In spite of the efforts made by the authorities to keep me happy, I just couldn't get used to being without my own mother and father. I had never been without them before. I was also worried about what was happening to them under Hitler. I decided to try a few more days, but I only got more and more depressed. Although it was not easy to decide, I had to go back home.

4

GOING HOME

One morning, without any baggage, I picked myself up and left for the train station. Arriving there, I stood back away from the visible part of the platform and waited for a train, any train. When the train was ready to leave, even though I didn't know where it was going, I jumped on and sat down. After riding for an hour or two, I found out that this train was going to Gomel, a big city. When the conductor asked for my ticket, I spoke to him in Polish. He only spoke Russian. Though I already knew how to speak the language a little, I continued speaking to him in Polish. He finally turned away from me and said to the other passengers on board, "He's a refugee from the now-occupied Poland." He let me go without even knowing where it was I was going and without a ticket.

When I arrived in Gomel, I had something to eat. I then took a train to Minsk, the capital city of Byelorussia. Arriving in Minsk the next night, I slept at the train station. When I awoke, I saw many Polish people, mostly Jews, going to the main building of the Byelorussian Communist Party headquarters. I went along, too. When we reached the front of the building, I couldn't believe my eyes. Thousands of people were sitting in the middle of the street, and Russian militia were trying to move the demonstrators to the sidewalk. The streetcars and traffic were stopped for a mile. It seemed the demonstrators were there for days. They were demanding that they be allowed to go back home, home being occupied Poland. Late in the afternoon a gentleman appeared on the steps of the headquarter building, claiming to be a member of the Byelorussian Communist Party. He explained that a state has no right to make decisions that involve travel outside the country and that the Soviet federal government was the only one that could issue visas or handle problems of this kind. He also said that he sent a telegram to Moscow asking for help, and the moment he got an answer, he would come out and tell us their reply.

In the meantime, I walked around and listened to all kinds of conversation. After a while, I stumbled upon an interesting conversation between three young men in their late 20s. They had decided to try to cross the border. That is the old border between the original country of the Soviet Union and the newly acquired territories. From Minsk to the border was only a ten- or twelve-hour train ride. The rest of the day, I followed those three guys around, for they already knew when the train was leaving. Naturally, I kept my distance.

After sleeping at the train station near the guys, I bought a pass that enabled visitors to get onto the platform to say good-bye to the people that were leaving. I did not know where or what town they were getting off at, so I couldn't purchase a ticket to any specific destination. When they boarded the train, I slipped into the same car but stayed a little behind. The closer to the border we got, the emptier the train became. The few people still left on the train kept looking at those guys. It made them very nervous. Nobody paid any attention to me though. A kid is a kid. Who cares?

The three guys got off at a station that was only about twenty or thirty kilometers from the border. I got off there, too, and stood at the other end of the car, waiting to see in which direction they were going. They took off into the woods, I right behind them. Once they were deep into the woods, they noticed that they were being followed. They hid and when I got close, they surprised me. "Who are you?" They demanded. I said, "I want to go with you. I want to go home."

"This kid is crazy. You cannot walk in this deep snow for twenty or thirty kilometers." "Yes, I can. Don't worry. I will keep up with you. Don't worry." They had to let me go with them.

After about fifteen kilometers, I was frozen cold, tired, and unable to continue. I sat down in the snow, which was about six feet high. I gave up! I was ready to freeze to death. Going through all this, I became disillusioned with life and the world. I could fool anybody, but not the Russian winter.

The three guys stopped. One said, "We cannot leave you here. You will die." They sat down next to me and did not know what to do. After a little rest, I felt better. I told them to take me to the railroad tracks and I would give myself up. I'd try to lie my way to the other side of the border. They agreed to take me back to the tracks, then showed me which direction I should go and then they left.

I moved slowly down the railroad tracks, wearily dragging myself along. After about a half-hour, I saw a big German shepherd running towards me at full speed. I was scared to death and happy at the same time. That meant the guards were close. The dog jumped on me and hit me in the chest. I fell to the ground. He then stood with his front paws on my chest and howled. A few minutes later two Russian border guards came on skis. Seeing me, they were speechless. What in the hell was this kid doing here in pants above his knees and half-frozen shoes?

They finally called the dog off, picked me up, and asked, "What in the devil are you doing here?" I remained silent. The border guards put me on a sled and took me to the guardhouse.

Before they even asked me where I was going, they realized that my shoes were frozen to my feet. There was no way that I could get them off. One of the guards immediately called for a doctor. He used the kind of telephone that you had to turn a handle to make a call. A few hours passed before they could take off my shoes. The doctor arrived soon thereafter. I was given hot tea and a sandwich, and then they inquired as to where I was going.

I told them, "I'm going to Kapcevitch in Byelorussia."

"Why?" "Because my brother is there. I lost my family in the war and my brother, being the only relative I have, is in Kapcevitch."

"Why didn't you go to the authorities and tell them? They would send you there with no trouble."

"Well, I didn't know where to go, who to go to and I have nowhere to stay. I cannot wait." I told him my name, but he kept on calling me son.

"Son, we are not allowed to let anybody cross the border. We have no authority to let you go. If we are caught, we will go to jail. Son, you would not want that to happen, would you?"

"But, nobody would know." They kept on explaining to me that their hands were tied, and I kept on insisting that they could let me go.

The next morning the three guys that had helped me were caught. They had gotten across the border already, but were apprehended in a house they slept in overnight. When these guys were brought in, I looked the other way. One of the guards was no dummy. He said to the guys, "Why did you leave him behind?" They saw me turn my head in the hope that they wouldn't give me away. Luckily, they said that they didn't know who I was and that they had never seen me before. I guess that was enough for the guards. Although they had tried to trick me, it did not work; so they had no choice but to be satisfied with my story. The three fellows were taken away. I don't know where.

After a few days, I was given new shoes since the old ones had to be cut off my feet. While held in the guardhouse, I took note of the train schedule: The 11 A.M. train went deep into Russia, and the 4 P.M. train went to Brest Litovsk. Once again, the guards decided to trick me by telling me that they were sending me to Minsk, and there I would be taken care of until my brother was sent for.

In reality, they were preparing to send me to Baranavichy, which was located in the new territory on the other side of the border. I really felt that I had overdone it, convincing them to let me go to my brother. I was worried, but when I was told that tomorrow, at 4 P.M., I would be put on the train to Minsk, only then did I realize that they were lying and that they were sending me where I really wanted to go. I pretended to be very happy and I thanked them for their efforts to reunite me with my brother.

When the 4 P.M. train arrived, the guard gave the conductor an envelope with some documents in it and told him to take good care of me. The conductor held on to me. As the train pulled out, the guard shouted, "I'm sorry son, we have to send you back." At that moment, I pretended that I wanted to jump off the train and started crying and screamed, "Liars, Liars, Liars!" It is a good thing the conductor held me tight. And so, I was on my way to the other side. I had my way across.

The conductor told me that upon our arrival in Baranavichy, I was to go to the stationmaster. He would give the stationmaster the envelope, and in a few days I'd be sent to my brother. Once in Baranavichy, I did not go to the stationmaster. Hiding on the side of the station, I could hear the conductor calling my name: "Goldberg! Goldberg! Goldberg!" I remained there until the train left. Spending the night at the railroad station, I boarded a train to Brest Llitovsk the following day.

The reason for my wanting to go to Brest Litovsk was that it was only one to three kilometers from the border, that is the new border between Russia and Germany. How or where do I cross the border over the frozen river Bug, which is wide and full with snow?

It was December already, 1939. I went to the open market where many speculators went back and forth smuggling watches, bracelets, and other things from the German side to the Russian side. No matter how bad a situation is, people are always looking to make a fortune.

Luck being on my side, I noticed a guy pulling out watches from his pocket and selling them to some Russian soldiers. Soldiers paid any price you asked. They were the best customers. I didn't let this man out of my sight. I had a feeling that he was going back to the other side, as he told one of the soldiers that he didn't have any more watches, but he'd be back in a few days with more. I had to take a chance.

That evening I followed him to a house. I stood outside, half frozen, watching and waiting for him to come out. About 2 A.M. he finally came out from the house. He walked very briskly. Although I stood at a distance, it was easy to see at night with the white blanket of snow giving light to everything that moved. When he approached an open field, there it was, the frozen river. He turned around quickly and when he did, he noticed that I was following him. He stood in place and waited for me to come closer. When I reached him, he asked, "Where are you going, kid?"

"I'm going home to Warsaw to my parents. Will you take me across the river with you?"

He was a little upset, but he had no choice but to take me along. Firmly, he said, "When we are on the other side, I'll take you into a house and then I'm leaving. I'll pay the lady for the night. In the morning you are on your own." I agreed to his terms, and we crossed the river with no mishaps.

The lady of the house was about forty-years-old, and with no man around, it didn't take her long to come into my bed. I guess a thirteen-year-old boy was better than nothing. When I got up in the morning, the lady very cheerfully made me breakfast. She then told me in which direction to go. I thanked her and left the house around 10 A.M.

It didn't take me too long after crossing the border, having only gone about two kilometers, to meet up with the first German officer. "Halt!" A very common German expression. "Where are you coming from?"

Hesitating for a few seconds, I then told him the truth. "I'm coming from the Russian side and going home to Warsaw to my parents."

"Are you a Jew?"

"Yes Sir."

"Where is your schande band?" The band of shame. It was a band worn around your arm with the Star of David on it.

"Sir, I don't have one. As I told you, I am coming from the Russian side."

"Do you know the law?"

"No Sir." "You could be shot on the spot for violating the law. This is not Russia. Don't you forget it! What is your name?"

I told him Heinrich Tzimbolknop.

"Well, Heinrich, I will give you a schande band. You have to wear it on your right arm, up high, so it is visible. If you are caught without it, you will be shot. No questions will be asked."

I guess he was good-hearted, or perhaps I just caught him in a good mood. He took me into a barracks full of German soldiers and introduced me to them. "This is Heinrich. He comes from the Russian side." I was given coffee and a sandwich. I was not hungry, but I was afraid to say so.

After I finished with my second breakfast, the soldiers began asking me questions about Russia. They found in me a Russian "expert" on arms, economy, culture, et cetera. "Do the Russians have butter?" they asked. "If they do, nobody knows about it." I hit the right spot. They all became hysterical. They laughed until tears came out.

"Heinrich, is it true that the Russian tanks are made of plywood?"

"Yes, but they sure do look real." I did it again. They couldn't stop laughing.

"Is it true that the Russians don't have white bread?"

"Yes, but that's not a problem. You put a little flour on pumpernickel and it's white bread." I was a regular comedian.

"Do you think we could beat them in a blitzkrieg?"

"Not just in a blitzkrieg, but in any krieg. If you saw them you would know why."

After a few more questions, the circus was over. They showed me the road that would take me to the train. It was about forty or fifty kilometers to a large city called Siedlce. It was 12 noon when I hit the road; me and my Star of David schande band. After walking, hitchhiking and walking and hitchhiking, I finally arrived in Siedlce. It was approximately 7 P.M. A train was leaving for Warsaw between 8 and 8:30 P.M.

On the railroad station platform there were many German soldiers. I don't know why, but I decided to move my Star of David armband all the way down to my wrist. Just then the loud speaker announced that the ticket window for the Warsaw train would open in 10 minutes. A line of about fifty to sixty people had formed already. I was one of them. Five minutes before the ticket window opened, from nowhere appeared a high-ranking German officer. I knew he was high-ranking because several soldiers followed him.

The officer instructed all Jews to leave the queue (line) and move to the left. With my Star of David near my wrist, I put my arm behind me and leant against the wall so it was not visible. Once all the Jews stepped out from the line, except for me, they were taken away. It was a group of ten or so small children with their parents.

Then an officer walked over to the line and started questioning each person individually. "Jude?" "No, Pole." "Jude?" "No, Pole." He kept moving down the line until he came to me. "Jude?" "No, Pole." He was ready to move on when one of my right-sided neighbors shouted out, "No! He's a Jude!" The officer asked me again, "Jude?" I answered, "No, Pole." He continued to ask me the same question over and over again. Six or eight times. "Jude?" "No, Pole." He finally gave up, at least so I thought.

The person standing next to the one who said that I was a Jew said, "Leave the kid alone."

"Okay, but why is he lying?" the man kept on repeating. Well, you can't blame a person who likes the truth and nothing but the truth. Of course not!

If you think for one moment that this officer gave up, you are in for a surprise. The German officer started back up the line from the other end now, requestioning everyone. "Jude?" "No, Pole." "Jude?" "No, Pole," and so on, and so on, until he was back in front of me. Then, firmly he asked, "Jude?" I replied as before, "No, Pole." The same question and reply was passed back and forth about ten times. Still not sure that I was telling the truth, he stood looking at me trying to determine whether I was a Pole or a Jew. The Germans could not differentiate between the two. Only the Poles had that gift. At least my neighbor was quiet this time.

The officer decided to take me into the railroad stationmaster's room to see if I had been circumcised. He didn't have to go through all that trouble because when I moved, my Star of David became visible. All I remember after that was being hit with the handle of a gun and being kicked so hard that I flew across the station. I lay there unconscious.

The next morning when I came to and opened my eyes, I was lying in a room, my clothes full of blood. A man wearing a red cap was wiping the blood from my head and face. He was the stationmaster, a Pole. He asked me how I felt. I wasn't sure myself. I was still in a daze. He took me home, and when his wife saw me, she screamed, "What happened?" He told her what the bastard had done to me and that he thought that I was dead.

I remained at their house for a few days until I felt better and was able to continue my journey. They gave me new clothes and even bought me a ticket to Warsaw. They also made sure that I stayed out of sight until the train was ready to leave the station. Finally, I was on my way home.

The train arrived in Warsaw after the curfew began. The curfew hours were from 9 P.M. to 6 A.M. The railroad station was overcrowded with people, who were all trying to get home, too. A few minutes after my arrival, an announcement in Polish came over the loudspeaker. "Anyone who wishes to go home will receive a pass, and groups will be formed according to the district where you live." Since it was curfew, we were only permitted to go in groups. After looking around, pushing left and right, I found the group going to my district. I couldn't have been happier.

The group had twenty men and four women. We left the railroad station together from Praga, a part of Warsaw divided by the river Vistula. We walked quite a distance before reaching the Kierbedzia

Bridge. We were stopped several times along the way by the German soldiers. After checking our passes, they allowed us to continue. The guards stationed on the Praga side of the bridge also verified our passes, and then motioned for us to cross over the bridge. When we finally reached the other side, we were told to halt! Another routine check, so we thought. But this time the guards collected our passes and told us to wait.

Within a few minutes, ten German soldiers came and escorted us to the German headquarters, a building I had been in many times before as it used to be the Museum of Natural History. Nobody knew what was going on.

We were taken into a big hall with a table where four officers were seated. They called the first man over. "Hey, you. Come. What is your name?" The man answered in Polish, "I don't understand German." The officer repeated the question again and again in German, then hit the man in the face and called him a Polish swine. I couldn't stand by and watch this brutality any longer. I had to intervene. I finally said in Polish, "The officer wants to know your name." The officer then turned to me and asked, "Do you speak German?"

"Yes sir," I said.

"Come here. I want you to ask each person their name and where they live."

Once my job as interpreter was finished, the German officer began questioning me. Then, my trouble started. "Do you know who the leader is?"

Not knowing what he was referring to, I answered, "The leader of what?"

"Don't play dumb, kid. I know why you were on the bridge."

"Why?" I asked.

"Germans are not dumb. You got those passes to walk after curfew hours illegally, and you tried to blow up the bridge." After he said that, I knew what was waiting for us.

This German officer had planned this whole masquerade, probably in the hopes of getting a promotion out of it. Capturing us before we blew up the bridge would bring him much recognition. He insisted that I, being only a kid, was just a front to make the group look innocent. "You cannot fool a German officer," he said.

We were all locked up in basement cells without any windows. The basement used to be a storage area for stuffed animals. The darkness and cold surrounded us. The only lights that shone were the ones in the hallway.

The next morning an investigation was held. I was the sixth one to be called. They told me that the five before me were shot for not collaborating with the investigation. We never did see those five guys again. I was offered a deal. If I could find out who the leader of the group was, I would be set free. The German officer gave me his word. Whatever that was worth. He gave me four days. "I or another officer will call on you everyday. If you haven't discovered the leader by the end of the fourth day, you will be shot with the rest of your friends."

When I was returned to the cell, I told the others what the German officer wanted me to do. I could imagine how all my cellmates felt, wondering who I would sacrifice so I could go free. Some got down on their knees to pray, some walked back and forth and some began talking to me. "Heinrich, what are you going to do?"

"I don't know. I don't know. No matter what I do, we are all going to be shot, including me." We all knew it and there was nothing we could do to prevent it.

The first two days when I was taken to the German officer's room, I didn't know what to do or say. I asked him to give me more time, although I really didn't know why I needed it. I guess I was just stalling for time so we could all live another day. As George Bernard Shaw said, "I don't want to die old, but I would like to postpone my death for as long as possible."

On the third day, while I was accompanied through the hallway to the German officer's room, a door opened and another officer called, "Helmut, come in here for a minute."

"I'm busy now. I'll be there in a few minutes."

But the officer insisted that Helmut see him then. He told me to go on to his room, Room 102, and wait for him there. I knew the way because I had been there twice before.

When I reached Room 102, I decided not to enter and continued walking. I didn't know what to do, but I knew that I couldn't get out of the building without a pass. There were guards throughout the building and at the front gate, too. I continued walking when all of a sudden, an idea hit me. I opened a door. An officer was sitting behind a desk. "Excuse me, I'm looking for Officer Gruber." I had noticed his name on a door while walking through the hallway.

"Can I help you?"

"I don't know if it's ethical to tell you."

"Why? You can tell me!"

"Well, Officer Gruber and I had an agreement."

"Sit down, kid ,and tell me. Maybe I can help you."

Hesitating and pretending that I didn't want to tell him, I said, "I will tell you our agreement only if you can do better than Officer Gruber."

"Listen, kid. I am a higher ranking officer than Gruber, and that means I can do more than he can."

"I don't really know if I should tell you." I aroused his curiosity still more by hesitating and pretending to be fearful of telling him.

He said, "Come on, kid. Don't worry. I promise, nothing will happen to you. Just tell me."

"Okay, Herr Schmidt. I used to give Officer Gruber the names and addresses of rich Jews, and he used to give me ten percent of whatever he appropriated from them."

"What is your name?"

"Heinrich."

"What nationality are you?"

"A volks deutsche." A volks deutsche is a person of German descent or one who is willing to become a German and work for the Reich.

"Listen to me, Heinrich. I will give you fifteen percent, but you must promise not to tell Officer Gruber."

"I'm not stupid," I said. The greed got to him.

While we were talking I could hear Helmut, my investigator, calling my name. I was scared. Luckily, Officer Schmidt thought it was Gruber calling me, so we both pretended we did not hear. Shaking hands, I pretended to get up to leave, but then sat down again and said, "Oh! Herr Schmidt, I almost forgot. I need a pass to leave." I gave him the name of Goldstein with the address from where we used to live, Dzika 35. Handing me a pass, Herr Schmidt said, "Don't worry. When they see my name, you won't have any trouble."

Holding the pass in my hand, I began trembling inside. I managed to say, "Auf Wiedersehen" and left his office.

Once in the hallway, I was afraid of meeting my investigator. I didn't dare run, although I wanted to. That would only draw attention to me. I just walked briskly in the hopes that no one would notice me. After leaving the building, I walked as close to it as I could so as not to be seen from a window. When I reached the gate, they took the pass from my shivering hand and opened the gate for me to go through. I saw a streetcar coming. Now I ran and jumped on it. With all my nervousness, I lost my balance and fell and broke my arm. It didn't hurt, though. I was too full of anxiety to even think about my arm.

After passing several stops on the streetcar, I got off and started walking home. Finally, I arrived at 42 Dzielna, Apartment 12. When I rang the bell, a woman opened the door, but the woman was not my mother. "Where is my mother?" I screamed.

"You are Chaim?"

"Yes. Where is my family?"

"We bought everything from your parents and they left for Russia. Brest Litovsk, I think."

When she said Brest Litovsk, I fell down and started crying hysterically. She took me in until I was able to compose myself and decide what to do now. Imagine what I went through. I had been in the same town, Brest Litovsk, and now I would have to make the journey back.

My father's sister, Ita, used to live only ten houses from us. Now with my arm in pain, I decided to go to my aunt. As I walked, I hoped that she hadn't left with my parents. What would I do then? A broken arm, no money, no relatives. Arriving at her home, I was so happy when my aunt opened the door. When she saw me, she got all excited with questions and questions: "Have you seen your parents? What are you doing here?"

I interrupted her. "Aunt Ita, please call a doctor. I'm in pain. My arm is broken."

The doctor came and put my arm in a cast. It was to remain on my arm for six weeks. When I told my aunt how I broke it, she said, "Thank God."

"I should thank God?" I yelled. "Which one? The God that got me into trouble or the God that got me out?"

"Chaim, don't talk like that. Don't ever say that again."

For the first three days I didn't leave the house, but spent most of the time sleeping. When I finally did go out and walked down the street, it looked as though dead people were walking around. People wearing their schande bands on their arms walked about in a daze. German soldiers, with their polished boots and beautiful light green uniforms, patrolled the streets in pairs, smiling and joking.

You didn't have to be on the street too long to see German soldiers loading people's furnishings on trucks and taking families away. They would go into any house and take whatever they wanted. If too many questions were asked, the whole family would be taken away, never to return.

Being only a child, I was horrified as I witnessed one of the most brutal incidents. It happened just around the corner from where we used to live on Smocza Street. A man ran out of his house without a coat into a small grocery, which was in the next building. Since he did not have his coat on, he did not wear his schande band. He was noticed by a

German patrol. One soldier said to the other, "Did you see that Jew without a schande band?"

"No! I didn't," replied the other soldier. "I will teach that Jew what it means to break the law." He then took his carbine from his shoulder and prepared the gun for use. They waited for over five minutes. When the man ran from the store to his house, with one bullet the German soldier put him to the ground.

Then a little boy who must have been his son, fell on top of his body, crying. One more shot was heard and the six- or seven-year-old boy was dead. The "good-hearted" soldier explained to his friend why he shot the boy. He hated to see a child suffer as an orphan. His friend agreed with a smile. No matter what one says about the Germans, one must agree that this was a "humanitarian" act. The only problem with this was, the Germans had too many "humanitarians" among them.

If you were to examine the situation from a German point of view, they "liberated" over ten million Germans who lived in Poland and many millions in Czechoslovakia and other countries. One must agree that it was a "patriotic" deed that the government went to war with the world to liberate all the Germans, no matter where they were. It was not Hitler's fault that the Germans lived all over the world. A government that protects its nationals is a great government. At least, so they thought. The only problem was that the other people objected violently, but one cannot blame the Germans for that. I'm just glad that I was not a German. Had I been, I might have been accused of being a traitor to my people for disagreeing with their official government line.

In the weeks I was in Warsaw, I saw plenty of brutality against the Jews and the Poles, but the incident when the child lying on top of his father was shot, has remained with me and very often is a part of my nightmares.

Bulletins with maps were put up showing where the ghettos were going to be. Most of the people hardly reacted, but it made me very uneasy and nervous. A few days later a new bulletin was posted with an announcement. All Jews from the age of thirteen to sixty, must register and receive a labor card. The registration was to be held at police stations and would be done in alphabetical order. I decided not to register and to leave the city, but Jews were not permitted to use the railroads anymore.

I decided to go to my old neighborhood and look up the few Christian friends I had from my school years. I found one of them, Stasiek. After we embraced and shed a few tears, I asked him to get in touch with my other two friends since I needed their help desperately.

Meeting with everyone, I explained to them about the new ordinance registering the Jews and creating the ghettos. I told them that all I wanted from them was to buy a ticket for me and to accompany me on the train to Siedlce so I might not be noticed. I would walk the rest of the way to Brest Litovsk.

I wouldn't blame them had they refused, since I knew they were frightened. Being caught aiding a Jew would cost you your life and that of your whole family. I didn't know if they were aware of the punishment that they might endure, but this was the German law.

After we sat together for a while and talked, I asked about my Halina, the girl that I had eyes for. I also inquired about other classmates from our schooldays. Before parting, I told them that they could not tell their parents, should they decide to go with me to Siedlce. My fear was that their parents would not allow them, thirteen-year-old boys, to make a sixty-mile trip with me. I did a lot of talking until I finally persuaded them to accompany me.

We planned to meet one week from this day at the same place, the place being Plac Parisowski, a bombed-out building. We were to meet at 9 A.M. Hugging each other and saying good-bye, we each went our own separate ways.

I told Aunt Ita of my plan and asked her to leave with me, along with her two daughters and son-in-law. Instead of listening, they tried to talk me out of leaving as it was so dangerous. They wanted me to stay with them. After hours of arguing, I decided it was useless and I'd just leave on my own without their knowing or saying good-bye.

A day before I was ready to leave, I went to see Uncle Shiye, Father's younger brother. I also tried very hard to convince him to take the family and leave Warsaw. It was of no avail. They only gave me a million and one reasons why they could not leave.

I removed my cast a week ahead of time and made myself ready for my journey back to Brest Litovsk. I left the same day the letter "G" came up for registration. While I walked to meet my friends, I was wondering if they would be there or if it was just a promise. I wouldn't have blamed them if they didn't show up.

Much to my happiness, when I arrived at Plac Parisowski, Zbyszek and Wacek were there. They told me that Stasiek could not make it. I then took off my schande band and we walked to the railroad station. Wacek bought three tickets to Siedlce.

The two-hour wait for the train made me very uneasy and jittery. When we boarded the train, I sat next to the window. My two friends sat next to me so as to broaden the distance between me and the other passengers. Hopefully, they would not recognize me as a Jew. While on the train, we talked very little, but listened to one of the other passengers who was telling stories of German brutality.

Immediately upon reaching Siedlce we walked out of the railroad station. With tears in our eyes, we kissed and wished each other to someday have a country with no Germans and no Fascists. We then parted. They went back to the railroad station, and I began walking. I walked about seven kilometers to my Uncle Velvul's house. He was my Father's oldest brother. He lived in a small village by the name of Broszkow.

My uncle was an Orthodox Jew and dressed like Orthodox Jews did. He had the usual long beard and wore only black clothing. When he saw me, he was in shock. "Chaim, where did you come from? Come in, come in."

My aunt and uncle were alone in the house. Sitting down at the table, I told them where I was going. It was not necessary for me to tell them why. My uncle told me about the mass graves of Jews in the next village, only two miles away. He also told me that he could not leave because his son, Usher, and his daughter, Frieda, were supposed to come home, and then they would try to leave as a family. I couldn't tell him not to wait, but to run, for it might be too late. It's not easy to tell a father to run and save his own life and leave the children behind.

I stayed with my aunt and uncle for two days. My uncle made a small map for me and told me not to go on the main road since it was too dangerous. When I was ready to leave, he introduced me to a farmer who was going in my direction, at least for part of the way. I kissed my aunt and uncle both good-bye and left with the farmer. I did nothing but cry for the next few hours.

The farmer was a plain man without much schooling, but even he knew what was in store for the Jews. He said, "You know, and your uncle knows too, that all the Jews will wind up in a mass grave. So run before the bastards get their hands on you." Then he asked me if I was religious. I was afraid to say no, since I didn't know this man, so I just said, "I don't know what to believe." The farmer answered, "Son, if there is a God, it is now that we need him. Not later. Forgive me for speaking like this, but this damn situation is so serious, it could shatter a stone." He then went on to tell me that he had known my uncle for almost forty years. "He's a man who worked hard all his life and probably, once he's gone, no one will even say a prayer for him."

The time passed quickly. When we reached the point where the farmer was to let me off, I thanked him and said good-bye. He showed me how to continue and informed me that I still had almost a day's walk in front of me. I walked through narrow little paths in the forest for almost two days. I didn't sleep because it was too cold and much too dangerous with the German soldiers always on patrol. My feet were aching, but I had to go on. Once you have had frozen feet, they annoy you very quickly in the cold.

On the second evening, I came close to the place my uncle spoke of. Here I was! There were lights on my left, lights on my right, and lights straight ahead. One of those villages was on the Russian side, but which one? I waited until it got very dark and then started for the village on the left, according to my uncle's instructions. He hadn't mentioned anything about the other villages I saw. I guess he probably had forgotten to tell me.

Setting forth, I finally arrived in the village about two hours later. Now, almost three o'clock in the morning, I still didn't know whether I was on the Russian side or the German side. Walking in snow up to my chest, cold and hungry, I was still afraid to knock at just any door. What if the empty field that I had crossed was not the river Bug, which was the border between Germany and Russia? If I was back on the German side, that would be the end of me.

I found a barn and decided to hide. I slept with the cows and hay full of manure. Sleeping for awhile, I was awakened by someone talking to his horse. I listened, trying to find out what language he spoke, but was unable to understand his mumbling. I got up and walked closer to the gate. He heard me and shouted in Yiddish, "Who is there?" Little did he know how happy I was to hear those Jewish words. "What are you doing here?" he screamed.

"Nothing, Mr. Jew. Nothing. Nothing," I kept saying.

It was barely dusk, so he could hardly see me. When his wife heard the commotion and came out with the kerosene lamp, they were both shocked. "It's a little Jewish boy. Come over here. What are you doing in my barn?"

"Sir, I'm coming from the German side."

"Oh, my God! You stupid kid. Why didn't you tell me? Come inside before the Russian border guards see you." His wife cleaned me up and gave me something to eat. She also told her husband to keep quiet with his many questions until I had finished my breakfast.

"Now son, tell me where you are going."

"My parents are in Brest Litovsk and I am anxious to see them." I hadn't seen my parents since November, 1939, and now it was March, 1940. My parents had no idea where I was because I didn't tell them where I was going when I left home. I also told him briefly of my many travels back and forth across the border in search of my parents. He told me that the following day he was going to Brest Litovsk. I jumped for joy when he offered to take me along. I slept the rest of that day and all through the night without even waking to eat. We departed the next morning right after breakfast.

It took a little over three hours by horse and buggy to arrive in Brest Litovsk. On the way, he asked about the Germans' behavior, and I told him a few stories. He said that I was a smart kid for running away. Arriving in the city market place, he gave me a few rubles and wished me good luck. I thanked him very much and started to walk around.

I walked around for hours looking for a familiar face. From nowhere, right in front of me, appeared an old neighbor from Warsaw, Mr. Rosenbush. He and his family were friends and neighbors of my parents. "Chaim!" he screamed aloud. Everyone turned around to look.

"Mr. Rosenbush, do you know where my parents live?"

"Do I know where your parents live? They are our next door neighbors. We came from Warsaw together. Let's go home. Your parents are worried to death about you."

5

REUNION AND
RESETTLEMENT

Mr. Rosenbush and I walked for about a mile. When we came before the door, he told me to go in by myself and surprise them. The house my parents lived in was located in a beautiful garden. It looked like a villa with a big yard. All the greenery was covered with snow. You could see that before the war, it was once a rich man's home.

I walked over to the door, knocked twice, and Mother opened the door. She burst into tears and so did I. After hugging and kissing her, I said, "Mother, all I want right now is a bath and some rest." I was full of lice and filth.

My sister, Sally, was in school. My father and oldest brother, Abraham, came home later. Father was full of joy and happiness seeing me there. He asked me about my brother Shlomo. I gave Father the address where Shlomo and I lived in Russia, and later that evening he sat down to write him a letter.

The Rosenbushes visited that evening, and I extended regards from their parents and sister who were left behind in Warsaw. Their parents were glad that at least the daughter and her husband were safe on the Russian side.

Mr. and Mrs. Rosenbush visited our home almost every evening. They discussed the political situation and also tried to convince my parents to return to Warsaw. I was outraged with such discussion, since I had just come from Warsaw and knew what was going on there. When I took part in the discussion and tried to tell them of my experiences and the things I had seen, I was accused by Mrs. Rosenbush of making up those stories. Her logic was that I liked Russian songs and was trying to discourage my parents from returning since I wanted to stay on the Russian side. She also said that all children make up fantastic stories.

Since it was still winter in Brest Litovsk, my father, brother, and I went out to get firewood. It was one of the necessities of life that you could not buy. We took down fences, steps, and anything else we could get our hands on. One evening we dismantled the wooden steps to a second floor apartment and then later wondered how the people would get down from there in the morning.

We were considered Polish refugees by the Soviet government. Spring was coming and with it came a Russian offensive. They sent out politruks, political educators and agitators with the purpose of informing the people as to the reasons of the new moves of the Soviet government.

A young politruk came to our house more than once to explain to us in detail what the alternatives were. We had one of two choices. We could accept Soviet passports and move at least a hundred kilometers from the border or we could return to Poland although it was occupied by the Germans. An agreement was made between the Soviet government and the German government to establish a commission allowing people to go to either side because families had been separated due to the war.

The politruk's purpose in coming was to convince us to stay in the Soviet Union. He tried to impress on us that should we decide to return to German-occupied Poland, Hitler would put us all in concentration camps. It was very hard for him to understand how Jews could choose Hitler's Germany over the Soviet Union. He repeatedly asked my mother if she would want to lose her children to concentration camps. My mother's reply was, "No! Of course not, but you must talk to my husband." "Talk to my husband," she kept repeating, as if she had no voice in the decision.

The politruk explained that Hitler was no friend of the Soviet people, and the reason for signing the agreement with Hitler and Germany was only to delay the war between the two nations. Before leaving, the politruk told us that he would not return again and that he hoped we would make the right decision. My guess is that twenty to twenty-five percent of all the refugees chose to take Soviet passports and move away from the border. Mr. and Mrs. Rosenbush won over me, in spite of all my efforts and explanations of what was happening on the German side. Father chose to register to return to German-occupied Poland.

At the end of March or the beginning of April the German missionaries arrived in Brest Litovsk. All the refugees were very excited as if something good had just happened. Notices of the commission were placed all over the city, stating when the registration for the return to Poland would start. It also informed us that a German officer would come and talk to the people in front of the mission the night before registration. He would explain to refugees the conditions under which they could return.

My father, Mr. and Mrs. Rosenbush, and I went to listen to the officer's speech. It was about eight o'clock at night when a German officer came out and stood on top of a table with a microphone. When he saw over ten thousand people before him, he couldn't believe his eyes. His first words were, "Hitler's Germany does not like Jews. All those who want to return will go directly to concentration camps. Do you still want to go?" The whole crowd, with one voice answered, "Yes! Yes, my Herr. Yes!"

When I heard that answer, I cried. I just couldn't understand what happened to those people. Did their brain cease to function or were they in a state of unconsciousness? Today, I am still dumbfounded over their choice of Germany under Hitler.

Of course, Mrs. Rosenbush came up with an explanation as to what was really happening. She said, "It's just a scare tactic to keep us all from leaving the Russian side. If it were true that we Jews were going to be sent to concentration camps, he never would have told us." It certainly is amazing how smart some people are. They think they know all the answers.

Most of the people stood there all night just so they would be the first to register, although they were given two weeks time in which to do so. My parents along with the Rosenbushes, registered within the week. Upon entering the building, you had to register with the Germans, and before leaving, you had to register with the Russian officials. We did not know their reason for doing this. My parents and the Rosenbushes were accepted by the Germans for return to Germany.

My brother, Shlomo, returned to Brest Litovsk just about the same time my parents were preparing to return to Germany. Despite all that was going on, we were all very happy to see him. I was especially glad because I knew that he would side with me. My oldest brother, Abraham, remained quiet as if the decision Father made would not effect him.

I told Shlomo of some of my experiences on the German side, but I didn't have to convince him of the situation there since he had experienced plenty on his way from Warsaw to Brest Litovsk in October of 1939. When I told Shlomo what the officer at the mission said about all Jews going directly to concentration camps and Mrs. Rosenbush's interpretation, he went wild. As a child of thirteen, I could not speak up to Mrs. Rosenbush, as Father would not stand for children speaking back to grownups, but Shlomo was an adult. He confronted Mrs. Rosenbush and told her off for speaking so stupidly. In his rage, he passed a remark which hurt her very badly. He said that she didn't have any children and that we had more to lose than her. This upset Mrs. Rosenbush because she had always wanted a child, but was unable to conceive.

Shlomo also accused Mrs. Rosenbush of presenting a forged letter to our Parents that stated life in Poland was normal and good. Mrs. Rosenbush left our house in tears. She never expected that my brother would be so rough on her. Shlomo then turned to my father and told him, "If you insist on going back to German-occupied Poland, Chaim and I will not go." Nothing could make us change our mind. Naturally, Mother started to cry. She said to Father, "Maybe the children are right. Perhaps the German officer was telling the truth." My brother won. We did not leave for Poland on the date assigned to us by the German mission. And neither did the Rosenbushes.

The Soviet government started to take action, first against single persons, mostly all the single men. They rounded them up one by one and sent them to various labor camps. Most NKVD commandants did this work at night so as not to alert the population as to what was really happening.

It didn't take too long for us to find out what our destiny was. One morning, about 3 A.M.., there was a knock at the door. When Father asked, "Who is it?" the answer came, "This is the NKVD. Open up." When Father opened the door, an officer and four soldiers stepped in.

"Are you the family Goldberg? Are there six in your family, four children, a mother and a father?"

"Yes, comrade." Our reply instigated a fury in the officer.

He said, "I'm not your comrade. Jews who want to return to Hitler's Germany have no comrades."

At that moment, Mother said something to Father in Yiddish. Whatever Mother said, it irritated the officer even more. The officer was Jewish so he understood Mother. Raising his voice, he told us not to say anymore. The officer said that he was ashamed of us, Jews who wanted to return to Hitler's Germany. He said that if he had the power, he'd do away with us. He told us that we had one hour to dress and that we could only take some soft things with us.

In a calm voice, Father asked the officer if he would allow us to take along our sewing machine, as this was not one of the items he told us we could take. Father asked him over and over again; but the officer, being very arrogant, told us that we were fortunate that he was allowing us to take our clothing. When our possessions were loaded on the truck, we found Mr. and Mrs. Rosenbush waiting for us. Since they were a family of only two, it took them less time to collect their belongings.

While riding in the truck to the railroad station, Mrs. Rosenbush began taking her anxiety out on me because she knew that I couldn't answer her back. She wouldn't dare start up with my brother again. This was the worst fifteen minutes I had experienced since my return from the German side. Mrs. Rosenbush didn't shut up until we arrived at the railroad station. We were all taken to the freight part of the station so we wouldn't be seen by the other passengers travelling from the main terminal.

After an hour or so, the sun started to rise and we could see thousands and thousands of people gathered together with military guards all around us. When Father and I observed other families with bicycles and beds and sewing machines and anything else that they could carry, we were very much upset because our Jewish officer had restricted us to only soft items.

Father was very concerned about having to leave the sewing machine behind, since it might be our only means of survival. We felt that we were destined to go to Siberia. With our sewing machine, we could exchange clothing for food. Father spoke to my older brothers in hopes that one of them would go and retrieve the sewing machine. It would be a great asset to us. But under no conditions would they go and risk being shot. Father turned to me, the youngest, and said, "Chaim, would you go? You are my only hope." I had no fear of the Russian soldiers, so I told my father that I would do it. Father reached into his pocket and gave me some money.

Before leaving, I went over and spoke to one of the soldiers, inquiring as to how much time we had before everyone was to board the train. He told me that we could expect to wait at least another two hours. As I started to run, a Russian soldier fired a warning shot. Ignoring it, I went on my way without fear or hesitation. I knew what had to be done and I did it. I always did what I felt was right, no matter how old I was. Just recall the five-year-old boy fighting for a whistle.

After running for a while, I came upon a man with a horse and buggy. I offered him payment to help me get home so that I could get the sewing machine and then to bring me back to the railroad station again. He knew of the NKVD operation. He told me that his neighbor had been taken away in the middle of the night, too, and he hastened to help me.

After picking up the sewing machine, I made a quick stop at my girlfriend Bella's house. When I rang the bell, it was about 7 A.M. Mr. Scheinblum opened the door and asked, "What are you doing here so early in the morning? Don't tell me you have a date." I said, "No, sir. I came to say good-bye." I explained to him what had happened to us. He tried to talk me into staying with them, but I couldn't. I explained to Mr.

Scheinblum, "If I would stay behind, Mrs. Rosenbush would harass my family to no end. She would say that I stayed behind to remain a free man while sending them all to Siberia, since I was partially instrumental in their decision not to return to Hitler." I kissed Bella good-bye, said good-bye to her parents, and left.

When I returned to the railroad station, more than half of the people had left, including my family and Mr. and Mrs. Rosenbush. I immediately went to see the head of the NKVD. I told him that I had received permission to go and get the sewing machine, and that my family was to remain here for another two hours, but now they were gone. With a smile on his face, he answered me, "Don't worry son. You are all going to the same place."

"Siberia?" I asked.

He said, "You'll find out when you get there." I had no choice, but to sit and wait until I was put on the next train. Hopefully, I would meet my parents at my final destination.

Well, here I was, all alone with the clothes on my back, a few rubles in my pocket, and a sewing machine. I found a family that had a girl approximately the same age as me. I made friends with her so that I wouldn't be alone, and I would have a family to travel with. I was also able to take advantage of the mother's good nature, as she volunteered to do my wash.

After waiting for almost an hour, we were boarded onto the train. The train we were travelling on was used as a cattle car, not a passenger car. We had to use the Russian meadows and fields as relief stations. Stops were not made at the regular railroad stations in order to avoid our being noticed by the Russian population, but were made a few miles before or after the city. You have to imagine: men, women, and children relieving themselves, without embarrassment, one next to the other, surrounded by armed guards.

We received food once in the morning and once in the evening. In the mornings we were given bread and cheese and hot water, and in the evenings we sometimes ate bacon or ham, bread, and drank hot water.

We traveled for almost three to four weeks until we arrived at a city called Kotlas. The city lies on the river Northern Dvina, in the Republic of Komi ASSR (Komi Autonomous Soviet Socialist Republic). In Kotlas, we were put on a large boat and were taken to the capital city of Syktyvkar which lies on the river, Vychegda. We were put ashore a few miles before the city. Hundreds of families were left here on the empty fields, surrounded by beautiful tall trees. It was already June, of 1940, so we were able to sleep in the fields with just a blanket to cover ourselves.

There was a huge building within walking distance. It was the resettlement headquarters, run by the NKVD. I went into the headquarters to inquire as to the whereabouts of my parents. I was told that I had to go to a settlement and work through the commandant there, a member of the NKVD.

Every day families were dispersed to settlements. They were loaded onto trucks and then they disappeared into the thick forest. I stalled for time, hoping that once the exiles were gone, I could find out where my parents had been taken. I didn't want to go to the settlement and work through the commandant there because I felt more at ease and more confident working directly with the headquarters.

New ships arrived every day from Kotlas to Syktifka, and along with them came new people—some local and some displaced. On the fourth day when the ship arrived, three women with blankets wrapped around them came off the boat. They sat down within twenty-five feet of where I was sitting with my new family. After about an hour of listening to the three women speak, I heard one of the women mention a son that she called Chaim. I went closer to get a better look at these three women. I didn't recognize any of them, figured that "Chaim" was a common Jewish name, and that none of them was referring to me.

Anyway, I stayed close, continuing to listen to their conversation as if I had a feeling that one of the women knew me. After a few moments, one of the women mentioned my name again and the incident of her son going to get the sewing machine. At that moment I felt as though an electrical shock penetrated my body. I screamed, "Momma!" Mother looked around. When she saw me, she fainted. I still didn't recognize her as my mother, but I knew she was. After I revived Mother with water and calmed her down, her first question was, "Chaim, do you have the sewing machine?" I had to laugh. Then tears filled my eyes. I pointed a finger to show Mother that the sewing machine was standing only a few feet away.

Mother is five feet, two inches tall, and when I left her she weighed about one-hundred-twenty pounds. Now before me stood a woman weighing only seventy to seventy-five pounds, holding a blanket and having only the dress she wore. Under no conditions could I have recognized this woman as my mother if she hadn't mentioned the incident with the sewing machine in Brest Litovsk.

While travelling on the train for more than two weeks, Mother had decided to eat a piece of ham. The next day she became very ill with dysentery. Arriving in Kotlas, Mother was immediately taken to the hospital by ambulance, carried in the blanket she still had with her. Father was permitted to go with Mother to the hospital, but was not allowed to stay. He was told that once she was well, she would be sent to rejoin the family. Father was then taken back to the ship to be with the rest of the family.

I recalled a trick Father once played on Mother. Father thought that Mother imagined that pork would make her sick, so one day, he purchased pork chops and told Mother that they were veal chops. Once prepared by the maid, Mother ate them. That night, Mother became very ill and was up the whole night with diarrhea. She was unable to work for almost a week. To this day, I don't think that Father ever told her what he had done.

Mother, who had been sent from the hospital in Kotlas to the headquarters of the resettlement in Syktyvkar, was now here. I ran immediately to the office and told them that I had found my mother and that she was promised to be reunited with my father upon her release from the hospital. Now I could accompany my mother instead of being sent to a settlement. The officer's answer was still the same, "You'll both have to go to a settlement. Then you can continue your search for the rest of your family from there."

The next morning about fifty families were loaded onto three trucks. Within ten minutes we disappeared into a thick jungle. We stopped twice to tend to our bodily functions and to nibble on the sardine sandwiches they had given us, which were to hold us until we reached our destination. We traveled on a one-lane path made of dirt and rock, just wide enough for these trucks. Though we only traveled about one-hundred-fifty miles, it took us over eight hours, due to the horrible road conditions. This was the first time since we had left Brest Litovsk that we did not have any armed guards watching over us. However, it would have been too difficult to escape into such terrain.

We arrived in a settlement called Dolgays, meaning "long one." A commandant in an NKVD uniform received a list from the truck drivers with everyone's name on it. He called everyone's name out so as to be sure that we were all there, since we were his responsibility now. He introduced himself by telling us his first name only, Konstantine. We were to address him as Commandant Konstantine and not Tovarish (meaning comrade).

Mother and I were taken into a large barracks that was to house all those who had just arrived. Each family was given a section partitioned off by plywood halfway to the ceiling. There weren't any doors. Mother and I and the sewing machine received one of these sections. Straw mattresses lay on the floor for us to sleep on.

I immediately went to Commandant Konstantine and explained to him, that since we were separated from the rest of the family, we didn't have any household items. We only had the one blanket that Mother had been carrying. We needed pillows, clothing, and anything else that he could assist us with. He listened very compassionately and went to fetch whatever he could. He gave us two pillows, one sheet, and another blanket. I think he got them from his own possessions. For a man that first impressed us as being rough and tough, he certainly was very good to us! He even told me that once our papers arrived, although it might take anywhere from one to two months, he'd help Mother and me locate the rest of the family.

The settlement consisted of about thirty or more houses made from logs, similar to a log cabin. Volga Germans lived in these wooden abodes. For generations, these people had lived on the Volga River in the southern part of Russia. In the mid-30s, Stalin sent these people into exile in Komi ASSR to live out their lives. The only ones that would be allowed to leave were the children, when they reached their sixteenth birthday. Under Soviet law, you were considered an adult at the age of sixteen, and children were not responsible for the deeds of their parents.

The commandant was not a Russian but a native Komi. Except for the commandant, all the other natives lived in villages away from the exiled. They spoke their own language called Zyranski.

The settlement was located in the middle of the tundra. A country-style store in the settlement was run by a Komi. We could purchase clothing, food, and almost everything necessary to live. Naturally, you needed money, of which we had none. All men and women above the age of sixteen had to go to work. But the only work available was lumberjacking. Children between the ages of seven and sixteen were driven by horse and buggy to school, about two miles from the settlement. I didn't attend school since I had to find a way to earn some money to keep Mother and me going until we rejoined the family.

The commandant, noticing that I had stayed behind, came to look for me. When he came into the barracks and questioned me as to why I did not go with the other children, I told him to look at my mother and to tell me if I could leave her here all alone in her frail and weakened condition. How could I sit in school and learn? He then reached into his pocket and gave me twenty rubles, which would supply us with enough food for a week. He told me that he was giving me this money so that I could go to school. I promised him that I would. I hugged him around his waist and called him "Diadia Koscia," meaning Uncle Koscia. Koscia was short for Konstantine. The next morning I attended class with the other children.

To ensure that the twenty rubles would last longer than a week, I visited Uncle Koscia's garden every night and helped myself to his potatoes. I'm positive that he knew that I was the one taking his potatoes, but he never said a word. When he saw the potatoes cooking in the pot, he just smiled and went on his way.

I noticed that the storekeeper spoke very little Russian and was having trouble communicating with the Jewish exiles, since they didn't speak too much Russian either. I confronted the commandant and told him that I could be a big help to the storekeeper if he'd allow me to work there. I could speak German, Russian, Polish, and Yiddish. All I wanted in return would be some food. Then too, I wouldn't need his potatoes anymore. The commandant burst into laughter. He took me by the hand as if I was his own son, and we went to the storekeeper. The commandant knew that legally a thirteen-year-old could not be hired. He spoke to the storekeeper in his native tongue for about five minutes, a language that I did not understand; after some hesitation and complaints, the storekeeper agreed to allow me to work there in exchange for food.

Every day after school, I'd go to the store to clean and sweep and help those who spoke Yiddish get the supplies they needed. After I had worked there for only one week, Mother gained ten pounds. I felt it was very important for me to learn the native language, Komi Zyranie. The storekeeper helped me a lot. It was just as important for him as it was for me that I learn the language so we could communicate more freely. Within four weeks I had conquered the language and could communicate quite easily with the storekeeper. Not only did I learn the language, but spoke it without any accent. Little did I know how easy it was for me to pick up a new language with little effort. The commandant was thrilled. He agreed to speak only Komi to me in order to help me improve my vocabulary. He said, "Son, you are a smart kid. You will never get lost in this world." I said, "Thank you, Diadia Koscia."

After being there for almost six weeks, I started to put pressure on the commandant to locate the rest of the family. All he could do was apologize, since he was in touch with the headquarters in Syktyvkar, but they kept telling him to wait. Once he even made the call to the headquarters in front of me so that I could listen and hear their reply for myself: "There are many people that need help. You'll just have to wait a little longer." Though I was anxious to see the rest of the family, I wasn't worried anymore. Mother had gained twenty-five pounds and was looking well. I hope the commandant was as nice to the other people as he was to me.

Another week had passed when one day a native man came over to me and handed me a piece of paper. The note said, "I am in the village of Krasovy." An address was written there which I cannot recall now. It went on to say that I should come to see him. It was signed Father—Leo Goldberg.

That night I walked seven miles to the village Krasovy and met Father. Well, you have to imagine for yourself, the happy reunion. With my crying voice, I asked Father, "How did you know we were here? How did you get here?" He told me the story as to how he came to learn of our whereabouts.

Father had asked the commandant in charge of his settlement for a pass to travel, since exiles could not travel without one. He wanted the pass to go to the hospital in Kotlas to see Mother. The commandant refused and told him, "If your wife is alive, she will be sent here, and if she passed away in the hospital, there is no use going." Father argued and argued, but the commandant just wouldn't listen. He was not a Diadia Koscia.

Father decided to go to the hospital anyway, without a pass. He left the settlement during the middle of the night after the commandant took the headcount. This was done nightly to make sure that no one had run away. Upon Father's arrival at the Kotlas hospital, he was told by the head physician that Mother was well and that she was sent to Syktyvkar. Father left Kotlas and headed for Syktyvkar.

Entering Syktyvkar at night after the headquarters had closed, Father learned that his oldest sister and brother-in-law were there. He was very happy that he would have a place to spend the night. Much to his surprise, they turned him away since he could be arrested as a fugitive, and they could be implicated for harboring him. Though Father's brother-in-law tried to convince his wife to let him stay, she, Father's sister, wouldn't hear of it. She insisted that he leave. If someone had cut off his arm, Father wouldn't have felt as much pain as he did then. Father was forced to seek refuge at home of a native, a stranger.

In the morning, Father went straight to the resettlement headquarters. While waiting to see someone in charge, he spoke about Mother and not knowing where she was. Fortunately, a woman from our settlement was there to be reunited with her family. This woman told Father that there was a woman at her settlement fitting his wife's description, but this woman was not alone. The woman had a son with her and a sewing machine. Father shouted with joy. "That's my son! That's my son!"

Feeling a bit relieved, Father did not wait to see anyone from the headquarters, but went outside to find a truck going in the direction of Krasovy, a village close to our settlement. There were no passenger buses here. Upon finding a truck headed that way, Father had to bribe the driver, since he didn't have a pass. The commandant from Father's settlement had notified the authorities and a warrant was out for his arrest.

After Father finished his story, I took the address where he was staying with the rest of the family, and I went back to my settlement. When I arrived, the commandant was sitting in our partitioned-off space, waiting for me. He asked if I had been to see my father; he had been notified from headquarters to look for my father and arrest him. I told the commandant, "Yes, I had."

He then asked, "Where is he now?"

I replied, "You really don't expect me to tell you."

"Knowing you, no, but I must perform my duty and ask." I did tell him, though, that Father was on his way back to the settlement and that I had his address. I gave it to the commandant. When he left, only then did Mother know that I had been to see Father. Her excitement was indescribable. I told her that Father was in danger of being arrested, but knowing Father, she needn't worry.

Luckily, Father met the same truck driver that had taken him to Krasovy and now left with him to return to Syktyvkar. Arriving there, he went directly to the headquarters to speak to the head of the NKVD. Father told him the whole story and gave him our address in the settlement Dolgays. The head of the NKVD shouted at Father so loud that it could be heard on the moon. He also threatened him with a three-year jail sentence. Father stood before him in silence and hoped for mercy, as all he had done was to search for his sick wife. Then it was as if an angel came down and put some sense in the chief's head. He gave Father a transit pass to go home. It was a miracle in Father's eyes that he was let off so easily.

Leaving Syktyvkar, Father traveled back to his settlement by boat. The first greeting he received in Ustiu Sopiu (this is the name of father's settlement) was from his commandant, "Mekie." Father showed him the transit pass he had gotten at headquarters, but it didn't matter to Commandant Mekie. He was still outraged at Father's disappearance. He screamed that Father was lucky that he had this pass, otherwise he would toss him in jail and throw away the key.

Mother and I were happy that we now knew where the rest of the family was and that our commandant was preparing the papers for our departure. At the same time, though, we worried about Father's ability to get back to his settlement without getting caught along the way. It took Commandant Konstantine eight days to get our travel passes and to prepare all the other papers we needed. Our destination was settlement Ustiu Sopiu.

The day of our leaving, Commandant Konstantine bid us farewell and told me that he was going to miss me, since he had gotten so used to having me around. I gave him a great big hug, thanked him for everything, and told him that I wouldn't return for any more potatoes. With tears in my eyes, I boarded the buggy, and Mother and I went on our way.

6
COMMANDANT MEKIE

We traveled to the village Krasovy, where we were placed on a truck and taken to Syktyvkar, the resettlement headquarters. Here I turned in our travel papers and in return was given tickets to board a boat to continue our journey.

We stayed overnight at the headquarters, as we had arrived there late in the afternoon and no boats were leaving then. The next morning Mother and I and the sewing machine were escorted to the boat. We traveled for a whole day, arriving the following morning in a small town named Kam. We only had fifty more kilometers to go to end our journey.

In Kam we were met by an NKVD officer who loaded us on a truck and told us that we were going to a village called Uran. It was located just across the river from Father's settlement. The river Vychegda separated the native Komis from the exiles. In a little over two hours, we reached Uran. Here, we had to walk a quarter of a mile to the bank of the river. Reaching the bank, we found an old man there sitting near a fire, baking potatoes. This man was a government employee. He helped Mother and me into a small boat and rowed us across the river. Once on the opposite bank, we had to walk less than a quarter of a mile to the settlement. With Mother by my side and the sewing machine on my shoulder, we set forth.

Everyone knew who we were the moment we entered the settlement, due to the commotion caused by the commandant when Father had returned. Everyone was excited to see us. Some ran to hug and kiss us while others ran to locate Father. They found him at work in the forest. Hearing the good news, Father immediately left work, along with my two brothers. The joy of the family being reunited again, along with the sewing machine, was so great! It's beyond description. Even Commandant Mekie came to greet us. Meeting him, I knew he was not a Diadia Koscia, and my first impression of him was correct.

This settlement differed from the one we had just left in the way that it did not have any Germans housed here. The only people living here were Polish Jews. It was smaller in size too, but was located in the tundra as the settlement Dolgays was.

The log cabin we lived in had three rooms and was partitioned off with plywood, halfway to the ceiling. A family of five people, Lehrer, shared the cabin with us. They occupied one room, we the other, and both families shared the kitchen. Naturally, there was no privacy. We could hear their disagreements, and they could hear ours.

The morning after our arrival, Mother and I awoke to the commandant wanting to speak to us. He informed Mother that she would have to go to work. I said, "Absolutely, no! My father and brothers are working and that is enough." He then turned to me and said, "You can rest until the end of the week, but then you too shall go to work."

After he left, I said to Mother, "You see, I told you he's no Diadia Koscia. He gave me twenty rubles just so I would attend school and not have to work. Now, Commandant Mekie is trying to make me do just the opposite by forcing me to go to work."

After several days of observation, I noticed that children up to the age of twelve, including my sister Sally, were going to school across the river in the village of Uran. I knew I had a battle on my hands, but I was determined to fight. I received no encouragement from anyone, including my parents. Everyone told me not to start trouble with the NKVD, but I was strong-headed and knew I was right; I decided not to give in under any circumstances. If I could fight for a one cent sugar whistle when I was five years old, then I surely could fight, at the age of thirteen for what was legally my right to be able to go to school.

When Monday arrived, the commandant came to our house to send me off to work. I blew my top. I screamed at him, called him a stupid son-of-a-bitch, and told him of his ignorance of the law of the land. I threatened to have him put in jail for breaking the law. He wasn't going to get away with this, especially with me around. I screamed, "All children up to the age of sixteen must attend school, and you, Commandant, cannot change the law." He pulled a gun on me. I knocked it from his hand and told him that he could not shoot me since I was a minor. Mother was crying and begged me not to fight with him. She was afraid that he might just shoot me. He left the house, but before doing so, said that he would return the following morning and I would then be forced to go to work. Realizing that this was not going to be an easy fight, I decided to write a letter to the DA's office.

That evening Father and my two brothers came home, Mother told them what had happened. Of course, Father tried to convince me to give up the fight. I told Father that I had stood my ground against eight hundred Christian children back home in Warsaw, and here, one on one, I was not about to give up. I also told Father that I had already written a letter to the DA. With a smile on his face, Father said, "It will never get past the commandant. All letters in or out of the settlement must go through the commandant's hands." At this point, I explained to Father that I spoke Komi fluently and that I would not need the services of our beloved commandant. I would give it to a native who would mail it from the village.

Tuesday morning I left the house before the commandant arrived and went into the forest. Mother couldn't speak Russian too well, so she could only tell him that I had gone. The commandant probably assumed that I went to work and left the house feeling that he had won the battle. Little did he know.

In the forest brigades, Komi and Polish Jews worked side by side but kept in their own groups. I picked out one of the Komi workers who looked friendly, went over to him, and started speaking his native tongue. He looked at me in astonishment and stood there speechless.

Finally, he asked, "Who are you kid?"

"I am a Komi born in Poland. My parents spoke Komi at home and so I learned it." I don't think that he would have believed me had I told him the truth; I had learned the language in only two months. I don't even think that my own Father believed me.

"What do you want, son?"

"I have a letter to the DA's office which I want mailed from outside the settlement." When he questioned me as to why I wanted this letter mailed to the DA, I told him that we'd like to establish our identity as Komi so that we could leave the settlement. He hesitated for a few minutes, but I assured him that no one would ever know that he mailed the letter. It was our secret. After thinking for a few moments, he agreed and took the letter. I thanked him and left.

I managed to avoid the commandant for several days; but when he checked with the leaders of the Jewish brigade, he discovered that I was not working anywhere. He decided to come to the house after working hours, instead of his usual morning visits, to catch me at home. Friday evening he barged in while we were eating supper. Without waiting for us to finish our meal, he asked me, "Where are you going every morning? I know that you are not going to work, and I know that you are avoiding me. Just how long do you think that you can keep this up?"

I answered, "Commandant Mekie, I never promised you that I would go to work. Besides, I've mailed a letter to the DA's office, and I want to wait until he comes before I do anything." Hearing this, he went wild. "How did you mail that letter?"

I said, "You don't really want to know."

Naturally, he said, "Of course I do."

"But I'm not about to tell you."

After much screaming and yelling, he pulled out his gun, and again threatened to kill me. "I won't let you grow up. I'll kill you. You are a troublemaker. You violated the law and you are under arrest."

I said, "Kiss my ass, you ignorant bastard."

The commandant was shaking with rage and that scared my father, for he felt that the commandant might just shoot me. Father stepped in between us and told the commandant that I would go with him. Not wanting to contradict my father, I went with him. He put me in jail.

The jail was a log cabin with bars on the windows set away from the settlement. Knowing that the commandant took a headcount every night after 11 P.M., I waited until midnight and then raised up the roof, climbed out, and went home to bed. I told Father not to worry, since there wasn't too much that the commandant could do. I was a minor, and the commandant could not bring charges against me. I waited earnestly for the DA's arrival.

The DA arrived about eight days after the letter was mailed. The commandant, being aware of his arrival, did not put me in jail that day. When the DA came, I was called into the office by the commandant. While I sat in the waiting room, I could hear the commandant and the DA discussing my case, since the door was ajar. They weren't afraid of someone overhearing them because they spoke Komi, which no one in the settlement knew except me.

The DA's first question to the commandant was, "How did he get the letter out without it going through you?" The commandant, having no idea, was reprimanded for not being able to oversee eighty people. The DA explained that if I was able to send a letter to him, then I could also get a letter through to Moscow and that would put both of them in an awkward position. He also went on to say that I was right and that the commandant should allow me to go to school.

The commandant said, "All the children here go to work and they don't complain. Why does he have to be different?"

The DA replied, "He knows the law. The others don't. That's the difference." The commandant agreed to let me go to school. He asked the DA for his support. Now, ready to see me, the commandant called me into his office.

The DA's first question was, "Young man, tell me, what do you really want?" I told him that I wanted all the children in the settlement up to the age of sixteen to be allowed to go to school. Nothing else. The DA got a little annoyed with me speaking out for all the other children, since the Soviet government does not like one speaking for a group as if we were organized. It didn't matter that we were only children.

The DA said that he would see to it that I could attend school, but the remainder of the children would have to speak for themselves. I explained to him that there were only five girls who were of age to attend school and that I would not go by myself. I insisted that they go with me.

The commandant began screaming and yelling at me. "You are in exile. You have no rights. You are lucky that the DA is allowing you to go to school. If this isn't satisfactory, then you can go to work like all the others."

I turned to the DA and in a calm voice said, "Would you explain to this imbecile."

"Please, no name calling," interrupted the DA.

"Would you please explain to the commandant that I am not in exile, my parents are. The only reason I'm here is because I want to be with my parents. The law of this land is plain and specific. Children are not responsible for the deeds of their parents. I want the commandant to remember that and not call me an exile."

The commandant said in a loud voice that he could put me in jail for ten years for mailing that letter without going through the proper channels. Meaning, without him seeing it first. I ignored his remark and continued speaking to the DA. I informed him of his duty as a law enforcement officer to carry out the law of the land, even though the commandant might be his friend and probably was. I assured the DA that if I didn't get any satisfaction from him, I would go above his head. That roused him a little. He said, "Are you threatening me, too?"

I said, "No! I'm just informing you of my rights. I will not give up."

After arguing back and forth for another half-hour, I stood up and spoke their native language. I told them that I had heard their whole conversation while waiting to be called in and that it was no use pretending to protect the commandant now. Of course, they both turned white. They didn't expect me to know their language since I was in Komi for only a few months. The DA stood up and told the commandant to send all the children to school and to forget about the whole incident. I felt victorious for having won, just as I had felt when I received my penny whistle from the six-foot, four-inch bully storekeeper.

I couldn't wait for Father and the girls to return from work so I could tell them of my victory. Father just couldn't believe it. He was relieved that it was all over, because he feared something bad would happen to me, as the commandant threatened me nightly. When I told the girls that they'd be attending school Monday morning instead of work, they were so excited. They prepared their clothes over the weekend and set out for junior high school, bright and early Monday morning. The whole settlement came out to see us off except for the commandant, who hid himself in embarrassment.

7

LIFE IN THE SETTLEMENT

Crossing the river in a boat, a horse and buggy awaited us on the opposite bank. It was to take us to the town of Kam, which was about ten kilometers from our settlement. There we were met by the principal who showed us to our quarters, one large room with six beds. A sheet hung around my bed to separate me from the five girls. Our food was provided by the collective farm, free of charge. School was from 8 A.M. to 4 P.M., Monday through Friday, and 8 A.M. to noon on Saturdays. At two o'clock on Saturday afternoon, a horse and buggy would come and pick us up and bring us back to the settlement. Since we were given so much food at the school, we'd save some of it and take it back with us to our families. The girls had difficulty making friends with the native children at the school, but I, speaking their language quite well, blended in with no problems. Their friendship helped me master the Komi language even more.

When I came home on weekends, my brother and I would go to the village across the river to buy food from the natives. The village was very small, and the store did not carry too much of anything. To my surprise, the storekeeper only opened the door to people who spoke the Komi language. Having taken the time and initiative to learn this language turned out to be a great asset. The biggest surprise of all was when the storekeeper wouldn't take any money from me because I was a kid and he felt sorry for me. I was able to get supplies such as butter, eggs, potatoes, onions, and fish. Fish was the main food, as it was plentiful. The rivers and streams offered them abundantly.

The village people called most of us Polakias, which means Polish. The word Jew was unknown to them since most Jews were concentrated in large cities, not in a settlement next to the Arctic Circle.

I had a problem with my own people when they found out that I could go into the village and get food. They all wanted to go with me so they could get into the store. Every time I went, I used to take a few people with me, and sometimes I would make extra trips in order to take others. The only people who did not ask for my help were Mr. and Mrs. Rosenbush.

At least there was one thing Mr. Rosenbush could be thankful for from living in Komi, his improved health. His ulcer cleared up within six or seven months, and he could have eaten rocks. The climate was fantastic, the air was pure, the pine trees were beautiful, and the cold was conducive to activity and motion.

When summer came and school was out, I decided to get a job. I wanted to help my family since there would be no more food to bring home from school during the summer recess. I went to the commandant and told him I needed work. He was surprised, but gave me a job, to tie pieces of cut lumber together and take them by horse to the edge of the river. When the river rose later in October, the lumber would float away to be collected elsewhere.

This was my first experience with a horse except for the time when I slept in a barn in manure. I took the horse from the stable and rode him about a mile down the road. On the way to the forest for the load of lumber, the horse stopped. First I tried to the cajole him. The horse just looked at me. Then I hit him and nothing happened. I kicked him. Nothing. I hit him. Nothing. I was in such a state that I sat down, and tears began rolling down my face. Just then, a native came by. Noticing me sitting there crying, with the horse standing by, he asked me what was wrong. I pointed to the horse and said, "It's the commandant's fault. He gave me a dead horse. He gave me a dead horse!"

The man said nothing to me, but grabbing the reins, spoke sharply to the horse. Sure enough, the horse took off. "You must speak to animals with authority, kid. Speak like you're the boss." I quit crying and I quit blaming the commandant for the horse's behavior. He had not really given me a dead horse, but he had let me learn a lesson: speak with authority to get action. I had no more trouble with the horse and worked at the job of hauling lumber all summer.

Living near the Arctic Circle, in time we got used to the "white nights." They were called white nights because there wasn't any darkness for approximately three or more months. You could see the sun set on one side of the sky, and at the same time, you could see it rise again on the other side. A bell rang through the forest when it was time to go home from work. Even the horse knew then that it was time to go back to the stable; nothing could stop him. I learned fast not to have a load of lumber on him at quitting time.

At home during the white nights, we put sheets or blankets over the windows to keep out the light so we could sleep. For about another three months of the year, however, the sun never rose. A duskiness covered the sky for three or four hours during the day. Then the sky began to get darker and darker. At night, the sky was a deep shade of black. One learned to live in the darkness, just as we had learned to live in the light. Kerosene lamps were used for light while working in the forest and at home.

After living in the settlement for almost ten months, the people began to feel hopeless that the day would come when they'd be allowed to leave. They decided to join together and refused to go to work, although a strike in the Soviet Union was unheard of. Monday morning everyone was going to say that they were not feeling well. At least ninety-eight percent did. I tried to find out from my father what the strike was all about, but he didn't know. No one seemed to know what they were asking for. When Monday morning arrived, the commandant went berserk, screaming that the people could not do this and that everyone was going to be shot. Since there was only one nurse in the village, she could not, by any means, take care of all the so-called sick people.

By the following weekend a general and two high-ranking officers arrived from Moscow, their chests full of medals. A meeting was called, and all the people were told to attend. The meeting was held in a hall large enough to accommodate the whole village of eighty or ninety people, in a recreation hall where people could gather to play chess and enjoy other activities.

The three officers, and the commandant, looked red-faced and helpless, opened the meeting. The one who seemed to be the general stood up and asked us what it was we wanted. What were the people on strike demanding?

One of the strikers got up and said, "The people feel that they are going to die in this place. They want to leave."

The General explained that "we" had asked to come here because we had registered to return to Germany, and when Germany refused to accept us for whatever reason, the Soviet government did not consider us a good element, and therefore, wouldn't permit us to live among the Soviet people. The only way that we would be released was when a Polish government was established that was willing to take the responsibility for our future. "If you continue to strike," he said, "you are going to be starved to death. So the smart thing to do is to go back to work and wait until a Polish government can help you."

He then went on to tell us that the Soviet government was willing to help make the waiting period a little easier. If any of us wanted a cow or a goat and land free of charge, we could have them. We could also build our own log cabins. The materials would be free and we wouldn't have to share space with other families, so this was a special attraction.

There was a question-and-answer period. Most of the people wanted to know if this was an indication that we would never leave. The general assured us that this would have no effect on our future, but most people didn't believe him. Most people wanted to know why the Soviet government was being so good to us. He explained that after we left, there would be others to take our place. The houses would be of use to us now and to the government later.

We were told that the ball was in our corner, and it was up to us to decide what we wanted. We were to register our decision with the commandant. The meeting closed, and the officers left the settlement. Discussions went on for the rest of the day. The upshot was that the people were not going to take anything from the Soviet government because they were fearful that it would mean that they would have to stay here permanently. My brothers and I convinced our father, though, that we should take some land. I also argued for a goat, but to no avail. Father was afraid that the rest of the people would resent us for getting too much.

Two days later I went with Father to the commandant's office and told him that we would like some land. We planned to plant potatoes and onions. Potatoes grew fast. It seems that nature works with the climate. Crops grew faster here and were ready for picking sooner than in a less harsh environment. Having our own land would give us a feeling of independence.

We were given a large parcel of land right beside our living quarters. We could have had as much land as we wanted as it was in abundance. At this time of year it was too late to start a garden, but in the spring we were given small potatoes, onions, and such to start growing.

The strike ended and everyone went back to work, waiting for a Polish government.

At the beginning of September I went back to school, leaving my horse behind without regret. I had trouble in school with the teachers. One of my objections was the way capitalism was taught. It's the same way that socialism is portrayed in this country—all negative. My objections got me into plenty of trouble. I knew something about capitalism first hand and could not accept, or let others accept, the teachings without speaking out.

The second time that I was called into the principal's office, he warned me that if my behavior continued in this manner, I would be expelled from school. He also notified the commandant of my behavior. When I came home from school, my family had been informed of this already. They were very hurt, but not surprised. They knew I was a rebel.

When I was confronted by the commandant, I told him that I did not like capitalism, but I had lived under it long enough to know the good and the bad sides. When the subject was taught in school, I felt both sides should be told. He said to me, "You were taught and learned the Russian Constitution. You might be an expert at that, but you are too young to be an expert on capitalism, too!" Of course, there was no use arguing with him. He wasn't too bright anyway, and there is no point in having words with someone who cannot think for himself.

One day around the beginning of October, we left school later than usual. I don't recall why, but when we arrived at the river crossing, the old man that operated the boat, was not there. The girls and I decided to make a fire and wait in the hopes that he might return. After waiting for about two hours, I convinced them that I could take us across. We hopped into the boat.

When we were within two or three feet of the riverbank, I told the girls to get out of the boat and walk the rest of the way. They didn't want to get their feet wet, so they begged me to get closer to the land. All of a sudden, from nowhere, came a huge chunk of ice that forced the boat away from the edge. In foolishly trying to break the chunk of ice with the oar, I wound up breaking the oar instead. The ice was forcing the boat down the river, and having only one oar, I was left helpless. The ice finally bypassed the boat, but now we were at the mercy of the powerful river current. It swept the boat swiftly down the river. My one oar was of no use. All I could do was try to slow it down, or within hours we would have be in the North Sea. Naturally, the girls were hysterical.

After being swept down the river for about thirty miles, we were rescued by another boat. The police were waiting for us on the riverbank. I don't know how they knew what had happened, but we didn't care. We were only too glad to see them. Probably, the girls' screams were heard by the local village people, and they alerted the police. All the hands on the rescue boat and the police were laughing at us since they knew the treachery of the river. It certainly was no job for an amateur.

The winters were very harsh. If you spit, the spit turned to ice before it hit the ground. Fortunately, we were in an area where there was very little or no wind. The thick forest protected us. A three-foot wide path with eight to ten feet of snow on each side led us from the settlement to the river. It was like walking in a kind of tunnel. Even that seemed a little warmer, being protected by a wall of snow.

I didn't wear shoes, but valenki. Valenki were made of sheep's wool and were like a boot coming up to the knee. A far better thing than shoes. They were lifesavers. One always got them two sizes larger. After we put on socks, we wound cotton strips over our feet, round and round, and then put on the valenki. I could not have survived without this apparel keeping my feet warm. Having once had frozen feet, as I explained earlier in my story, it was even more necessary for me to be careful to keep my feet warm. I must do this even today. The moment they get the least bit cold, they begin to ache.

Before the onset of winter, my brother Shlomo tried to leave the settlement. Although we were living in Russian Siberia, he was hoping to get back to the Russia that was really Russia to him. He only got a few hundred miles when he was arrested. If he had known the native language he might have made it, but speaking only Russian made him an immediate suspect. I probably could have made it because I was adept and had learned to speak like a native. He was given a nine-month jail sentence, but was released in six months.

In July, 1941, Hitler attacked Russia. There was a quiet satisfaction that ran through the exiled people. They began to think that they would be able to leave. There was a renewal of excitement, a desperate excitement, of not knowing what was going to happen next.

About a month later, a Polish government was established in exile in London. Several weeks passed. One day a high-ranking officer came to the settlement. A treaty had been reached between the Soviet government and the Polish government in London. General Sikorski was the prime minister in London at this time. Within a few weeks, we were told that we would receive papers from the Soviet government enabling us to leave. The only unhappy person was the commandant. He was going to lose his power and control over his people. His crown would be gone.

Three weeks later the NKVD officer arrived with a secretary and two other men. We all received papers equivalent to political asylum. We were asked if we wanted to put in Pole or Polish Jew. Most of us put down Pole as we found that that would be to our benefit. I had my papers state: Birth—Polish, Birthdate—February 24, 1926. Since I did not know my actual birthdate, I chose this date because I think it was the day Lenin died.

The majority of people left within a few weeks after receiving their ID papers. Transportation was supplied by the government: cattle cars. They were worth the money we paid, which was nothing. We waited to pick our potato crop. Having about ten sacks of potatoes, we gave away half of them to neighbors and friends.

My family moved from the settlement into the village. Since I spoke the language, I went to the director of the collective farm and told him that we could help harvest the crops in exchange for food. We needed food more than money. Money was an uncertain commodity, but food could always be exchanged for other things. We were given a house to stay in while we worked. It did not take me long to find a girlfriend right next door. I slept more at her house for the three weeks that we were there than in my own.

When it was time to leave, they gave us a horse and a wagon. We had sacks of potatoes, tomatoes, onions, and radishes. We left loaded with so much food that we needed two wagons, one for the food and one for the family. We were now on our way to the Kam railroad station about ten miles away. It had all worked out well for both sides. We got the food we needed and the collective farm got the help they needed, since most of the men had been drafted.

8
KAZAKHSTAN

Keeping our food with us, we boarded a train to Kotlas, which was a few days' journey. We arrived there early in the morning. Here, many cars were put together. The people traveling were not only exiles, but Russians, too, all interested in getting to Central Asia, further away from the battlefield.

In each railroad car there was a wood stove so we could prepare food for our meals. We found our family sharing a lot with others as we could not sit and eat while others around us went hungry.

We did not know where we were going, except towards Central Asia. A war was on and not to be forgotten. Military transports had priority over all else. We were often shunted aside and stopped for long periods of time. Sometimes we would get out from the car and exchange food with people for other things we needed. Though the trip was long and monotonous, we did not mind. We were free, and that compensated for all the difficulties we went through.

After many weeks, we wound up in Kazakh SSR, more commonly known as Kazakhstan. This was Central Asia, a Soviet Republic consisting of predominantly Moslem people. My family decided to leave the train in Kyzl-Orda, once the capital of Kazakhstan. The population was about fifty thousand, but had increased to two hundred and fifty thousand within a few months. This large influx of people was due to evacuees being sent here from all over Russia. The citizens were sent to safe places before the onslaught of the Germans. Kyzl-Orda was a safe place far, far away from the war. Not only did the Russians evacuate people, but factories and universities as well. Whole buildings were dismantled and rebuilt in safe areas. We had Simfropolski, a medical college from the Crimea, brought to Kyzl-Orda along with all its students.

While my mother and brother Abraham waited at the railroad station, Father, Sally, and I went to look for a place to live. After walking around all day, we finally found a house. The man who owned it lived only a couple of hundred feet away. He rented it to us for thirty rubles a month, which was very, very cheap. The house had three rooms, a stove, and an outhouse. It was made of lime and straw, as were ninety percent of the city homes. They were built this way because of the intense heat in the summer. Sometimes it got as high as 120 degrees, if not more. The houses built in this fashion stayed comparatively cool. The other ten percent of the houses were big brick homes, mostly owned by Russians exiled in the thirties when the Russian purges took place.

The basic food here was watermelon, cantaloupe, and dynia, which was like a cantaloupe, but huge in size. They could weigh anywhere from five pounds to fifty pounds. We noticed long strange strings of some kind of food hanging from the houses, and we asked our landlord about it. He told us, "That is dynia drying. We use it in the winter for food. It can be eaten as is or made into marmalade and such."

Everything that grew in Central Asia was sweet to the taste—onions, potatoes, everything. The sun was hot in the growing season, and this accounted for the sweetness of all foods, which seemed strange to us. We exchanged food with our landlord at first for local foodstuffs. There was no refrigeration, so it was healthier not to eat meat in the hot seasons.

The Kazakh people were nomadic until the early thirties when the Russian government moved to put a stop to their way of life. The older people were not formally educated, but the younger ones went to school. Most of the higher positions were held by Koreans, Jews, and the Russians. Only a small percentage were held by local Kazakhs because of the majority's lack of education.

The Koreans were moved from Manchuria, refugees from Korea when Japan occupied it. The Russians moved them away so that it would be easier for the Soviet government to catch any infiltrators, as the European eye found it difficult to differentiate between the Japanese and the Koreans. The Koreans brought the culture of rice with them, and it became one of the main crops of the area. The Kazakh took very fast to the cultivation of rice. Along with potatoes, rice became one of the main dishes.

The Korean homes were well heated. They devised a kind of central heating system in the floor. Their houses had a stove under the floor and ducts with vents leading from the chimney. This system kept the floors quite warm. Thus, it was no hardship to sleep on mats on the floor. This also accounted for their use of low tables and no chairs. Koreans are a bright and intelligent people.

Father went out to the local markets to see what he might be able to do in buying and selling, to speculate. My two brothers got jobs in the rice factory, which employed over a thousand people. The rice was prepared here for shipping. Of course, they filled their pockets with rice to bring home, as many others did too.

A few months after our arrival, the Polish school was established. All of the teachers were Poles and Polish Jews. Their salaries were paid by the Soviet government. My sister attended this Polish school, as she was about ten years old at the time. I did not go to school, but liked to go to the college just to listen to the lectures without being obligated to write or do lessons.

Noting that the Koreans ran the show here, I decided to learn their language. The way, of course, was to get a Korean girlfriend. Even though I was only fifteen years old, it was not too difficult. One day at a dance, I befriended a girl named Vera. Vera was her Russian name. She was the same age as me. I liked her very much and started going to her house quite regularly.

The first time I was invited to Vera's house for dinner, soup was served. I had no idea why everyone at the table was looking at me and waiting for me to take the first spoonful. Swallowing the first spoonful, I realized why. I could not catch my breath. The soup was full of pepper. Having waited anxiously for my reaction, all of them burst into hysterical laughter. From that day on, pepper in any amount was never a problem for me.

Vera and I saw each other quite often, but it was always in her home or with other people around. We never had a chance to become intimate. Besides, I was too shy to make any advances on such a young girl. Perhaps she wouldn't have accepted them anyway, but now I will never know.

Vera's mother was a very quiet, timid woman, much different from my own mother, who was very joyous and always giving of herself in an outward manner. We were a family full of fun, even in bad times. Wittiness, joking, and just enjoying each other were a part of our everyday family life. The quiet home of my girlfriend was strange to me. Although Vera's father had been killed by the Japanese, I knew that this did not account for their retiring ways. Vera's family was just different from ours.

In a short time, I became a part of the family. Eating supper there almost every night, I got to know them all well. Vera's brother, Keisha, who was in his mid twenties, became like a brother to me. He was the director of a government printing house where they made passports and other important documents. He used to take me with him to meet some of his friends, and we'd all go dancing together. Though I was younger, I was like one of them. Jokingly, Keisha would tell his friends, "Watch out what you say. This Polack speaks Korean already." It had taken me close to three months to learn to communicate in Korean.

Although I liked to dance, I was too shy to ask the girls to dance with me and was afraid of being rejected with a no. I felt comfortable and had more success with older girls because they made the advances instead of me.

One day out of the blue, Keisha gave me ten bread ration cards. Normally, a person only received one ration card for the entire month, which allowed them to purchase one kilogram of bread a day. This is equivalent to two pounds. Now with these additional ration cards, I could purchase eleven kilograms of bread a day. Naturally, this was far too much bread for any one person to consume, so I'd trade the bread for other items that my family or I needed. I would barter for such things as shoes, salt, or wood for heating and cooking.

The wood here was a very hard wood called saksaul. It comes from a wild tree with no leaves that grows in the desert. The wood looks like the roots of trees or great chunks of driftwood. Being such a hard wood, it could scarcely be chopped with an axe. We'd take chunks and strike it on the ground, or hit wood on wood in order to break it. This wood burned hotter and better than coal.

The Kazakhs would go into the desert with their camels or donkeys, load the wood, and bring it back to sell in the open market place. In the winter, heating was vital in a place which got as cold as twenty or thirty degrees. The cold, though, was not as bad as in Siberia. It lasted about three months—December, January, and February—and then it would start to warm up again.

In the summer, the natives dressed in fur hats and cotton-lined long sleeve jackets. Those who wore fur-lined jackets turned them inside out, wearing the fur on the outside. Heavy boots were a part of their dress, too. Their warm clothing was supposed to protect them from the sun.

The Korean men mostly dressed in European-style clothes, a very fancy dress: suits and ties. They were the elite, holding high positions, and they dressed accordingly. It took me almost a year to be able to distinguish between a Kazakh and a Korean. The way their eyes were shaped made the difference.

Kazakhs, who were Moslem before the Soviets established power, had more than one wife. When the Soviets made monogamy a law, the Kazakhs were very upset. Those with more than one wife were permitted to keep them, but were not allowed to take any more. The Kazakh women wore the typical long Moslem-style dresses except they were made from flower-printed cloth. Some of the women kept their faces veiled, too. A lot of the girls wore a flower over their ear to signify their marital status. A flower over the left ear meant the girl was single, a flower over the right ear meant she was married.

The Korean women were more modern, of course. They wore make-up, high-heeled shoes, and lovely European-style dresses.

The Polish Jewish population had a lot of problems with the Buchara Jews. They are Sephardic Jews who spoke the native language and Hebrew. They looked exactly like Arabs: dark hair, dark skin, and a hooked nose. Now I do believe the Jews and Arabs are brothers. We looked European, so they did not consider us to be Jews. They said that we were Germans; we spoke German and even acted as Germans. Intermarriages and two thousand years of living in different climates had produced different types of Jews. Since we were not allowed into their synagogues, we had to establish our own. After a while the Buchara Jews realized that we were Jews, too, and we were able to build a closer relationship with them.

Kim Keisha gave me two dozen ration cards the next month. He told me I could sell one dozen and share what I made with him. The other dozen was to be for my family. I sold twelve for a hundred rubles apiece and gave six hundred to Keisha and kept six hundred. This allowed me to dress nice, and our house had everything we needed: rice, flour, potatoes. Whatever we needed, we were able to have.

I told Keisha that if he brought me the engraving plate every month and paper, too, I would be able to make more and of course would share with him. He introduced me to his cousin, Kim Pen Sun, who taught me how to make the ration cards without messing the job up. After three lessons I was an expert. During the next month I made five hundred. Of course, I did not sell them on the streets, as it was too dangerous.

I made friends with another Polish Jew, Misha, and made sure I could trust him to sell them mostly to our own people. I gave them to him for seventy rubles and he sold them for a hundred. For about two months I made the cards and gave them to Misha. I established that I would give Keisha a thousand rubles each month for supplying the paper and use of the plates.

After a time, the whole transaction got me a little scared, realizing the penalty in time of war was death. I told Misha that I was going to move out of the house and that he should move with me into an apartment on the other side of town, far away from our families. We both moved.

After about six months I had a valise full of rubles—a stack about two feet high and three feet long. I was buying gold pieces and diamonds and giving them to my family. Of course, my visits to Vera's house were not as often in order not to be seen around there. Most of the meetings with Keisha took place at the dances. Of course, we spoke in Korean.

I met one of our fellows whose name was Deduk. He noticed that I was mingling with Koreans and speaking their language. He said to me one day, "I don't want to get mixed up in your business with the Koreans, but I would like to ask a favor. " I asked him what it was that he wanted.

"Government authorization for travel," he told me.

This required special documents which allowed a person to travel to any part of the country, as traveling during the war was limited. I was very hesitant to talk to him about it, because I only knew him from the dances and never really had any close contact with him. I told him I would get back to him. Of course, I had to check him out and make sure he was not one of the informers. There were informers even between our people. Every group had its quislings.

After a few weeks, he was considered on the level. I met him again at a dance. Now in the summer, these were held in the park with a live orchestra. In the winter, they met at the railroad club. I asked him what he needed the travel permit for. He told me he had friends that would like to travel to the Iranian border and into Iran, and from there to Israel. Palestine, as it was then.

I told him that if I were able to get the papers, they would cost five thousand rubles apiece. He said, "Money is no object." So I told him I would get back to him soon.

Keisha who told me that it would be no problem for him to get me the necessary papers. Whatever I felt it was worth to me was all right with him. A few days later he brought me a dozen. I gave him twelve thousand rubles. He was taken aback. He didn't expect to get that much money. Of course, I told him not to worry, that money was not any problem. I never told Misha about this business transaction. Having so much money and not knowing what to do with it, I gave Misha a key to my money trunk. And permission to take money as he needed it for his family. He had a sister who was married to a Polish lawyer and a brother back home who was like a CPA. I will never know how much money he took.

On the weekends I often slept at my parents' home. My brothers used to go through my pockets and take out money, and I always pretended I didn't know about it. I guess they were too embarrassed to ask me for the money, as I was the youngest. My parents were never aware of the extent to which I was involved in this illegal business. I took care to protect them, as I did not want to get them in trouble, should I be caught.

Misha had a girlfriend, Slava, who was a medical student in her third year. Misha was in his late twenties and Slava was in her early twenties. Slava was about five-foot-three, blonde, blue-eyed, and very sweet. I always wished she could be my girlfriend, but I guess I was too young for her. But she was a part of our family. She was like a second sister. She came to our house, helped with the cooking, and was a part of us.

I used Slava to help buy clothes and shoes for the college students who had none or had very little. They had been evacuated and most had no families with them. Slava never knew where the money actually came from. We told her that a Polish committee gave us funds to help that way. I bought at least two hundred pairs or more of shoes, dresses, socks, and stockings.

One day I saw a girl with torn shoes, and I asked Slava if she knew her. "No, but I know her name. Why? Do you want to meet her?"

"No. Find out what size shoes she wears. I want to get some for her."

Slava did. I went to the market place and bought shoes and then had Slava give them to the girl. I told Slava I didn't want to let on who had done it. A secret admirer, I told her, just say that. I could not have so much money without helping, and I did it this way. I gave Slava plenty of food and told her to share it with others who might need help.

I also helped the Korean girls who worked in the stores where bread was distributed. If they needed some extra for a party or some special occasion, they knew they could count on me to help with extra ration cards. In return, we never had to stand in the long lines waiting for bread. Sometimes the people would stand for hours and hours.

I had a girlfriend, Katia. Her husband was away in the war. Of course we did not go out together. There was a difference in our ages. She was in her early thirties. I used to sleep many nights at her house. She was Russian. She worked in a distillery factory where they made vodka. She lived alone in a small, three-room house. Very often Misha, Katia and I, and Misha's girlfriend would spend all night drinking and singing there. Of course, most young women had no husbands at home because they had been drafted. So if you were a clean-cut type you had no problem.

My brothers and I played soccer at a club named Kyzyl-Ordinsky Spartak.

Around the first week of March, I got up one night around 2:30 A.M. for no apparent reason. Misha was sleeping elsewhere; and just as if someone had told me to do it, I went to Misha's jacket hanging on a chair and looked in the pockets. I found ration cards. Not mine. I looked at them and could not believe my eyes. They were ones he had made himself, obviously forged. They were smudged and crooked. The discovery scared me. In spite of the fact that I had given him a key to the trunk and had told him to take what money he needed, Misha was making his own ration cards! And poor ones at that.

I got dressed and started at once for the house of a distributor I knew, Moniek. When I got there I pounded on the door. Finally, someone I did not know at all came and opened the door. "Where is Moniek?" I demanded. "He's not here. They have moved away."

After some hesitation, I was given the new address and I went there. And I pounded on another door. Someone I did not know answered, but I pushed him aside and went in yelling for Moniek.

Before he even appeared, I did a strange thing, as if I had been told where to look. I went directly across the room to where three suitcases were piled one on top of the other, each one smaller than the one below it. I pushed them aside, and without pausing, pulled free one of the lime bricks from the floor and uncovered Moniek's supply of forged ration cards.

Moniek appeared and couldn't believe his eyes. "How did you know where to look? You couldn't know. I just moved here." I waved that aside and showed him the cards Misha had given him. "Look at these. You are going to sell these? We'll all be in trouble. They're bad cards! How could you miss it?"

He had no answer. I took all the badly made cards I found and left, tearing them up and throwing them in the garbage cans. And hoping without much hope that these were the first and last of them.

9
ARRESTED

As soon as I opened the door at home, two policemen were beside me. They had been waiting at a neighbor's house for my return.

I asked calmly what I could do for them.

One said, "Plenty. We have a warrant to search your house."

"Let me see it."

That surprised them, but they showed me the warrant. "What are you looking for?"

They gave me a stare and said, "You should know."

They found about a dozen or so ration cards. And that was enough. I was only one person. What was I doing with so many cards? Then they asked about the trunk. "What's in there?"

I showed them. They couldn't believe their eyes. A pile of money! They figured it was counterfeit, too. But no, it looked right. How had I come by so much money? Not honestly, for sure. They put a seal on the trunk as they had no authority to remove it. Nobody would touch it with the seal.

I was arrested and taken to the police station, about a five-minute walk from the house. I was immediately taken up to the investigating officer, Bykovsky. A typist took down the words of my first interrogation. I was very, very nervous, knowing full well what the penalty was for what I had done.

The first thing they wanted to know was if I had family here. I told them Hitler killed them. All of them. I knew this would give my family time to hide whatever they might need away from the house, should the police find out and go search.

I told them I did not know anything about Misha, but they told me he was under arrest. I told them I had bought the ration cards they found. Misha and the whole group were arrested. I didn't know how many there were right then, but later found out that about twenty-five people who had been coming to see Misha had been caught.

They put me in a cell with five other people. About eight or nine at night Misha was brought into the same cell. Which was not a smart move on the part of the investigators. Misha looked at me and asked me if I was mad at him.

"No, I knew it was going to happen sooner or later, but never expected it to happen because of what you did. Why did you do it? You had the key to the money, anything you wanted. You were my partner. Why? What in the hell made you do it? You made garbage. Such bad cards even the blind could tell they were fake."

"My sister," he said. "She wanted to make money, too. I was helping her."

I said "Misha, we must think what to do now. It's too late to go back over it. What shall we do now? We have to say we just started. We have to tell the same thing, so they'll buy the story."

Of course, the poorly made card had done us in. A woman had brought it to a store. The storekeeper reported the card and who had used it. She told them she had got it from Misha's brother. Thus, our arrest and present predicament.

Under pressure, Misha involved Kim Pen Sun, who had supplied him with the paper and plate. He, too, was immediately arrested. You have to understand how Kim Keisha felt, seeing his cousin arrested. He felt he would be next. All the people that Misha dealt with were arrested. He talked under interrogation and got them in trouble.

At the same time, Father had been under investigation for over a year. He had told a neighbor whose husband had been killed that the Germans were not as bad as reported. He knew them from the First World War, and they were intelligent, not so vicious. It was propaganda. The woman reported him to the NKVD as spreading anti-Soviet, pro-Nazi propaganda. The NKVD were trying to find out if we were Jews or Germans, secretly spreading Nazi propaganda. Many Germans claiming to be Jews had been arrested. It was a deadly war, and such tactics had to be stopped.

About a month after my arrest, Father was also arrested. They had plenty of informers to verify that he was a Jew. He was charged with violation of statute 58.10, which is spreading anti-government rumors. In a short period, he was sentenced to ten years' imprisonment. He was told he was lucky, lucky he was a Jew, or else he would have been shot. He went to a prison camp in Karaganda, which is also in Central Asia.

Our investigation seemed to go according to our plan. Mr. Bykovsky accepted our word that it was the first month of our adventure. We felt very good that we had put something over on them. Little did we know that this was not the end.

When his report reached Moscow, the officials didn't buy it. The main reason was that they wanted to make sure there were no political reasons behind our acts. This was at the same time that the prime minister of Poland, Sikorski, was killed in an airplane on the way to meet Soviet officials for a conference to establish a Polish army. Rumor had it that all of his party were killed because he was considered too friendly with the Soviet government.

The money I had was the reason for the investigation of political connections. The officials did not know why I had it or what purpose I might be using it for. But with the death of Sikorski, General Anders became the new prime minister. He was a right-wing extremist. And he put up a hard line against the Soviet government.

The Soviet government's reaction was fast and drastic. The Polish consulate was closed, and many from the consulate were arrested. In addition, thousands of others who had non-citizen papers were forced to take Soviet passports or go to jail. Many of them complied, but others chose prison. A new Polish consulate was established, and all new people were hired. A Polish army was formed in Russia, but according to the treaty Russia had with Japan, no foreign armies could be formed in Russia. Anders' anti-Semitism became a part of his policy. Very few Jews were accepted into his army. Thousands of Poles, maybe five percent Jews, were assembled and sent to Iran. There the official Polish army was formed. Most of them wound up in England. They fought from there. The relationship between General Anders and the Soviet government was worsening, and the Russians stopped the Polish mobilization completely.

About two weeks after Bykovsky's report was sent to Moscow, a young man in his thirties arrived. He was a sharpshooter, an investigator of high class. The first thing he did was downgrade Mr. Bykovsky for letting Misha and me share a cell. We were immediately separated. After the investigator put pressure on Misha, he spilled his guts. He told the new investigator that it had been going on for several months, which was not what we had agreed to say. He told him everything.

Then the same investigator started to work on me. I was not as easy as Misha had been. That frustrated him. After questioning me for the twentieth time, demanding to know where I got my paper and plate, I told him that all Koreans looked alike and I could not identify my supplier. Half the Koreans were named Kim, I told him, and that was all I knew about the man. That got him really mad. He screamed, "You think we are playing games?" He hit me in the face with his fist.

I jumped up and grabbed an ink pot from the desk, which was made of marble. I threw it out a big picture window. It made a huge crash, glass flying all over the street below. He was taken aback, to say the least. I screamed, "You do not touch me. If you touch me again, I'll demolish the whole office. Under Soviet law investigators have no right to use force or violence. It is not my fault if you are incompetent," I added, for good measure.

That really got him mad. He decided to use a different approach. He promised me that if I cooperated I would not get a death sentence. All they wanted was to know who had supplied me with the materials. No way, I thought to myself.

But because I had mentioned the name Kim and that he was about five foot six, he asked if they were to bring the man before me, would I recognize him. I said yes. The next few days about a thousand "Kims" were paraded in front of me, all about five-foot-six or seven. After that I said, "He probably left town. I don't see him here anywhere. They all look alike."

For two weeks I was not allowed to receive any parcels. Prison food was not the most exciting thing, so we used to get food parcels. But not for me, unless I cooperated. But there were ways around that. Under the names of others in the cells, I got my parcels anyway.

Keisha spoke to my sister Sally. Knowing what was going on, he asked her if she thought he should leave town because he feared arrest. She told him she would get in touch with me and let him know what he should do. She put a note in the parcels that came in. I put a note in one of the containers being returned outside. I told my sister under no condition should he leave. I would not tell on him under any condition, and if he left it would only look suspicious. Keisha was not to worry at all.

Slava had told my family what was going on with me and Misha. She visited them often. And her source was Mr. Bykovsky himself. She made friends with him and took him out to dinner and out dancing. From him she learned about what was going on. He told her that Misha, Kim Pen Sun, and I would get the death sentence, no matter what. Newspapers, radio reports, and union meetings all demanded that our sentence be death. But amazingly, in none of these reports or meetings were we ever called foreigners or Polacks.

The sharpshooting investigator finally gave up. After three months, the investigation was turned over for trial. And a public trial it was, in a huge auditorium. We had a Korean judge and two distinguished citizens, one sitting on each side of the judge. I don't know what power they had, but according to Soviet law they could override the judge on the sentence. I don't know if it ever happened, but that was the law. Of course, this would not be the first law the Soviet government had ever violated.

From obscurity I became the leader of all twenty-seven people on trial. I was singled out as the leader. Realize the situation—a sixteen-year-old boy suddenly the leader of lawyers, CPAs and professors. The funny part was that I hardly knew them. They were Misha's contacts and relatives. It was not easy to convince the judge and his two aides that I did not know them or ever had any dealings with them.

After six weeks, twenty-three people pointed to me, not to Misha. Misha was the only person who did not stand up and speak against me. He took the blame, since the investigators had it on record anyway.

Union delegations and other distinguished citizens turned over petitions to the judge. They accused us of denying people bread by selling it on the black market. Unfortunately, they were right. We did harm them. Thousands of pounds of bread had been illegally distributed.

In the Soviet legal system, political cases are held in a closed courtroom. Even family is not allowed. But all other trials are open to the public. When there is a recess, you are allowed to sit with your family and talk. So every day for about an hour, I would sit with my mother and sister. Of course, Slava was in court every day talking to Misha and me. She told us that she was called by the prosecution as a witness. Though the state provided us with lawyers, there was not much they could do since the case was pretty clear as to what had happened. Only five people went free, as the state could not prove any connection; they did not have enough evidence to convict. The lawyers drilled on that.

Two days before the final court hearing Slava was called to the witness stand. She had been told by Misha and me to cooperate with the prosecution; no matter what she would say, it would not alter the decision of the court. But she defied us and did what her conscience told her to do. She said we had committed a crime against the state, and the state had a legal right to do what it had to do. But to her, we were the nicest people she knew.

While she told the court how I had helped the girls and how I spent money to help poor students, the DA interrupted her, warning her that she was a member of the Komsomol, the young Communist Youth League. Her mother was a hero of the Soviet Union as a guerilla leader. She should watch what she says. She could be expelled from school and lose her membership in the Komsomol.

But she couldn't be threatened. She insisted that she had never had better friends. In a rage, the DA removed her from the stand. Of course, she was expelled and removed from the Komsomol. Being friendly with criminals who had admitted their guilt and refusing to put them down as common criminals was her crime.

When called, I was the last to speak to the court, as everybody else had already spoken. All except Misha had made me look as if I was a conniving, shrewd, calculating monster; that I made them do what they did not want to do. Since they would never do such things, it was my power of persuasion. That's what they all said. The most amazing thing was that I hardly knew any of them, hardly spoke to them. They belonged to the aristocracy, were lawyers, CPAs, and so on. They were twenty years older than me. I hardly knew them. They were of high society and would never have associated with me. Being lawyers and so on.

It was the fear of what they had done. Like animals caught a net. They were fighting for survival.

When my name Chaim Leibovich (as my father's name being Leibo, my name was Chaim Leibovich Goldberg) was called, I really didn't know what to say. To say "I'm not guilty" did not make much sense. The only thing that was not true was that I was the leader of the so-called organized group of criminals. But denying it would not do me any good, since more then twenty people pointed their finger at me. The only thing I could do was to take advantage of what my so-called "friends" had said about me, that I was the "brain" of this so-called organization.

I stood up and said, "Dear Judge, and my two distinguished citizens, I'm going along with what my friends say about me. There may be some truth in what they say. Let's see, we have here lawyers, accountants, and other Polish intellectuals; and here I, with my almost-high school education, made them do whatever I wanted, and those poor Polish intellectuals could not resist. My advice to this great court is that I should receive a light sentence. And all my so-called 'friends' should be shot. Nobody needs intellectual idiots. I could bring good ideas and do good for the country. In other words, I could be an asset to society and pay back many times over for the damage I did to this country."

I knew my speech would not change anything, but after sitting in court for almost six weeks with everyone lying through their teeth about me, I had to say a few words of my own. I guess it was for self-satisfaction. I felt it would have no effect on the results. But if I didn't say something, I would not last much longer. I would bust. The judge and his two distinguished associates had a mild smile.

After my speech, the court recessed so the judge and the two distinguished citizens could come to a decision. Of course, as always, I sat with my mother and my sister. The most difficult thing for me was to try to explain to Mother what was going to happen to me.

I asked Mother and my sister that they should not cry now or when the sentence was pronounced. I told them I would be sentenced to death, which would be commuted to life, changed to ten years, and that I would be home in about two years. I didn't know why I said it. It was the stupidest thing I could have said. But it was what I said.

My mother said, "Why do you talk like this? You try to make me feel good?"

I said, "Mother, I don't know why I said it. But I did. I told you, cry now but not when the sentence is pronounced. Because if you do, then I will cry, too."

"They are going to shoot you and you tell me not to cry!"

"Cry now, not then, when the sentence is read, when they say what will happen to me."

I didn't know how long it would take, sitting in court holding their hands. I didn't know when I would get to do it again. I liked my sister very much. She was not the same little spoiled brat who made us suffer and feel inferior to her. She had become a loving, caring sister over the years.

The DA had already asked the court for three to five years for twenty-five defendants, and death sentences for Kim Pen Sun, Misha Nachmanowich, and Chaim Leibovich. We knew that was what the sentence would be. There was no question about it. I had looked it up. The minimum penalty for our crime in time of war was the death sentence. I knew it before, when I moved away from our house, not to involve my family.

The court was called into session. For the last time I squeezed hands with my mother and sister. Slava, after kissing Misha, slobbered all over me, too. The other person in the courtroom was Misha's sister, Genia, the only one of his family who was not arrested for participating in the whole scheme. I don't know why, but she was not arrested. I was really surprised.

We went to our seats, and the judge and the two citizens took their places. He raised his gavel, the court was in session, and the judge began. First, five people were acquitted for the lack of evidence, and then he sentenced those who would receive one to five years. And then, death for Kim Pen Sun, Misha, and Chaim. We were to be shot. After the sentence was pronounced, four policemen drew their guns at the three of us sitting next to each other and said, "Do not move. If you move, you will be shot."

10
PRISON AND LABOR CAMP

After the court was cleared of the other defendants, the three of us were taken to a different prison from the others, the NKVD prison. Misha and I were in one cell. Kim Pen Sun was completely separated from us. The cell had no beds and a tiny little window at the top of the wall near the ceiling. We could not reach it to look out. In our cell was a man sent there for being a German spy, which he was. Also to be shot. He told us what his job was: to spread anti-Semitism in Russia. He apologized to us, for his job was to spread hatred of Jews. Being in a similar situation but for a different reason, we showed no bitterness towards him. But we were not too friendly, either.

Karl was a typical German. Every night and every morning he had to do his exercises. He explained to us how the Soviet system worked. He was a Volga German. I don't know how he knew what he explained to us, but he said, "If you are taken out of the cell and not asked to take your clothes with you, you will be walked out to the courtyard and be shot from behind. When they tell you to take your clothes, that means your sentence was commuted." He said he was sitting in this cell already for over sixty days.

According to Soviet law you cannot be shot until your appeal goes through the Supreme Court of the republic where you have been sentenced. If denied, your appeal then goes to the Supreme Court of the Soviet Union. If the Supreme Court denies your appeal, then it goes to the Supreme Soviet. That's the Soviet government. Then if denied, it must be signed by the president of the Soviet Union. At that time it was Kalinin. So that is the whole process which takes months before you are actually executed. We had already been told by our lawyers how the system worked.

I particularly felt that I was too young to die yet. And I felt I would have my sentence commuted. The funniest part was that every night I could hear the music from the dance in the park located close by. We never knew a prison was there because it was surrounded by trees. From the outside, the prison looked like a beautiful villa, a mansion. Imagine sitting in a cell hearing music and people dancing where you had spent so many nights with friends while waiting for the death sentence to be carried out or changed.

Of course, Misha looked at me and apologized for what he had done. I had no bitterness towards him. "I guess we all make mistakes," Misha said, "but this is the most costly one I ever made." Nothing I could say would change anything now. I didn't really hate him for what he did. I was just surprised, for I considered him a smart fellow who had finished high school in Poland. His whole family was highly educated. They came from a rich family who owned a lot of lumberyards back home. But when you take a donkey around the world and bring it back, it is still a donkey. In other words, when you send an idiot to college, you bring back an educated idiot. It is an old Russian proverb.

Misha was in his mid-twenties, eight or nine years older than I was; I thought he had more brains and could resist his sister's temptation. He had everything he wanted, money and everything. He did not know where to stop. His sister's greed was greater than the sack of money that I let him share with me.

When we had been taken out of the courtroom, we walked about five to ten minutes to prison. My sister, Mother, and Slava followed to see where we were taken. That way, in case they wanted to get in touch with us, they could. They did not know that under the death sentence there was no communication with the outside world, including your family. One day my sister made up a dinner and came to the prison and walked over to one of the guards. She told him that her brother was in prison and that she had brought dinner and wanted to give it to him.

The guard looked at her and said, "Where is he?"

She said, "In the death cell."

He said, "Dievushka (little girl), there is no such thing as a death cell."

She said, "But I was in court when he was sentenced to death and brought here."

He said, "Little girl, take your food and go. There is no death cell here. You are in the wrong place."

Of course, Soviet officials will not admit to anything that sounds cruel. In tears, she left. I did not hear her because the doors are steel, with little windows opening only from the outside. To hear what she said or to hear anybody outside, I would have to have my ear glued to the steel door.

The cell we were in was the first one in the hallway on the right. On the left was the warden's office. We could hear the telephone; when it rang we put our ears to the door to listen. They used to scream very loud. It was an old fashioned phone you cranked, so we could hear what the warden said. It was a little consolation that we could hear something.

Other prisoners were taken out twice a day for walks except those sentenced to death. It was the same prison my father was in, the prison was for those sentenced to death and for political prisoners.

About two weeks after Misha and I were put in the cell, Karl, the German spy, was called out and told to take all his belongings. We do not know what happened to him. In spite of his story to us about the belongings, we still did not know if his sentence was commuted or not. How much truth was in what he told us we did not know. It was hearsay.

Misha and I did not talk too much to each other. We did not know what to say. We talked mostly of whether or not we would be executed. Would they do it or not? The Supreme Court of Kazakhstan denied our appeal after twenty days. The warden told us it was denied. The case was moved to the Supreme Court of the Soviet Union, and we would know the result in a few weeks. More weeks of waiting.

The food was better than in the regular prison, more nourishing. Nothing to go wild about, but it was good enough. Food was not one of our bigger concerns. We could read books (they asked if we wanted books) or play chess. Of course, we took books. I had no patience to play chess, but books were something to occupy the time. I read: *Leon Feuchfanger*, *The War of Judea*, and *Josephus Flavius*. Also, *Goethe*, *Lermontov*, *Pushkin*, *Turgenev*, and *Gogol*—we could finish a book in a couple of days. One of the books, I think, was *The Rubiyat*, by Omar Khayyam. *Turgenev* was one of my favorites.

When you are in the death cell, you have no contact with the outside world. You have the warden to talk to. He would ask us if we needed or wanted anything. The warden realized that I was not too calm, and he came to the window and tried to talk to me. He told me nobody my young age ever had the death sentence carried out. He tried to give me a pep talk. I didn't take him too seriously. He felt sorry for me, I thought, still a kid, just sixteen, not an old man yet.

On the thirty-fifth day, after midnight, the phone rang. After about thirty days, I couldn't sleep at night anyway. I put my ear to the door to listen. Misha stayed asleep. I heard the warden talking loudly, as they usually did with the old-fashioned telephones. "Moscow, I'm listening. Yes, Moscow. Chaim Leibovich, Misha Danziger, yes. Kim Pen Sun, yes." Our three names were mentioned. Well, you have to comprehend the electrification that was going through my body, not knowing what was being said, death or commuted. Did they say, "Take those bastards out and shoot them," or "They are commuted to live?"

Misha was sleeping. I woke him up and told him that the warden just received a telephone call from Moscow and he better get ready. He said, "Ready for what?"

I said, "For one or the other. To live or to die."

"One or the other. To die or to live," he repeated. "I hope it's the last one—to live. That it will work for us."

After about five or ten minutes, I could hear the warden's footsteps coming towards our door. He told us to take our things. We slept on the floor—a mattress but no bed. The only time you could leave was to be taken to the bathroom, but only when nobody else was out. You could not be seen by anybody.

We walked into the office shaking and nervous, looking right into the warden's face, waiting to hear what he had to say. He started to smile, and that relieved some of our nervousness. "Okay, kid, your sentence is commuted to life." I didn't know how much that meant. The laws had been changed in time of war. So I didn't know if it meant fifteen, twenty, twenty-five years. We knew it was more than ten years. He said we would have our papers when we arrived at the labor camp.

We were taken that night, for everything is done at night in the Soviet Union. You never see cars or trucks with bars taking prisoners. Everything is done at night.

We were taken by penal truck with bars to the general prison. Kim Pen Sun was not with us and we didn't know if he was commuted or not.

We were taken to a huge hall where prisoners were gathered before being sent to individual cells. The reason we were being held was that a transport was being formed that night for a group to be sent to labor camp. Now the cells were full; but when the transport left, we would be assigned to the newly emptied cells.

Outside you could hear the footsteps of hundreds and hundreds of people. I stood by the window to hear the names being called. The window was only three feet from the ground but was barred. The warden or transport director was calling out names of people who were going to labor camp. Of course I did not know what to expect. After hearing hundreds of names, I heard "Label Myorwitz Goldberg."

The name of my father! An electric shock went through my body when I heard my father's name called for the transport. I knew Father had been arrested, for Mother had told me during the trial, but I thought he had already gone, receiving ten years for his crime of spreading anti-Soviet propaganda. But he was not gone. They had waited until more people were accumulated for the trip. I thought to myself, "What I would not give to go together with my father."

After calming down from my excitement and sweating, I knocked lightly on the window. A guy said, "Who's that?"

"Do me a favor," I said. "See if you can find my father, his name is Myorwitz Goldberg. He was just called. See if he can come to the window and talk to me."

He recognized my voice, that I was a kid. For somebody older, he might not have done anything. It was in the middle of the night, and the window was frosted. He found my father and brought him to the window. I said, "Tata?"

He replied, "Who is this? Chaim?"

"Yes."

He said, "What are you doing here?"

"Well, I was just commuted from my death sentence."

He became hysterical. I said, "You don't have to cry now. It's all over. I'm commuted."

"So what is your sentence?"

"I don't know yet. At least I'm alive and have a chance to come home. And I promised Mother I would come home in two years."

He said, "Stop talking like a kid. You are a grown man already. I can't understand. Sultan, who was in your cell for the last day of your trial, told me you were sentenced to ten years."

"I guess he did not want to tell you the bad news, to hurt you. He lied to you. He did not want to make you suffer, as you could not have done anything for me anyway."

When the roll call was finished, they were all taken away for transport. I said goodbye to my father and said that as long as we were alive we could hope that we would all be together again as a family. We both had hopes for it.

About half an hour after they were taken away, we were taken for showers and put in cells. Misha and I were again in the same cell with about eighteen others. The food was not as good as what we had had in the death prison. The NKVD receives better rations than ordinary people, and we were now ordinary people. We were in prison for three weeks. The lawyer told my family about the sentence commuted to life. He said I would probably be sent to camp, and they would probably receive a letter from me soon.

Three weeks later we were assembled in the middle of the night and sent to Turkistan to a coal mine called NKVD. I don't know if it was run by the NKVD or for them. After traveling for two nights and two days, we came to a huge labor camp. After arrival we were registered and assigned to a barracks, Misha and I still together. We became more friendly. He felt less guilt and realized I did not have such a grudge since our sentence was commuted. But he didn't understand that I never had a grudge against him. I was sorry for him and sorry for me. I never showed or felt any hate for him.

The labor camp was huge, over ten thousand people at least. About half of them were deserters between ages forty and fifty and seventy to seventy five percent native Moslems. The others were minor criminals. Political prisoners and murderers are usually sent deep into the Tiga, the tundra in Siberia where you cannot escape even if they let you go. You would die of hunger before you reached a railroad.

Do not compare the labor camp I was in with the labor camps of political prisoners. There is a big difference. The prisoners are treated differently. One-time offenders with minor crimes are in the regular labor camps. Ours was a major crime, but we were treated as minor criminals. It was, after all, our first offense.

Political prisoners suffer more for two reasons. First of all, they are in camps with more discipline, a harsher environment; and they feel they are innocent, which makes it more painful to demand certain rights the Soviet government guarantees. These rights are broken more often by the government than by the people. For example, the Soviet constitution says if anyone wants to criticize the government, the government must provide a free press and free distribution of the complaint. But if anybody tries to do what the constitution guarantees, I would like to see them after their complaint is printed.

The labor camp was huge. About three thousand were women there for petty crimes. Many prisoners were Moslems fanatics. You couldn't find younger deserters. The guards were draftees, older, over forty. The younger ones were sent to war.

We were all assembled in the yard where the commandant explained to us the law and rules of the camp. The commandant was very tall, six-foot-six, in an NKVD uniform. We could write as many letters as we wanted, and they would not be censored, he said. We took that with a grain of salt. But everyone must work, unless he was not well, and he must have a doctor's note for that excuse. There was a hospital in the camp. There were doctors and nurses. Eighty percent were free citizens and lived in town about five miles away. Some were prisoners. The commandant told us we would get paid every month, minus deductions for room and board. He showed us a store where we could buy bread, cigarettes, chocolates, and other things with the money. About six months later the store closed due to lack of supplies. The army needed the supplies, the commandant told us.

He told us there was a club, a soccer team, ping-pong, and chess; and after work we had a right to use all the facilities. After work and on Sundays. Our work was twelve hours. starting at seven in the morning and ending at seven in the evening, with an hour for lunch. We got breakfast in the morning at six, which consisted of half a pound of bread, some vegetables—tomatoes, onions—and once in a blue moon, a piece of ham. For lunch we had to provide our own, any way we could, by buying from other prisoners, or the store while it was still open. Supper was after work between seven and eight. It was soup and half a pound of bread. In the beginning we had meat in the soup, but it got scarcer and scarcer as time went by. The explanation from the commandant was always the same, that the war came first.

The whole camp had only three Jews, Misha, myself, and a young fellow who worked in the coal mines. We were assigned to work on a Kammenny carrier, which is a huge mountain of different kinds of rock. Before that, we were given two days off so we could get acquainted with the camp and the camp ways, and have it explained to us that it was different from other places. There were no beds, but bunkbeds to sleep on in the barracks. The mattress was straw with straw pillows. No sheets, only blankets. You had to write home for sheets; and if you had them, some of the characters would try to take them while you slept. You had to tie your shoes together and then to your wrist, or others would steal them and sell them to those with passes to town who would then resell them. The passes were given for good behavior. You slept in your clothes for the same reason. It was no picnic, but it was better than sitting in a death cell waiting to be shot.

I knew I was guilty of my crime, so I had to accept the punishment that was meted out to me.

After I said goodbye to my father, I had a vision or recollection so strong of our time in Warsaw. I saw Father on a Saturday morning lying in bed with all the children surrounding him while Mother was making breakfast. Father was reading us stories in Yiddish from Shalom Aleichem, Bialik, and others. It was a delight to learn from Jewish literature, with humor, describing Jewish suffering and making fun of old-fashioned Jewish life and tradition. It bought tears to my eyes thinking of those days.

After we had been in the labor camp a few days, we wrote home and told our families where we were so they could send us parcels, which we started receiving a month later. Misha's sister was all alone and everything had been taken away from his family, so the parcels I got I shared with Misha. In a few months everyone thought we were brothers. Pretty soon parcels would be given to him "for his brother." Nobody knew we were just friends; I had forgotten all that had gone before between us.

We had to try to survive. Without saying anything to Misha, I went to the chief surgeon, Nicolai Nikolaivich, with some complaints about my knee, my arm, little things, but never asked for a certificate not to go to work. I did this just to talk to him. I did not have any true complaints. He did not feel any suspicion about the reason I came to see him. When we were talking, I told him what I was in labor camp for. I did not tell him about my death sentence, but that I had ten years, that I was young and foolish and had made a mistake. He listened very patiently to me, as he was in his fifties, slightly gray-haired. He explained to me the Soviet law, which I already knew, that if you get sick and need lengthy treatment, you could be released with only the chief surgeon's permission. Of course, I had asked him and led him on. I already knew what the law was, but he didn't know that I knew, and I never told him. I'm not an expert in Soviet law, but those that I could use or could be used against me, I knew very well.

The surgeon explained that if I needed lengthy treatment, all I needed for immediate release was his signature. I told him my sentence was ten years, not twenty-five. I did not want to scare him off.

I went to the commandant to find out what my sentence was. The commandant looked into the papers and told me it was twenty years. He told me to write a letter to the president of the Soviet Union. He provided me with an envelope and told me what to write: about my mistake, my background, and how young I was. He felt my sentence would be shortened if it was understood about my background and position.

Misha and I both wrote and sent the letters to Moscow to the president. It took less then two months before we got a reply; it was that our sentence was cut in half, to ten years. This made us feel a little bit better. I did not tell Misha about talking to the surgeon. I knew his sister had no money, and in case I worked something out and his sister could not pay, it would make me feel bad to leave him behind. This way he might believe that I had a certain illness, as the commandant would have the signature of the chief surgeon.

I talked to the chief surgeon when he was alone and told him the sentence was ten years. I would like to leave camp between one and two years, I told him. I continued going to him, which gave him a chance to compile a record of my illnesses, a medical record to prove need for continuous treatment. About six months later, I wrote to my mother and told her what I had achieved in the labor camp. Of course, the letter was mailed on the outside, as I did not trust the mail from inside. I told her I could leave the camp for twenty thousand rubles, and that my brother should come and bring ten thousand rubles with him. The other ten thousand the doctor would receive after I was free.

After eight months, my brother Shlomo came to the camp with ten thousand rubles. When the time came, I was hospitalized. And fooling around with the nurses at night, I was healthy. The others were sick. Misha came and told me my brother was here. I told the nurses to call the doctor, and the doctor gave me permission to leave the hospital. I went and visited with my brother on a Thursday, and he told me that he came with the money but he was afraid to go to the doctor's house. I told him that there was nothing to fear; it was what the doctor had suggested. I told him just to go, just leave the money, you don't have to talk, just leave the money, and go get the train and go home. And then write to me and tell me what happened.

Shlomo was too chicken to do it. My brother Abraham would have done it. I don't know why they sent Shlomo, knowing how he was. He was afraid the doctor's house was being watched. So he just went home again with the money. I did not know it. I went back into the hospital. I told the doctor that my brother was here with the money and that he should receive it within the next few days. He explained to me that he was getting the papers ready, and that they had to be sent to some medical authority to verify the findings, which usually takes between two to six weeks. After that I would be able to leave.

Two days later, the surgeon told me that nobody came. It was hard for me to believe that my brother would have come all that way and then gone home again with the money. A few days later I was released from the hospital. I felt betrayed, thinking that the surgeon had received the money and pretended as if nothing had happened. Then I received a letter a few weeks later saying that my brother had gone home with the money, because he was afraid to leave it, in case the house was watched.

After about a year or more in camp, I stopped getting parcels from home. This surprised me. The food was getting worse and worse. The war was not going too well, so the parcels were very important. A big help. The soup got thinner and thinner, and the commandant said the whole nation was having a bad time with food. It was true. So the parcels meant a lot. I knew something was wrong, but I didn't know what. I feared the worst. That somebody in my family was dead.

I had to go back to work. The commandant, thinking since I had to go to the hospital so much (so he thought) and since I was young and ill, gave me an easier job. I was made a kind of foreman, overseeing others and not having to do the actual labor myself.

This was all-important to me. I did not have to work so hard. I did not get so tired, so at night I could sneak out and go to the women's barracks. It was convenient, how they lay next to one another. What could I do? One would ask the next, "Is he a good lover?" I tried my best, and they did seem pleased with the results. They had to teach me, and I was a good pupil, one of the best, and willing to learn every night if possible.

All the same, I was depressed, remembering how my chance for freedom had vanished because of my brother's cowardly refusal to act on my behalf. Misha, not knowing what was going on, did not feel so bad. And Slava, his girlfriend, came to see him. That helped him even more, of course.

Labor camp was really like living in a village, surrounded with barbed wire. We could not leave, but we had a kind of freedom. We did not sit in cells. We went to work, we had entertainment, we could write out, receive company.

I told Misha to tell Slava where I worked outside of the camp. She could come there, and I could talk to her. Of all the guards who took us to work and back, one was especially nice. The rest were strict. I would sit down near this one and he would talk to me, although it was forbidden. I always attracted more attention, being small and looking younger than I really was; and most people wanted to know what I was doing there. And the guard was curious, too, like most other people.

I told him the story. He felt bad and said don't worry about it, the war will be over, there will be amnesty, and you will go home. I really felt encouraged that someone would talk like that to me. He was like a father figure. I knew that he would let me talk to Slava. When I saw Slava from far away she waved a handkerchief. I went over to him and asked, "Citizen guard, would you allow me to leave to see my girl? I promise I will not run away." I had to go down a hill where he could not see me.

He said to me, "Let me tell you, son, if you run away, I would have to serve your sentence. I know you are not going to do that to me. I have a wife and three children. I'm taking a chance but I have faith in you. And I trust you. You are not a bad kid."

I thanked him very much and told him he would not be sorry. I went over and talked with Slava for about an hour. She told me she did not know what had happened to my family. They moved out of the house we had lived in and moved to a completely different neighborhood. She told me she did not know the reason. She was not too inquisitive. I really did not know what had happened. I could not imagine, because when my father and I were arrested, I knew we had left money in diamonds and gold. Mother could have sold any one item and had enough to live on for years and years.

Slava left and I stayed sitting by the road, doodling with a twig on the ground, thinking it was good that she had been reinstated in school and was back in the Komsomol, when a truck came along. Suddenly a voice called to me from the truck. It was the driver. "Chaim, what are doing here?" It was none other than our neighbor Lehrer's son, from our time in Siberia! From Komi ASSR. He was working on a collective farm not too far from the labor camp.

I told him I was in a labor camp. He asked for how long and I told him about nine years more. He said, "Come on and get in the truck, and I will take you to town and you can forget the whole thing."

I was very tempted to do it, but I remembered what the guard had told me. That he had three children, and that if I ran away after he had given me permission, he would serve my sentence. I don't know if it was true or not, but I was afraid to take a chance. He was too nice to me. He talked to me like a father. I told Mr. Lehrer, "I can't do it."

"Don't be stupid. To hell with him."

"No, I can't do it. Because if I don't go back I would never forget what I did, and it would bother me the rest of my life!"

Mr. Lehrer shook his head and said, "You are as stupid as you always were. Doing things when you didn't have to. Fighting the commandant. But here, to save your own skin, instead of saving the guard's skin, you will sit in labor camp nine years, eh? Smart, right?"

I couldn't answer him because he was right. Maybe I should have gone, but I couldn't. When I came back I told the guard the story. He almost had tears in his eyes when he said, "Oh my God. You—I don't know what I would have done in your place."

I said, "I hope you never have a chance to be in my place."

Then he started to smile. "I knew I could trust you."

I said, "You could. I couldn't. I was very tempted. But I decided not to."

He looked at me and said, "Forget about the whole thing. I didn't let you go, you didn't run away. You saw Slava. That's all over and we are the only two who know it."

Of course, I sat for hours thinking what would've happen if I had done it. I guess I will never know because I didn't. It was very difficult for me after seeing Slava and thinking of my brother and what he could have done. I was really depressed for a long time.

Of course, Misha suffered too. He and I shared my parcels and he used to wear my clothes, as I told you, and nobody knew we were just friends. They thought we were brothers.

At least one good thing happened. A couple of months later I received a letter from the President of the Soviet Union which said our sentence was commuted to ten years, instead of twenty-five. Of course, that would give us some joy, but still, the eight-and-a-half years left was still a long, long time. I was also told that with good behavior you could cut off two-thirds of the sentence, which would mean that instead of ten I would have to do six-and-a-half. That would give me a little over five years.

My hope was what the guard told me, stating that after the war, there would be amnesty for all who had served in prison for reasons of the war. In war, conditions are not easy, and people do things that under normal conditions they would not do. That at least kept my hope up.

In the meantime, the Russian front kept moving closer, liberating territory after territory occupied by the Germans. Slava told me when the Crimea was liberated that the whole college was to return to her home town of Simferopol, where the university was. She also told me, which pleased Misha and me very much, that she was reinstated in the Komsomol Young Communist League. She was also back in college and had only a year-and-a-half left to become a doctor. Of course, that meant a lot to us, since what she did was really heroic on her part. It didn't do us any good, but it still made you feel good just listening to her, what she said making the DA go wild and berserk. I guess it was some kind of heroism, and it did mean a lot to us.

In August or September of 1943, the commandant called me and Misha and Lazar into his office, and said he wanted us to take over a shift at the coal mine from seven to five. Coal miners work two hours less. We had to work ten hours with a one-hour break inbetween. I looked at the commandant and smiled. I asked him, "Citizen Commandant, do you know how old I am?"

"Yes, I know how old you are. You are seventeen. I looked at your file."

"Don't you think I am too young to run a coal mine?" I asked him. "I come from Warsaw. The only time I saw a coal mine was in a picture or in the movies."

He smiled and said "Lazar could do it. He has already been there for three years. Misha, he is 28? He can do it. You? You could do it, too. I read your file. I know you can do anything you want to. You are a pretty bright kid."

I pointed towards the camp and said, "Look out there. Look how many people you can pick. Why me?"

He went over to the window, pointed, and said, "Look at them. The Kazakhs. Half of them are stupid morons. Illiterate. You think they could run a mine and you can't? If you think that way, you're not Jewish."

I started to laugh. He said, "There is not a Jew who cannot achieve whatever he wants. I have lived with plenty of Jews. And none of them was ever considered stupid. The old-timers were tailors and shoemakers. But you show me the new generation which does not have an education and still has a good, important job. We have Jewish generals. There is no question in my mind. You are going to do it and do a good job of it."

I did not want to spoil his image of the Jews, after that pep talk, though he might not be correct. I have met stupid Jews in my life. For example, the people who registered to return to Hitler's concentration camp, I did not consider smart. But I did not tell that to the commandant.

I was really scared because I was afraid of going down in a coal mine. The coal mine was split up into three sections. Each of us was to have a section. The people who were running the coal mine were not prisoners; they had been drafted. So we had to take over. They were with us one week to show us how to run the mine, and after that we were on our own. I was still fearful of the mines after I had been there a few months. After five or six months we were running the mine as well as the others had and produced as much or more coal than they had.

Every two hours or so, all the workers would stop for a smoke. They were prisoners but their right to smoke was not taken away from them. It was an unwritten law. The same thing had been done on the rocks, but that was done by brigades. Some worked and some stopped. But here, everybody smoked, and no coal came down while they smoked. It was supposed to be a five-minute break, but it usually took up to fifteen minutes. Pierekur—smoking time, like teatime in England. If Stalin himself had come down, he would not have told the men to stop and go to work. I got used to it after a while. Seeing the empty conveyors, I thought they should have been shut off, but nobody bothered and I did not want to try to start something new. It is like a law. You sit down, even if you don't smoke, and wait. You wouldn't dare try to continue.

During a break, I had a conversation with one of the deserters. I was very curious to find out why they chose prison instead of going to the army. They explained to me that I was too young to understand what war is. They did not know what I had already been through. They explained to me that when you go to war you have a fifty-fifty chance of not coming home alive, and a secenty-five percent chance of being crippled. Being in prison receiving packages from their wives was an easier way out, since they were positive that when the war ended they would all be free. "Don't think we are stupid. We pretend to be, but we know what we are doing. We acted dumb at the trial and we are acting now."

The days and the nights went past. Playing a little soccer, on Sundays going to a movie. Most of the movies we saw were military, heroically portraying the Russian people fighting Nazism, guerilla commandos, all kinds of things. A radio loudspeaker blared every time the news bulletins used to come on, stating what area was being liberated. They'd name some towns and so on. So we had a pretty good idea of what the front was doing, and we were always rooting for the Russians to beat the damn Germans.

There were two reasons why. First was the amnesty we all expected, and second, we knew what the Nazis were. We saw the atrocities shown in newsreels taken after the Russians had liberated places. We saw massacres of Jews, massacres of Russians, people who had been hung on trees and lampposts. It was inhumane just to look. I cried very often looking at those newsreels.

This was, I think, in January or February of 1944. I was around eighteen. It had been about two years since my arrest, but with the investigation and everything, it was about twenty months or close to it.

11
REUNITED

About this time the Russian army entered Polish towns, and amnesty for all Polish citizens who had committed no capital crimes was announced on the camp loudspeakers. I was really surprised that ours was not considered a capital crime. We fell under the amnesty. We felt that our crime was a capital crime, but the Soviet government bent over backwards to please the Polish people, and we were considered Polacks, not Jews, by the Russians. Misha, the other Jew Lazar, and I were called in by the commandant. He told us that as soon as the papers arrived, we would be free to go. But only under one condition: Misha and I were to never return to the town where we had been condemned. He explained to us that according to the town, we were dead, and if we came back it would ruin the image of the death sentence.

I understood his reasoning but I said to myself, "Where else can I go but back to my family? What would I do?" We agreed, however, that we would not go back home.

I think it was in June that the commandant called us in and said the papers had arrived for our release. He prepared papers, travel documents, and a ticket we asked for to Novo Sibitsk. It would take us in the direction where we lived and past that town. We could not tell him we were going back home. This meant we could get out at Kyzl-Orda on that ticket.

You have to realize the joy the three of us felt, as we were the only three Polish citizens in the labor camp. Everybody came over and wished us good luck and happiness and told us never to return. I promised them that—never to return. It had been approximately twenty-two months since I had told my mother I would be home in two years. Well, I still owed the Soviet government two months, since I came home in twenty-two months instead of two years.

When we got off in Kyzl-Orda, Misha went home to his sister, and I went home, too, because Slava had told me where my family lived.

When I saw the outside, I cried. One of the windows was shattered, and a pillow was shoved in to keep out the cold. The inside was dirty and dingy. My mother was standing in the hallway, looking a little bit better than she had looked when I met her in Syktyvkar in Komi. She was drably dressed,and had lost a lot of weight.

Of course, Mother did not expect me, but she knew of the amnesty from hearing it on the radio. She never believed it would happen to us. To others, but not to us. When I came close to the house I screamed, "Mama!" Mother collapsed and fainted when she saw me. When she came to, she said, "I don't believe it. But you told me you would come, and here you are. You told me two years, and here you are." I calmed Mother down, for fear she might get a heart attack. She did not look too healthy.

After that I walked into the house. My sister Sally was shabbily dressed, and not too happy in the face, either. I embraced and kissed her. I held onto Mother's hand, and thought back to the day I had to let it go in the courtroom before the sentencing.

The one-room apartment was dirty and dingy and had only two beds. Mother slept with Sally, and my two brothers were on the other side of the room. The room was about ten-by-twelve. A wood-burning stove stood in the middle of the room. When I saw everything, I cried inside. I didn't want to show Mother my disappointment. I couldn't wait to ask her about the gold and diamonds.

"What happened to the gold and diamonds Father and I left you?" I finally had enough courage to ask her what had happened. She explained that my brother had hid the whole satchel when they lived in the old place. He had buried it in the desert and put a little tree and a rock on it, not realizing that the desert winds would rip out whatever did not grow naturally, and even things that did grow, if they were weak. I did not even ask which brother did it. Even today I still do not know. It doesn't matter anymore. You can't bring the past back to change it and I'm better off not knowing which of my brothers did it so as not to harbor resentment towards him.

I told Mother, "Listen to me. Forget it. Things are going to change. We are going to move out of this dump. Let's wait a few more weeks until Father comes home."

When I asked my sister why she had to hide the gold, she said it was because of Moniek the stutterer, the same Moniek where I had found the ration cards that Misha made. He was not jailed, but he lost his profitable business and was looking to make an easy buck. He went to the police, got a hold of a detective, and told him that he knew I was in jail and Father was in jail, and that we had a lot of good things. Father had a sable coat, Mother had a lamb coat, a karakul, and there was a silver fox coat worth a lot of money. He told the detective that my two brothers would not do anything, they were not very brave, and that he should go when they were at work and confiscate the things worth so much money. Since Mother spoke very little Russian and my sister was in school, they would have an easy time taking everything. He could get away with it, and the two of them would share what he got.

On her way home from school, Sally met a neighbor who said to her, "Sally, you know what happened?"

"What?"

"Your mother was taken by a detective and two policeman. They cleaned out the house and loaded everything on a horse and buggy on the way to the police station."

She ran like wild and saw Mother trailing after the horse and buggy. She followed Mother into the police station. The detective was not too happy because Sally was only about twelve years old, and it was not easy to put something over on her. She was a little bit like me—pretty fast and, for a girl, pretty tough. She went in with Mother and insisted that everything that was taken should be listed. The detective tried to skip the fur coats, but she insisted they add them, too. He finally did it.

Sally asked, "When are we going to get our stuff back?"

He said, "First of all, there has to be an investigation to see if this was bought with illegal money. If everything is all right, you should get it back in a few weeks."

She told the chief of police what they did was illegal. But the detective had told him there were enough grounds for investigation. The chief of police doesn't always know what the hell is going on.

Being my sister and a tough little girl, Sally left the station and went to the DA to tell him the story. He said what they did was illegal. She asked, "What can you do about it?"

He asked, "What time do you get back from the school?"

She said, "Three o'clock."

The DA told her to wait a few days, and if by the end of the week she heard nothing, to go find out and see what was happening. If she did not get a satisfactory answer, come back and tell him. And that is exactly what my sister did. When the police detective told her not to rush, that these things take more than a few weeks, making excuses, my sister went to the DA again and told him.

He made a date with her and told her to be there at the station at four o'clock. He was to be there for something else, and when she saw him she was to make a big ruckus, scream and cry. And he would try to find out what it was all about, pretending that he knew nothing. That is what she did. She came a few minutes before four o'clock, saw the DA coming, and started to scream and cry and carry on, asking for her things back. Of course, mother was scared.

The detective said, "Dievushka, little girl, you can't come in here and scream and cry. Who do you think you are?"

The DA intervened and asked, "Little girl, what is the trouble?"

She told him the whole story as if he had never heard it before. "The detective came with two policeman, threatening my mother with arrest if she resisted, and they took all my stuff, all our things."

The DA turned to the detective and asked, "On what authority did you do this?"

"We had been told by an informer, Moniek Schwarzberg. He said that all the things they had were gotten with illegal money, with money from the brother and Father on the black market."

The DA said, "You cannot take the word of an informer without some proof. An investigation should have been made before you took anything."

My sister told them that my brother did not live in the house and that the money was from Warsaw. He lived separately, she said, he had his own apartment. And millions of rubles were confiscated from him and never given to the family.

The detective was put on the spot. The DA said that within the week he must have the evidence or return the stuff. He told my sister that if she didn't get the stuff back in a week to come and tell him and he would make sure the detective abided by the law. He told her this in front of the detective. They were protected by Soviet law as well as any other citizen. Just because Mother did not speak Russian; and the brother and Father were in jail paying for what they did, you could not just be harassed by anybody unless there was evidence for the charges.

"You did nothing," the DA said. "Or your mother. If you don't get your things in a week, you let me know."

Lacking one day, the detective and two policemen brought back everything on the list except Father's fur coat and Mother's. Of course, my sister asked for them. She kept going back to the station, but the detective had probably sold them, not expecting to have an investigation stop him.

The DA told my sister, "If you want to press charges, I'll go along."

But Sally was afraid. Afraid the DA might be transferred and a new DA might not be as helpful, or even be on the side of the police. So they settled for getting the things returned. She decided to let it alone.

Moniek, who was supposedly a friend, had tried to do this to us. He tried to destroy the rest of our home. This reminds me of looters in times of flood or fire, trying to get rich on someone else's misery. Fortunately, it did not work out too well for him.

Because of the fear that they might come back, my brother had buried the satchel of gold and diamonds in the desert. The satchel must still be buried somewhere in the steppes of Central Asia.

I don't know what my brother did or didn't do, but our home was not the same. I saw hunger. I told Mother, "Don't worry. You will never be hungry again."

My sister told me that my brother Shlomo beat her. I asked her why? He has a girlfriend and he wanted to marry her. But my brother had outbursts and was uncontrollable and the girl wanted to wait. She said she loved him but wanted to wait. As an excuse, or perhaps because as a little girl Sally used to make up stories and my brother and I would get beatings from Father, now he was getting even. But probably he was just taking out his frustrations on her.

Since Sally was his favorite child, the youngest and the only girl, Father used to give us advance beatings before he left the house, stating we would get the rest when he came home. We used to beat Sally anyway, knowing we would get the rest when he returned. Father used to have a rubber hose for the boys. My sister was never screamed at, forget about beatings. Whatever she did was okay. She was Father's little girl. (She still is, even today. But today we understand and have no resentment.) Mother was helpless to do anything about the situation. She was weak, too weak to do much more than cry.

The minute my brother came home, we embraced and kissed, then I told him, "You are my older brother, but if I ever see you put a hand on Sally, I will kill you. And I mean it literally." A few days later I came into the house, and Sally was crying. "What happened?" She told me Shlomo had hit her again. I went berserk and chased him for blocks. I screamed, "If I catch you, I'll kill you. I'll kill you at night when you are asleep. She went through enough without having this trouble from you."

He never touched her again.

I laid low for awhile. Then I went to see my Korean friends and they gave me money, which helped me to fix the window. We were still waiting for Father to come home, which was to be soon. We had plenty of food, with Keisha and the others helping. He was willing to help more, but I only took what we needed. So the Korean Polack was alive and kicking and back in the circle of friends.

Kim Keisha was now the director of transportation for the town. My friends asked me if I wanted a job. I told them no, I wanted to lay low, at least till Father came back. I was a little fearful to go back to work with them, although the case was past and dead. But there might be a problem, anyhow.

At my first meeting with Keisha in his house, his mother and sister jumped and kissed me. His mother said to Kim in Korean, "My second son came home."

I jokingly said, "Be careful. My mother might object to that."

About two months later, Father came home, late August of 1944. The town had very few men. The only men in town were Koreans, who were not drafted, I don't know why, some of the Polish Jews, and people over fifty-five. I found out a new Polish army was established under Wanda Vasileska. She was a Polish Communist leader at one time, leading the Communist Party for awhile.

The Polish government in Russia was called the Lublin Government. Now we had two governments, one in London and one in Russia. Russia did not recognize the government under General Anders in London. It would have created a problem—the army would have been a Jewish army, not a Polish one, because the majority would have been Polish Jews. Most of the Poles who lived in Russia were sent out by General Anders in 1942 or '43. Most of the citizens left were of the Jewish faith. The Russians used Polish citizens of Russian descent in the Polish army. Marshal Rokossovsky led the Polish army; although he was a Soviet marshal, he was of Polish descent.

After the army was created, the minute they entered Polish soil they started recruiting Poles.

Slava had already left, and the whole college returned to Simferopol. Many factories remained—they were never dismantled—but many of the people had gone back home. Thus the town, once half a million people, now had about a quarter of a million. It was a busy little town. Leaving the factories helped to industrialize Central Asia.

We had a joyful reunion when Father came home. Once again the whole family was together. I also found out Father had been in a labor camp called Karaganda. He was a tailor and made suits privately for the officers and private citizens of the town. He would send money home to Mother, which was a big help after losing all that we had. And most of the clothes were sold. They were not guarded in the factory where Father worked. That made it easy for him to send the money home.

After being home a few days, Father went to the market, speculating, buying, and selling. I took a donkey and a wagon and went to the railroad station to use it to transport luggage, coal, and whatever people needed. I still wanted to lay low, not to rattle things in any way. Of course, my Korean friends couldn't understand why I was not willing to accept more help from them. To most of the people of the town I was dead, and I did not want to be seen too often. I was stopped many times, mostly by women asking if I had a younger brother, Chaim. I told them yes. They expressed sympathy for what had happened to him. They told me that I looked just like him, mistaking me for my older brother. My hair had receded so I looked older. I let them believe I was my older brother.

After working a month or so, the Jewish Birobijan theatre arrived, a troop of over fifty. They came from Birobijan, a Jewish republic established in the early thirties as a solution to the Jewish problem in the world. It was near Manchuria. This was an answer to Zionism, a Jewish state. Birobijan offered a Jewish national life. It was not a big success because Jews did not want to move to a desolate area. Most liked to live in big towns. Even though they could have become store owners, the younger generation was becoming more and more assimilated and paid little attention to the Jewish national state. There was Jewish life there, but not as expected by the Soviet government.

When the Jewish theatre came to our town, they had a little problem. They had three Pullman cars full of decorations. I came home one evening to find a man sitting in our house. My father said, "There is a man waiting for you."

The first thing that came to my mind was that he was from the NKVD and that I would have to leave town, that I had no right to be here. I didn't say anything but waited for him to talk first.

As a joke he said, "I am not from the NKVD."

I gave a sigh of relief. He said, "I am the director of the Jewish Birobijan theatre. We have three Pullman cars full of decorations, and we can't get them unloaded. But we have to get them moved in the next few days, or we won't be able to open the theatre in time. We need time for rehearsal."

I asked him, "Why are you coming to me?"

He said he was told that I was the only man in town who would be able to help him.

I asked, "Who told you?"

He said, "I can't tell you the name."

I asked him, "Why don't you go to the mayor and ask for transportation?"

He said, "I went everywhere, including the police. And everyone gave me the same answer. The majority of the vehicles were taken by the army, and they are working with a skeleton amount. They cannot afford to give away trucks to anybody for even a few days."

"What do you want me to do?" I asked.

He said, "You could do it. You have the connections. And I am willing to pay for it."

"How?"

He said, "I'll give you a bale of beautiful fabric, about a thousand yards, worth thousands of rubles on the open market, as most of the stuff on the market is not of this quality. For the ten weeks we are in town we will employ you at a salary of about four hundred rubles a month."

Which wasn't too much on the black market.

"All of your family will have passes to the theatre every day and sit in the first row, which is usually reserved for dignitaries."

Of course I would have done it without pay, as I wanted to see some Jewish theatre. After he told me about the plays they were to put on, I was really excited. One of the shows was *Tevya the Milkman*, which here is known as *Fiddler on the Roof*. In Russia it was performed as a drama, not a musical.

I asked where I could meet him. I would tell him my answer tomorrow night. He said he would come back the next night, as he had no office yet. I went to see Kim Keisha, the director of transportation, and my best friend. Keisha took me to the mayor's office and when the mayor saw me he said, "Yes, Genadie?" (This is the Russian name they used to call me. There is no *h* in the Russian language so a *g* is used instead. Hitler is pronounced with a "G".) "I know what you want."

"You do? But how?"

"They were here. I could have given it to them, but I knew they were going to wind up with you. So you can make something for yourself."

I smiled. "That was a dirty trick. Thanks a lot."

"You know, we will never forget you, knowing what you did for Keisha and others."

"Let's forget about that. It is forgotten."

"We can never forget that. It is only two years, but we will not forget it. Ever."

He said they would get me four trucks, which would be at the railroad station at four o'clock in the morning. The theatre would have to provide the working men and should finish in one day. No matter how long it took to bring the decorations, the drivers would not leave.

That night the director came to the house. I told him he would have not two, but four trucks to move out in one day; but no matter how long it would take, the drivers would not leave until the job was finished. He should have his working crew at the railroad station at 4 A.M. sharp. He was very glad and shook hands with me and left. And we were very glad we were to have Jewish theatre for ten weeks.

About a month after I started working in the theatre, we found a beautiful place to move to, a brick house that was stucco or lime-covered. The inside had beautiful parquet floors, a beautiful kitchen, full bath, three bedrooms, even a basement.

Because so many people had left, there were plenty of places to rent. We moved in and felt like kings. This was a better place than we had had in Warsaw. It was a single house with a beautiful garden, oak doors with glass inserts, brass handles and custom built. The floors shone. I don't know what was used on them. The owner was a retired railroad engineer who had another house not too far away.

On the opening night of the theatre, the majority of the people were non-Jewish—Koreans, Kazakhs, Russians. It was a sellout for the whole ten weeks they were there. My family, of course, had the first row and the tickets were free. Also sitting in the first row was the mayor of the city and Keisha, also a big shot, the director of NKVD, the assistant director, and the chief of police and his assistant. And the investigator, Bykovsky, and the judge who sentenced me to death as well as the DA who carried on the trial. They were sitting right next to us.

I said to my father, "Dad, do you know who we are sitting with?"

Of course, he didn't believe me. A little bit over two years ago they were prosecutors and judges. Now we were sitting side by side enjoying the theatre. Even one of the Supreme Court judges was there, too. I pointed out the judge who sentenced me to death. My father said he couldn't believe it. It was like a fairy tale. And for ten weeks we had almost the same company. I don't know if they recognized me or not, but if they did they pretended not to know me.

"By some kind of miracle," my father said. "It is unbelievable. Now we are sitting together. People who make the law, enforce the law, and break the law. The same who sentenced me for a political crime and you for an economic one."

I think the happiest person at the theare was my mother. Her eyes were full of joy, having all the family once more enjoying life together.

I said "If we tell this to anyone, nobody will believe it. I don't know if I believe it. I have to pinch myself."

Every performance received standing ovations. The actors were fantastic. We had seen Jewish theatre in Warsaw, but none to compare with this. The people who did not understand Yiddish had programs to explain the meaning of the show. It was a high point for the life of that city to have such performances. When the ten weeks passed, I lost my job. The theatre packed up and left for another city. They were on a schedule.

12
"LIFE IS SWEET"

I don't know if it was a state or federal law that allowed us to produce anything we were able to, and sell to compete with the government. There was only one candy and soda stand in the city which belonged to a Russian. Abraham told my father it seemed a good idea to open one of our own. I approached the director of finance, who was a tall Russian and very strict. When Father and I met him in his office, he made it very difficult for us to get a license. Others had told me it might take a little time because he was very strict. I knew that we would get it in the end, but how long would it take?

When my father was in prison, he met a man called Moyshe Wulkan. He was arrested when the Polish mission, run by the Polish government in London, was closed down. The Soviet authorities tried to force him to take a Soviet passport. He was one of the heads of the Polish mission. He was an Orthodox Jew and was considered a Talmud "chochem" scholar—meaning wise man. He had been the head of the Jewish community in Aucshwitz before the war. In spite of having an anti-Semitic Polish government, he was very often called in by them for advice and consultations.

My father, though he was not an Orthodox Jew, knew the Talmud very well. And Mr. Wulkan, a man Father met in prison, became very friendly with my father in order to exchange ideas. I don't know what my father told Mr. Wulkan about me. They shook hands when they were separated and sent to different labor camps. He made my father promise that if they were ever free, he must bring me to him, that he had to meet me.

Mr. Wulkan was in his fifties and had a son about twenty years old, two daughters, Saba, about twelve to fourteen years old, and Runia, who was twenty-two or twenty-four. He and his son were arrested. If he had taken a passport, they would have been free. The Soviet government felt that his being the head of the mission would encourage others to do the same. But he did not take the passport. After the amnesty, he came back, but his son died in labor camp. Most of the children from the rich died, as they were unable to withstand the hardships. It was a big loss to him, as it was his only son. And to Orthodox Jews, it was very important to have a son.

When my father said to me that he had made a promise to Mr. Wulkan and that I was to go with him, I was not too excited because they were the Polish elite. In spite of being Orthodox Jews, they spoke only Polish in their home. I went with my father to meet him. I was very impressed with this man, his wisdom, and the way he thought. I spoke Yiddish to him. It was not that I did not know Polish. I speak Polish fluently, as well as any Pole. Runia, the oldest daughter, was the only one who sat and listened to our conversation. She had already been to college for a few years, and was highly intelligent. I liked her, but I made no effort to get to know her better.

As the Wulkans had no means of income, they lived by selling diamonds for ready cash. They were wealthy. Father suggested to me that if we got a license to open a stand, we could share it with the Wulkans. I had no objections to that. We decided that Mrs. Wulkan and my mother would do the baking, making cakes and jelly doughnuts. Soda was not too hard to make. It required food dye, ice, the saccharin and sugar, and only two flavors—lemon and orange. A few weeks passed and Keisha told me that he had arranged a meeting for my father with the director of finance. I don't know if Father paid him off or not, but we received a license a few days later.

While we built a big stand a short distance from the open market, production went into action. Mother and Mrs. Wulkan worked very hard. We bought candies from a Russian man who made them at home, even though it was illegal to buy and resell. Since they were homemade candies, people assumed we made them ourselves. My brother Abraham used to go to the Russian man to buy the candy, and he tried to watch how he did it, since they were made while you waited. After six weeks my brother thought he could make them himself. But every time he tried, nothing happened. I told my father that I would like to go and see how he did it. I went once, and the next day I made my own. Not only did I make the things he made, but I created my own variety. I wish I knew how to do it today.

Business went great, terrific. We had very little competition. We grossed over a thousand rubles a day. We used to have problems with Mr. Wulkan; in spite of his wisdom and knowledge, he used to get lost going from the house to the store. His Russian was very poor, so he had trouble communicating to find out where the store was located. It sometimes took two hours before he arrived, when it should have taken only twenty to thirty minutes. He had always been driven wherever he wanted to go; he never had to go on his own or even think about it. Even tying his shoe laces was a problem for him.

My brother Shlomo, disappointed that his girlfriend still held out on him by not marrying him, decided to go off on his own without waiting for the rest of the family. We all felt very bad, but there was not much we could have done. Mother and Father could not talk him out of it. After saying goodbye to everyone, he took his clothes. Father gave him money, and he left.

I was in the store from four to eight P.M. One day Runia brought cake from the house to the stand where I was working. She didn't leave but stood and talked to me for about an hour. She took the initiative and said, "How come you keep avoiding me?"

I told her I was not avoiding her, that she belonged to a higher society, afraid of being rejected, I was very cautious. She said that she would love to be friends with me. I bent over and kissed her, and after that day you hardly saw us apart. We used to spend nights till three or four in the morning sitting near the river Syr Darya, discussing books, philosophy, and other things that boys and girls talk about. I learned a lot from our conversations.

I also used to spend hours talking to Mr. Wulkan. His thoughts intrigued me very much. He was able to answer most anything. I asked him once, being a man who used to travel all over Europe, if he ever betrayed his wife? He was shocked by the question but came up with a very appropriate answer. "If a man betrays his wife and another man knows about it, he is no man." He also had a way of handling certain situations that would make some men furious. One day, Runia and I were alone in the house on the porch. We were kissing, and I had my hand under her blouse. Her father walked in on us and, instead of stopping and reprimanding us for what we were doing, passed right by as if he had not seen us. One minute later he came back, giving us a chance to stop what we were doing, and in a loud voice said, "In my house there are no secrets. If you say something, speak loud. It is not necessary to stay on the porch and whisper secrets." He did this so as not to embarrass his daughter or me. She said, "That's my father."

Mr. Wulkan's way of describing people was that every person is like the centerpiece of a fish. The dumber one was, the closer to the tail he was, and the smarter ones were closer to the head. If someone was stupid he called them a sardine, just a tail without a head.

Mrs. Wulkan was a beautiful lady, about five-foot-seven and slightly gray-haired. She was a little different from her husband. Runia sometimes would give her messages to give to me. She would gladly have seen me marry Runia. I had discussed marriage with Runia. We both agreed to get married, but we were going to have to work on Mr. Wulkan. During one of my long conversations with Mr. Wulkan, I said, "Mr. Wulkan, what would you have to say if I wanted to marry Runia?"

His answer was, "You are like a son to me. And I would do anything for you, but the only way I would let you marry Runia was if we were unable to leave the Soviet Union and have to live here. But should we be able to return home, I would want Runia to marry a religious person. This is the only objection I have against you." In a joking way he said, "You are almost a Jew. If you could become religious, I would give you my blessing."

I told him, "I guess you know me by now. Though I would do anything to marry Runia, I could not fake being religious."

He said, "I knew you could not fake it. If you would have done it, you would have done it sincerely." He knew, from my long discussions, my thoughts on religion in general. Not just Judaism, but all religions.

About a month after our discussion the whole Wulkan family got sick. A Chinese doctor, Mr. Chun Sun, came and told them that they had typhoid. The house had to be quarantined; nobody should come in and they could not go out. The hospital was overcrowded. There was no room there to take them, so they had to stay home. Mr. Wulkan offered the doctor money for the visit. Mr. Chun Sun got insulted. He told him if he ever offered money again, he would never come back. He was a very, very good doctor. He told them he worked for the state and the state paid him. He loved his work and that was why he helped people. "And if I wanted more money," he said jokingly, "I could have been a coal miner."

Mr. Wulkan answered him, "I'm glad you're not. I would hate to be treated by a coal miner."

The burden of baking fell on my mother, as we could not allow Mrs. Wulkan in her condition to do anything, because typhoid is very contagious.

When the doctor came back three days later, I was waiting for him outside. I asked him how they were they doing. He said they had high temperatures and were running out of food. It didn't look too good. Nobody was able to take care of them.

I waited till the doctor left and went into the house in spite of everyone inside screaming at me to not come in because they had typhoid. I ignored their warning. The first thing I did was to kiss Runia on the mouth. Of course, Mr. Wulkan turned his head away. He didn't like to see that. I told them I would stay till they recovered. I would cook and do anything they needed to have done. I would not go home. I would sleep on the floor. I had made arrangements with mother before I carried food to the Wulkans. Of course, my family did not know what my intentions were. They finally realized I was there when I did not come home to sleep. Mother used to bring food and leave it in front of the door.

Three days later when Dr. Chun Sun came, he was furious about what I did. He said in a few days that I would be lying with them, as typhoid was one of the most contagious of diseases. I jokingly said to him, "Doctor, I can't get sick. Who is going to take care of them? You don't want me to let them die, do you?"

"If I knew you were going to do this, I would have taken you for mental observation at the hospital, to make sure you are normal."

I told him I didn't know if being normal was an asset or a liability. You have to realize that what is going on in this world today, I would not call normal either.

Before he left he told me what to do, how many times to give them medication, and said as long as I was walking around, I might as well do it. I was there a little over a month. To my own surprise, I never got typhoid and brought them all back to their normal health. When the doctor came the last time, he couldn't believe that I had not been infected by the disease. He sent men from the hospital to disinfect the house before he would allow anybody to come in. Before I left the house, Mr. Wulkan kissed me on my forehead and said "I want you to understand that you are the only person except my own family I ever put my lips to."

Everything went back to normal. Back to long nights on the river with Runia. Runia had two years of college already and was very bright. We used to talk a lot. She helped me to get an education without going to school. Runia's younger sister, Saba, was a very close friend of my sister Sally, as they were approximately the same age and attended the same class at a Polish school.

After talking to my father, he suggested that we should open another stand, which would be open in the hours after we closed the first one. It should be in the park near the dancing area. I felt it was very good idea. We would only sell soda and buttered rolls. The next day I went to see my friend, Mr. Pack, the director of the parks. I told him I would like to have the spot near the entrance. There was a booth on the left side that sold entrance tickets. I wanted mine on the right side, with two windows, one facing the dance floor. It was no problem for him to agree as we already had a license for commerce. We had a carpenter a few days later start building a stand.

Two days later we got a visit, as usual at night, from two NKVD officers. They were waiting for me, as I got home very late. Of course, Father was all shook up, sitting by the house waiting for me. He had the same thoughts that I did when I saw them, that they wanted me to leave Kyzl-Orda, as I had not done as I was told by returning here.

When I came into the house they showed me their I.D.s, and told me to sit down, please, that they wanted to talk to me. They said, "Listen, Genadie, the spot you have near the dance floor, where you are building a stand, we want you to give it up. We need it for one of our men."

Of course, the whole family was not sleeping, being nervous, waiting to see what they wanted. I felt a little relieved that it was not what I had thought, that I would have to leave the town, but only that they wanted the spot by the dance floor near the entrance. I got a little braver and a little mad at them. "What right have you to come and tell me where I can or cannot have my stand?"

They tried in a very nice way to tell me I could have it on the other side, and said they would even pay to build the stand there. But after I insisted that the spot was mine and there could be no changes, they changed their tactics and started to threaten as to what they could do to me. I told them, "The only way that I would give you this place is if the director of the park withdrew his permission for me to build there."

They said they had already spoken to him and tried to put pressure on him to do it, but his answer was that the only way they could have this spot was if I gave it up voluntarily. Under no conditions would he deny me the right to have it on that spot. I told them, "In that case, you can say good night and leave before I throw you both out."

They had to leave and they said, "We will be back. This thing is not over yet."

I told them, "That's what you think. This is finished."

The next day I went to see the director of the parks. He told me, "You know that I would do anything for you. Under no conditions will I give in to their pressure. And the only way that they can have it, is if you give it to them. If you are willing to stand for your rights, I am willing to stand with you all the way."

A few days later our stand was finished. When the dance opened, their informer had to take the spot the NKVD had offered to me, which was on the other side, near the orchestra. Not very many people passed that way. No one wanted to stay too near the orchestra, which was very loud—trombones, saxophones. I was glad they did not approach my father about this matter. Because my father would have caved in right away and given up the spot as he knew what they were capable of.

Our stand was so busy we had three people working. We used to take in between one and two thousand rubles a night, which was more than we did the whole day at the other stand. Many, many times while I was working I looked across the park to see if I could see the prison that I spent thirty-five days in. It had been right there, and I had listened to the same music through that little, high window. The prison could only be seen in the winter when the trees were bare, but in spring and summer the leaves on the trees made it invisible at that distance.

In March of 1945 my Korean friends offered me a job as the director of supplies in a leather factory. The factory employed about twelve-hundred people. I accepted the job after having an interview with the director of the factory, Mikhail Mikhailovitch Griboyedov. He told me I had come highly recommended and that if I wanted the job I could have it. I took the job very gladly, as I only needed a couple of hours to make the candies. Everything else was made by the rest of the family. We also decided to give the Wulkans the store where we were partners, and opened yet another one near the college. My brother used to go every morning at eight o'clock to open the one near the college.

My brother Abraham, for reasons unknown to anyone, would never go out with girls, only married women. They were his thing. One afternoon I came to relieve my brother for an hour or two. A gypsy lady with a baby in her arms asked my brother if he would give her a roll for the baby, because the baby had not eaten for days. Abraham said to her, "I will give you six rolls if you will go to bed with me."

She looked at him and said, "You are very cruel. I don't want anything for myself. I ask for the baby."

"Well, I made you an offer. What's wrong with that?"

She said, "I'm a married woman. And I don't sell my body to anyone."

My brother said, "I like married women."

I intervened and took two rolls and gave them to the woman.

She thanked me for them and said she would like to read my palm. She said, "You have a long life before you. You have a lot of traveling to do," and she finished with, "You will never be hungry in your life." I guess she had the Bible in mind. Though she didn't say it, that is what I felt about casting your bread upon the waters. I was sure she did not see that in my palm. But I let her do it. It is a very funny thing, but even till today, I was never hungry again. It is funny, though, my brother ended up marrying a widow instead of a girl. I guess he was looking for an experienced woman.

13
GOING HOME II

Once a week the management of the factory had night duty. In case orders came in, somebody had to be there to take them. I was on duty the night of May fifth and sixth. The phone rang. When I picked up the phone I heard, "Hello, this is Moscow. Hello, this is Moscow." They usually repeat a few times as the phone connections are not good. "What is your name?"

I told them Genadie Leibovich.

"Listen very carefully to what I have to say. And repeat after I tell you, to make sure you understand what I am saying."

"I'm listening. I'm listening."

"The war has ended. There is a holiday tomorrow."

I repeated it to him.

"There is a celebration tomorrow. All factories are closed. Make sure there is enough vodka and food so when the workers come they can all get drunk."

I said okay and repeated the whole message. Before hanging up, he said, "I greet you with victory."

I immediately called the director and when he picked up the phone, the first thing I said to him was, "Victory greetings!"

He got all excited. He said, "What happened? What happened?"

I told him I had received a telephone call from Moscow only a few minutes ago and that tomorrow was a holiday. "Get your behind down here as fast as you can to prepare for the celebration."

The same telephone call was probably received at all the other factories in town, and in government offices. I was too excited to sleep anymore, although it was only two in the morning.

The next day about noon, I could hardly walk, I was so drunk. I couldn't hold my head up. Walking home, I saw the whole city was celebrating. There was Korean music, Russian music, and Kazach music dancing in the streets. I was hardly able to make my way across town. I was grabbed by many strangers, and I had to have a drink with them. I could hardly see, my eyes were bleared. I have never been so drunk in my life. Hours later I finally made it home. I slept the rest of the day.

A few weeks later a lot of the Polish people started to move back to Poland. Our family and the Wulkans got together to discuss whether we should return. We decided to wait a while, as we were making a lot of money that would help us not to go back poor.

My brother Abraham was a phlegmatic. Everything he did was done in slow motion. The only time you could see my brother doing anything fast was on the soccer field. Nobody would ever believe he was the same person. Mr. Wulkan used to describe my brother, saying that he was dead and the only reason he didn't lay down was because he didn't know it. "I hope he never finds out," he used to say. I never knew what Mr. Wulkan thought about me because he never said.

Just weeks after the victory over Nazi Germany, Russia entered the war against Japan. The minute they entered the war all Koreans were registered to go home to Korea. The Koreans were not upset about going home as they knew they would have high positions, since they were all Soviet-educated. And indoctrinated in communism.

We learned about the atom bomb that was dropped on Hiroshima and Nagasaki. After the Japanese surrendered, the Koreans started to move back to Korea. They probably knew they would run North Korea as the country was divided at the 38th parallel.

In June, 1946, we and the Wulkans decided to liquidate our business and go home. Before we left, we had to clear up with the tax department, since we paid no taxes the whole time we were in business. The Russian director of finance had died of a heart attack a short time after we opened our stores. The new director was Muhammad Babayev.

Father went to see Mr. Babayev. Of course, Father did not tell him the real amount we used to make each day, but whatever he told him for the two years, it came to ten thousand rubles owed for taxes. Mr. Wulkan's bill, because he only had one store, was about four thousand. When Father came home he showed me. I told him to give me the bill, and I would go back and see what I could do. I sat down with Mr. Babayev and spent about half a day, and we wound up with a figure that was a little over a thousand rubles. I had explained to Mr.Babayev that the figures were incorrect. Even though we bought merchandise from government sources, I explained to him, about ninety percent of the flour and sugar we bought was on the open market. Sugar was not five rubles a kilo, but a hundred rubles for a pound of sugar. To make the deal kosher, I gave him a gold pocket watch, a Swiss watch, Doxa. Mr. Wulkan's bill was down to about two hundred rubles. I told Father to go fast and pay it and get a receipt that the taxes were paid in full. So Father and Mr. Wulkan went the next day, paid up, and got their receipt.

Mr. Babayev turned around and said to my father, "Your son is the smartest Polack accountant I ever met. I wish you did not have to leave. I would give your son a job right next to me as an accountant. The watch he gave me will always remind me of him."

We sold our stands to local Russians, packed our things, and went to Moscow. We were there for two weeks. We lived on the ground floor of the Polish embassy. They told us that we would have to wait for a while to get our papers allowing us to cross the border.

In the meantime Runia and I went around town having fun. We went to the museums, Lenin's tomb, the movies, the theatre, and fancy restaurants. Traveling in the subway was an experience in itself. The whole subway is made out of marble, and there are crystal chandeliers. The trains used to come every two minutes and they were immaculate inside and out. We stared at the beauty of those subways. Each station had different statues. It was unbelievable, and it is very hard to describe the beauty of it. Each car had a section for invalids, and you would never find anybody in that section except those who belonged there.

One day Runia and I were sitting in a fancy restaurant, and the language we used was Polish. A Russian officer sitting by himself at the next table came over. He heard us speaking Polish, and he asked us if we would mind if he joined us. We told him no, with pleasure. His chest was full of medals, and underneath he had a golden star, which indicated he was a hero of the Soviet Union. He told us he had just come back from Poland a few weeks ago and that Poland was in turmoil. There was armed conflict going on between the Polish government in London and the Soviet government in power. He told us that when we got home we would have to be careful, as the country as a whole was not very safe. He told us a little story that we thought was true, but wound up being an anecdote.

He told us when he received his golden star as a hero of the Soviet Union, there were about twenty men receiving them. Standing between the men was an old lady in her late eighties with her kerchief over her head and to her shoulders. The president of the Soviet Union, Mr. Kalinin, walked to each of the men and shook their hands, pinned on their medals of heroism, the gold star, kissed them on both cheeks, and thanked them for their heroic deeds.

After the officer received his gold star for heroism, next to him came the lady in her late eighties. President Kalinin kissed her on both cheeks and hugged her. He thanked her for giving fourteen children who all fought in the war. "You are Mother Hero of the Year." He gave her a gold star and he moved on. On the steps going down from the Kremlin, after the ceremony ended, the old lady pulled the officer over and said to him, "Son, I want to ask you something."

He said, "Yes, Babushka, (grandma) what can I do for you?"

She said, "Please tell me where I have to put my golden star."

He said, "Babushka, I won mine with the chest. I pin it on the chest."

Of course we became hysterical. Only then did we realize it was an anecdote, not a true story.

Two weeks passed by very fast. We received our papers to travel home. We boarded the train from Moscow to Warsaw. The next day we arrived in Brest Litovsk, the old town. To get to Warsaw we had to change trains because the Russian's train tracks are more than a foot wider than the rest of the world's. I guess this created a lot of problems for the Nazis, as they could not use their trains for supplies to their army deep in Russia. They had to use trucks, which made them more vulnerable for attacks.

The Russian border guard treated us very nice. We had about ten suitcases, large, and he kept on asking, "What do you have here? What do you have here?" After pointing to all ten, he said, "I will open one and if you have told the truth, I won't open the others."

We were not allowed to take rubles out of Russia. And we had plenty of them. But we were not searched. We told them that we only had a few hundred rubles for the family. And he did not take that away from us.

Before we boarded the train for Warsaw, one of the officers said that the minute we crossed the border into Poland, we could not come back, no matter what. We told him, we understood what he said, but we were not running away, we were going home. We explained to him that we left a huge family behind, and we hoped to find them alive. He said he understood and hoped that we did, too.

We boarded the train for Warsaw and we had only entered Poland a few miles when we heard a young Polish boy screaming to another, "Franek, Franek, the Jews are still alive! The Jews!"

And Franek answered, "What the fuck are you talking about? There are no more Jews."

You have to realize how we felt. Being greeted so nicely.

I held hands with Runia till we arrived in Warsaw, which is many hours from the border. In Warsaw the Wulkans said goodbye to us and left for Krakow. Mr. Wulkan called me aside and said, "You remember what I told you. If we go back home, my daughter will have to marry a religious man."

I told him I knew that destiny gave me no choice. He took out a big diamond, over two carets, and said he wanted me to have it. I told him,

"I cannot accept that." What I did for their family was not for money. Besides, if he had to pay me, he would need more than that to make it up. "I know you don't have it, and I don't want it."

He felt bad and kissed me again on the forehead. We said goodbye to the rest of the Wulkan family, and they boarded the train for Krakow. We went to a barracks in Praga, which is the other part of Warsaw across the Vistula.

We exchanged the rubles on the black market. Most of them went to Russian soldiers going home. The next day I went across the river to see if I could find anybody or anything from where we used to live. All I could see was huge mountains made out of rubble and wild grass growing. I went to see the ghetto area, and not a single house remained standing.

The ghetto had been destroyed in the Warsaw uprising in 1943, when our Polish friends did not lift a finger to help. But I guess they got paid back. The Russians did to the Poles what they did to the Jewish ghetto. In 1944 the Russian forces were only ten miles from Warsaw, when the Polish army, loyal to the London government, had their own uprising, which would give them a victory by liberating Warsaw. Not the army of the Socialist government; but the Russian forces and the Polish army stood by and let them fight their own battle, which the Germans destroyed them in a few weeks, with the rest of Warsaw.

After the defeat of the Polish army, the Soviet and the Polish Socialist army, loyal to the government in Lublin, entered victoriously and liberated Warsaw. Of course, the government of London didn't expect this to happen. It was a miscalculation on their part, not knowing what the Russians were capable of doing and not doing.

After a few months, elections were held to see who would rule Poland, the government of London or the government of Lublin. In the few months we were in Warsaw there were many attacks across the country and pogroms against the Jews by the AK, Armia Krajowa. That was the army of liberation loyal to the government in London. The Western world, fighting communism, was not unhappy to use Jews as scapegoats. I guess they felt Hitler did not do enough.

What the Western world called freedom fighters, we saw as butchers and murderers of innocent people, women and children. When the election came, I don't know what the rest of my family did, but I voted for the Socialist government over two hundred times, using the addresses and names of those who had perished. We were taken by trucks to polling places and guarded by Polish soldiers of the Socialist government. No Russian soldier would walk alone as they too had been attacked by the AK.

We voted for the socialist government as our survival ticket. The Socialist government won a majority and created a real government, leaving the London government completely out.

After the elections, we left Warsaw and took the train to Lodz. On the way, near the town of Zdunska Wola, our train was stopped by members of the AK. They went from car to car, taking out Jews and Russian soldiers. They were all armed with machine guns, American- and English-made. The AK took away the jewelry and shot all of the soldiers. It is hard to describe what we felt just before they reached the car next to ours. We saw Western-style democracy in action. Holding up trains was a regular procedure by the A.K. So the Russians used to drive near the railroad tracks and be alert. We didn't know how many Russian soldiers came, but thanks to our good luck, they came shooting from both sides. We all lay down on the floor, and after it quieted down, we saw about a dozen AK soldiers dead, and about forty men, women, and children and three Russians dead. The Russian soldiers searched the pockets of the AK liberators. Some of them had dollars on them. The Russians did not know what they were, as they had never seen dollars or pounds before. But I knew very well what they were. Some of the Russian soldiers boarded the front, and some the rear, and the train continued to Lodz.

When we arrived in Lodz, we went to the Jewish committee and gave our names in case anyone would ask for us, for who had survived the holocaust, and they would know we were alive. We also checked the list to see if we could find anyone on it that we knew and that might still be alive. Murders and killings were to continue by the so-called western-style "freedom fighters." They were the leaders of the Western world who wanted that type of people to be our government, and probably called it a democracy.

Kibbutzim were organized by the Zionist organization to prepare the youth to leave Poland to go to Israel. After some of the kibbutzniks were massacred in cold blood at night by the AK, the Polish government and the Russian army provided all Jewish organizations with rifles and machine guns so we would be able to protect ourselves. You have to realize that Zionism and Communism are on opposite sides. It must be noted that it was the first time in the history of the world that we were allowed to carry arms provided by the government. I don't know if the Zionists paid or got the weapons free, but we saw it as an act of concern for a part of the population.

You have to imagine what it was like having a Jewish army next to the Polish army. Of course, pogroms continued. We decided to leave Lodz and move to the newly occupied territories that Poland had taken from the Germans, as we felt the AK would not operate over there. So we moved to Wilbrzych, Silesia. The Polish government picked all those who were members of the Nazi party or collaborators, told them to pack their things, and walk all the way to Germany. This part of Silesia used to be a part of Germany. Now it was under Polish rule. It used to be a part of Poland fifty years before that.

When we arrived, we could pick any house we wanted that had been left by the expulsion of the Germans. Of course, we took a beautiful house with a garden that some Nazis used to enjoy before. Zionist organizations were very busy with propaganda, convincing a lot of Jews to leave Poland and go to Israel. Our family was undecided what to do, as the AK operated near the border, and many Jews had been killed before they crossed the border into Czechoslovakia. We decided to leave Poland but we did not know where we were going to go. Of course, we worried as to what might happen to us.

The Zionist organizations used government trucks to take the people to the Czech border. The Czech government let them go through without any harassment, as they were also a Socialist government.

After a lot of people accumulated in Czechoslovakia, transports were formed to take them by train to Austria. Before we boarded the train, the Zionist who ran the show told us that we had to give up everything that showed we had any connection with Poland— documents, anything we had. The only thing we had were pictures from back home with the word Warsaw on them. The reason given to us was that while traveling to Vienna we were supposedly traveling as Greeks, so anything we had on us to contradict that might get us into trouble.

The Soviet authorities knew exactly what was going on. But the ordinary soldiers were not informed as to what was really going on. I was walking with my sister in Vienna at the railroad station—as you know, my sister is blonde-haired and blue-eyed. Two Russian soldiers looked at us, and one of them said to the other, "If this girl is Greek, I am a Chinaman."

And the other said, "You ain't kidding."

Of course, we started to smile and they said, "You see, they understand everything we say. They are Greeks and we are Greeks too."

It was so funny, Sally became hysterical with laughter.

From Vienna we were taken to Salzburg, which was in the American-occupied territory. We were housed in military barracks. After a few weeks we were taken by train into West Germany, where we were placed on an open field with tents. There were thousands of us. Each family had his own tent. There were UNRA officers—United Nations Refugee organization. The organization was run by American,

Belgian, and French personnel. From there, groups were assembled and placed in DP (displaced persons) camps all over Germany. Our family was sent to Wetzlar am Lahn, a town on the river Lahn. This is the town where Leica cameras were produced.

We were placed in a camp that had over six thousand people. It used to be an SS camp. There were ten barracks, two huge soccer fields, and a recreation hall. Food was supplied to us all the time by UNRA. The duty of the UNRA was if anybody wanted to be repatriated home, which many Russians and Poles did, they would prepare everything for them to go back home.

Most of the displaced people in Germany were slave laborers from German-occupied territories who were sent to Germany to work for free. After liberation, the UNRA helped repatriate, and those who did not want to go back were looking to be sent to different countries. The U.S., Canada, Australia, and Sweden were the main recipients of those who did not want to go back to their country for political or any other reasons.

You have to realize that a large number of those displaced persons, though not Germans, wore German uniforms and fought for the Third Reich. And after they threw away their uniforms, they passed as one who suffered as the others.

Ninety percent of our DP camp were Jews from various countries in Europe, and the other 10 percent were Poles. A total population of about sixty-five-hundred people. Our commandant, who represented UNRA, was a red-headed Belgian. Local militia was created, as the German police had no right to enter our camp. The only outsiders who were allowed into our camp were the American MPs. Others were stopped at the gate by the militia and questioned as to their purpose. As you know, where there are two Jews, there are usually three political parties. Everyone has a different opinion about everything. We had only about twelve different parties. Each party offered you jobs or to do whatever they were able to offer—you should join theirs. I never joined any of the parties. I don't like meetings. I do not like politics laid out by a leadership that I may not agree with, and I don't like someone else thinking for me. I will support any policies from the extreme left to the extreme right if I feel the policy will benefit the people as a whole and not necessarily me personally.

All my life, I always followed my own conscience and did what I felt was right, in spite of the feeling of the majority. I do not believe in majority rule, and I have yet to find the majority that was ever right. Most majorities would like to destroy the minorities. The reason I like the United States is because the Constitution guarantees the right of the minority. However, all governments violate their own laws it seeems. I feel that the founders of the United States Constitution were as afraid of the majority, as I am. In all of world history it was always the minority that brought progress to the nation and then was followed by the majority.

Not to be involved with any political party in our DP camp, I organized a sports club. We had a soccer team, a ping-pong team, and a tennis team. I was the captain and secretary of the soccer team. The president of the entire club was an old tennis pro from Lvov, Samuel Mincer. Abraham and I were on the soccer team. The Jewish Central Committee in Munich organized competition between DP camps, because we were not willing to play any German teams, as we had not too much love for them.

I don't know why I always attract non-Jews to be my friends. As usual, I do not care who someone is or where he comes from if I feel that he is a serious person. One of the fellows I attracted to be my friend was Zbyszek Galek. We became very close friends. He carried a gun and was employed by the U.S. military government in our town. I didn't know about the gun, but after a few weeks he told me and showed me his gun. He spoke English fluently and he was a survivor of the Bergen-Belsen concentration camp. The hatred for the Germans was at a high point. It was only a little over two years since the war ended.

I had a lot of problems with many Jewish people when I stated that I was not proud to be a Jew. But I was never ashamed of it. My reason for thinking that way was because you have to be proud only of what you achieve yourself, and not with what you are born into, as this was not by choice but a birthright. To know more about Germans as a people, I started to make friends with some of them. Most of the German friends I had were people who were or had close relatives in concentration camps. After mingling with some of the Germans, I found out that almost four million Germans were sent to concentration camps for opposing or speaking out against Hitler. It made it a little bit easier for me to think of the German people as good people, that not all of them were crazy followers of Adolf Hitler.

Whenever I went to town I always carried a one-foot-long bayonet at my side. If there was a remark from any German that was in nature anti-Semitic, or at least if I felt it was, I would beat the hell out of them. Of course, the Germans couldn't hate the girls. Even the Poles who hated the Jews used to like Jewish girls.

Zbyszek and I used to spend many nights in the hotel in town, though he was married and had a young wife and one child. He used to tell her he was on duty, as he worked for the military. One evening, late at night, Zbyszek and I were on our way home to the camp when we were approached by three Germans. They stopped in the front of us and told us to get off the sidewalk. "Juden should give right to the Germans." They may have gotten away with it with someone else who was bragging that he was proud to be a Jew. He might have given them the right of way. But they picked the wrong two fellows. In short, one German wound up in a hospital and the two others bleeding, and we continued walking on our way to the camp, as if nothing had happened.

The German police had no right to enter our DP camp. So the next morning the MP came to investigate what had happened last night. Of course, nobody knew except me and my friend. So they could get no information. After spending almost a day in questioning most of the Jews, including me, they left empty-handed. I guess they were not too crazy about the Germans, either, as they did not seem to be too upset.

If any German opened his mouth in front of me and made any remark about Jews, I reacted immediately. I never lost a fight. Of course, my father knew of my behavior and was a little bit worried that some day a group of Germans might catch me and get even with me. I did not worry about it.

One day Father and Mother went to the railroad station to go to Giessen, which was only about ten miles from Wetzlar. My sister and I walked behind and were talking. Being blonde-haired and blue-eyed, she was often mistaken for German, since they pretend that anybody blonde-haired and blue-eyed must be German. Two German fellows walking behind us were making remarks. "You see what the German girls are doing for chocolate and cigarettes. Even going to bed with Jews." Knowing what my reaction would be, my sister grabbed my hand and tried to stop me from doing what I usually did. I ripped my hand loose, and the two Germans behind me did not expect it when I turned and started hitting left and right. After one was bleeding from the face, they ran away. Father was upset and said, "You don't have to react to every German who makes a stupid remark."

I told him that I do what my conscience tells me. Hitler is dead and those who carry his philosophy should die too.

I don't hate Germans anymore, only those who carry Nazi philosophy and are still around.

Father and Mother never came to a soccer game as Father always considered sports in general as games that detracted people from serious issues. But when we played for the championship of West Germany, we were the leaders of northern Germany and played Landsberg, the leaders of southern Germany. It was for the silver cup.

The whole camp went to the game. Father finally decided to take Mother and they came to see us play.

I played outside right as I was the fastest man, I guess, in all the Jewish camp. I could run a hundred yards under twelve seconds. My brother Abraham played halfback in the center. As usual, the whole team was on the field, and my brother was walking in his slow, phlegmatic fashion. Everyone was screaming to start without him. As usual, he came five minutes late. We beat Landsberg one to nothing and won the silver cup. It was my header that got the goal for the team. It made the goalie run in a different direction when the ball came from the other side. It was very funny.

Some Landsberg players knew me from back in Warsaw as the kid who carried his brother's shoes so he could get in for free. They knew my brother, they knew both brothers, from back home as the soccer players who belonged to a team named Jordan.

I know it's unbelievable, but my father became a hardened soccer fan. He used to go with us on long trips to see us play. The camp provided trucks for us, and, of course, for the leadership in our camp and our president who was four-feet tall and a member of the Labor party.

From the committee, our club received plenty of camp cigarettes, coffee, and chocolate, as no money was available. Of course I did not smoke and I turned the cigarettes into cash, selling them to the Germans. The black market was a big business since most German stores were ninety percent empty. Coffee and cigarettes were in demand, as Germans are crazy about coffee. The black market was supplied by the American military. They used to sell trainloads of stuff to our people, and our people would retail it to the Germans. American military blankets for Germans turned into coats and pants. Green and pastel were for officer's pants so they were our big sellers. The stuff my brother and I received in our club (I, of course, received double for being captain and secretary of the club), we used to turn it over to Father, and he used to sell it in town.

After Father dealt with one woman for months and put a little trust in her, he started giving her credit. After she had accumulated a few hundred marks, she refused to pay my father on the pretense that she was robbed. Father came home very upset and said, "That bitch. Took all that stuff and don't want to pay." There was nothing he could do as the whole transaction was illegal.

I told my father, "Dad, don't worry. You take me there, let me see where she lives." I told her, "Gertrude, I'm not my father, and if you do not start paying back the money I'll make sure that you are not around too long."

I told Zbyszek what happened and that somehow we had to get her into trouble. American GIs stationed nearby did not receive American dollars but military script and it was illegal for any civilian to have the script. Zbyszek took me to the captain who was the provost marshal. We told him the story and I also said, "I don't care what it takes. That bitch must pay." Of course, my friend was the interpreter. We devised a scheme to have two GIs go up to Gertrude's apartment and throw five dollars of military script under the dresser while she was supposedly buying cigarettes from them. The next day they did exactly that, and the minute they left four MPs arrived, searched the apartment, knowing exactly where the military script was thrown, and found the script. Gertrude was arrested for the possession of military script. She knew exactly what I had done but could not prove it to the judge. The American military court sentenced her to one year in jail. She could not deny that she was doing black market business as coffee and cigarettes were also confiscated at the time of the arrest.

After nine months, when she was free, I went to her and I told her that she had to pay the two hundred marks to my father any way she could. If she was caught again, and I would make sure she was, a second offense would be three years. She realized she had started up with the wrong people and paid my father back the money she owed.

There was also one incident with some Orthodox Jews in our camp, of which there were not too many. They transported a truck full of cigarettes with thousands of cartons. It was stopped by German police and confiscated. My father had told me the story and asked me if there was anything I could do to recover the loss. Zbyzsek and I went back to the captain and told him that the German police were holding thousands of cartons of confiscated cigarettes. Under the pretext that the German police had no authority over the DP, the cigarettes were transferred to our town and the German police were told that it was now an American matter, and the Americans will handle it. They would find the guilty parties and prosecute them. The captain accepted a thousand dollars in cash from me and turned back all the cigarettes to the people they were taken from. Because of that, I became like a hero in the camp, but the credit should go to Zbyzsek as he was the one who spoke English and was able to do the talking. I was only the instigator of the whole thing.

I was never involved in the black market. I devoted all my time to sports and girls, and of course, did a lot of boxing, which I knew was very useful for whenever I needed to protect myself.

My mother had a very large family in London, including two sisters and a brother. After the first World War, my grandfather left Poland to settle in England. In a year, after he established himself with a job, he asked my grandmother to come, too, who at that time had three children, Mother's oldest sister Sophie, Mother, and her younger brother Sam. My grandmother refused to go to England. My grandfather remarried in London, and my grandmother remarried in Warsaw. She had two more children by the second marriage, and grandfather had two children from his second marriage, Barney and Millie.

Uncle Barney, a concert violinist in the thirties, came to play in the Warsaw Philharmonic. Mother and Father went to see him. They had a little trouble communicating, as he spoke very little Yiddish, but at least she met him and knew how her younger brother looked. Of course, by that time grandpa was dead and so was grandma. He looked exactly as his father had looked.

My father loved to write letters, and he was in constant touch with my Aunt Sophie in London. She lost her husband in the early thirties. And Father, without the knowledge of my mother, sent her money every month. I don't know if my mother would've objected to it, since we were not considered a well-to-do family then. While we were in Germany my Aunt Sophie and Uncle Sam came to visit us. Sam and Sophie were the two children that grandma sent to England in 1916 when she refused to go. She kept my mother, who was the youngest.

My Aunt Sophie and my Uncle Sam spoke fluent Yiddish so there was no trouble communicating with them. My Aunt Sophie suggested that I come to England to live with them. She suggested it because I had expressed doubts about going to the United States. I had mentioned that I had enough racism in my life, that it could fill more than one lifetime. She had told me that in England they did not practice racial discrimination, contrary to their behaviors in colonies. The first thing she did was to call me "Henry" instead of Chaim. I said, "I don't care what you call me, as long as you get me to England."

They left after two weeks, and we said goodbye between my parents and my uncle and my aunt. It was thirty years that they hadn't seen each other. My aunt also told us that she had lost one son in the war. Her remaining two daughters and one son, Lily, Fay, and Alex were well adjusted children that she was very proud of.

England had a mandate over Israel during the first World War and signed the Balfour Declaration that guaranteed a Jewish homeland, at that time called Palestine. The British had established a quota, which was approximately ten thousand Jews a year, if I'm not mistaken. It would probably take more than ten years before those Jews who were waiting to go to Israel would be allowed to go. So the Zionist organization established an illegal immigration to Israel. You may remember this from the story Exodus, when the British refused to allow transports to enter because the quota was already filled. I don't know what the official U.S. policy was, but they collaborated with the British intelligence in arresting many people who tried to enter Israel illegally.

So we had to watch out not only for the British, but also the Americans. The only people who did not collaborate with the British were the French. They were very often helpful to the émigrés. I guess the United States was too fearful that Israel might become a socialist state. Ben-Gurion, the main force in Palestine at that time, was the leader of the Labor party. Kibbutzim, which were communes, were widespread in Israel. You know how the U.S. is afraid of anything that Americans consider contrary to their way of life. They never did and never will understand that each people has a right to choose the government they want without outside interference, no matter how they came to power.

Of course, we had a right-wing organization, which the United States called terrorists. It was the Irgun Zvai Leumi, which was previously known as the Beitar. The leader was Zev Zabotinsky. He created his party in the early twenties in Poland. He believed the British would never leave Israel, only if and when the Jewish people were willing to fight and die for it. There were many battles in Poland between the Socialist movement and the Zabotinsky movement. It was the Irgun who paid the British back for what they did to anyone who fought for Palestine in the past. They did not kill indiscriminately. The Irgon or the Haganah would only kill an English officer (not soldier) if the British would kill any Irgon or Haganah member. I don't know if any civilian was ever killed by the Jewish underground army. You may remember the situation with the King David Hotel, where the leader of the Irgun, Menachem Begin, called the British and told them to evacuate the hotel, then the British headquarters. Of course, they started to laugh and considered it a hoax, as British headquarters were very well guarded. The British could not imagine anyone would have a chance to plant bombs in there.

At the exact time they were told the hotel would be blown up, it was blown up. I don't know how many British casualties there were, but it was their own stupidity for not taking the call seriously.

I was not annoyed when England called the Irgun a terrorist organization, but I was very much upset that the U.S. did not call them freedom fighters, but also called them terrorists. It would make you think twice about what the U.S. government calls freedom fighters. If you just compare them to the AK in Poland. The kibbutzim in Israel produced all Israel leaders, Ben-Gurion, Moshe Dayan, and others. Those were people with an ideal and would not do things for military gain, contrary to those in the U.S. who liked to get into government to better their economic situation. I know you remember Golda Meir, also a member of kibbutz. A kibbutz is communal life. You produce according to your ability and receive according to your need. Which is a Marxist slogan, and that of course disturbed the U.S. very much.

I remember after Israel became an independent state, President Truman asked Ben-Gurion, the prime minister of Israel, if he would help Israel to dismantle all kibbutzim. Ben-Gurion explained to Truman that kibbutzim are the backbone of Israel; and without them the country would never survive. It is true that only about twenty percent of the population at that time belonged to kibbutzim. As the Israeli question was soon to be brought before the U.N., all Zionist organizations in Germany worked very hard to recruit young Jews to go to Israel, legally or illegally.

In the beginning of 1948, two men came to our door in the middle of the night, and told me that I should go with them, as they wanted to talk to me. I don't know why they did not bother my brother. I was taken to the building where the Jewish committee was. When I came into the room, it was dark. When I sat in a chair, a big reflector light was shining straight into my face, for me not to see who the people were on the other side of the desk.

A lot of pressure and threats were made on my life, if I did not register to go to Israel. They explained to me that the state of Israel would soon be a free state, and it was no question in their mind that Arab states would attack. They needed every able person to fight for the survival of Israel.

As you know me by now, I don't give in under pressure to anybody, no matter if they are right or wrong. I told them that it was for me to make the choice, not them. And that I would have to think about it, that I will be the one to decide if I should go or not go. I also told them that their NKVD tactics wouldn't work on me. I had faced NKVD before. All threats are meaningless to me, I said, as I had faced that many times before. And somehow survived them all.

After half an hour or more of arguing back and forth, they let me go. I guess the Jewish people were desperate in recruiting people to fight for the survival of the state of Israel. I hate war even if it is the right war. To me war is destruction. Of course I was told not to say anything of what had happened to me that night, and I promised I would not.

Our soccer team became a very popular team as we were champions of Germany. A man, Harry Capel, had a sister in our DP camp. He wanted to play soccer with our team while he was visiting his sister, about a month at a time. He came from Hoff, in Bavaria. He played with us in one game. After the game he came over to me and my brother and said, "You know, it's amazing, on the team that I am playing with, we have one player who looks like you, and his name is also Goldberg." So we said, "What is his first name?"

"Shlomo."

Of course, we got really excited that we had finally found our brother who had left Russia before us. We ran fast to my parents and told Father we found our brother in Bavaria. We took the address, and Father immediately wrote a letter. A week later my brother came to visit us. And once more our whole family was back as a unit. And all safe out of Poland, the country that the United States had tried to build as a "democracy" on the blood of our people.

He was with us a whole month. He told us he was to get married in a few months to a girl named Esther Melman. He showed us a picture of her, and we told him we would be there for the wedding. A few days before the wedding, we all took the train and came to Hoff and met Esther's family. She had one brother, Samuel, and a mother and father. It was a three-day wedding.

At the wedding I met a girl, Viera, who had a German father and a Jewish mother. Because he refused to divorce her mother, as the Nazis demanded, her father was sent to a concentration camp where he died. The mother and daughter survived. She was a beautiful girl, about eighteen years old, and she really fell in love with me. We spent a few nights together and developed a very close relationship.

One week after the wedding, we all went back to our DP camp. I used to correspond with Viera, and she wanted to marry me. I was only about twenty-one years old but was already half bald and looked older than my two brothers. I had to have my father tell Viera my true age, as she also thought that I was older. It's very funny. I always looked younger than my age until the age of eighteen and then because of my baldness I gained about ten years. In one year it happened.

While in Germany, I attended a dental technician's school three times a week, and traveled by train at seven o'clock in the morning to make sure I was in class by nine o'clock. After a few months attending school, I took a job with a dental technicians laboratory, also in Geissen. After I finished school at three o'clock I used to work until eight. I told the lab that I wanted no money, that I needed practice to learn. They were very pleased to get free labor, and I had a chance to get some practice.

I had bought a bicycle a while back and used to perform all kinds of tricks like making a figure eight with no hands. I also rode into town which was on a hill, reading the paper or eating an apple, and very seldom using my hands. I was known to the Germans in town as the circus man. Once in a while I used Zbyszek's motorcycle, a 500 cc DKV. From riding behind him on the motorcycle, I took the motorcycle and drove it with no problems. It was as if I had driven it for years. The motorcycle belonged to the military government and had U.S. government license plates.

When we would leave the town to play soccer in other towns, the camp provided large GMC trucks. The whole town and the camp knew if we lost a game. We would usually arrive late at night and very few people knew of our arrival. But when we were victorious, there were four to five trucks when we entered the town. Russian military songs were sung very loud, as the Germans looked out the windows, wondering if the Russians were invading the town. After awhile they got used to it. Of course, we went to the camp and did not let down. We woke almost everybody up, and they knew from previous experiences that we had won.

The next day we were asked, "What was the score?", not if we had won. They knew that we had won from the way we arrived back.

I had a friend who lived one floor above us in camp, Milton Laks. He lived with his mother and had two brothers in the United States. They were trying to get them over to the U.S. He also became a friend of my family.

By now Sally was a beautiful girl in her demeanor as well as appearance. She was no dummy. She was very particular whom she went out with. My brother Abraham, as usual, did not bother with girls, only looking for married women.

One day me and another friend, Leon Lasser, went to town. Before we left, his father, knowing my reputation, that I don't hate girls so much even if they were Germans, said to us, "Chaim, make sure the girls don't bother you two."

Leon was not eighteen years old, a tall, handsome fellow. While we were in town, we saw two people from our camp walking on the street with two German girls. We jokingly said, "It's not nice for Jewish kids to fool around with German girls."

Two German fellows came from across the street and harassed the two Jewish boys, made anti-Semitic remarks, and tried to take the girls away from them. You know how I usually react in situations like that. Leon also knew that I probably wouldn't be quiet. He said, "Don't get involved. They are not your girls."

I told him, "It is not the girls, but the two Jewish boys who bother me, what the Germans said to them."

They had said, "Don't contaminate German girls," and that is what triggered my reaction. Those two fellows just stood idly. They probably belonged to those who were proud to say they were Jews. I, in fury, attacked. After hitting and tripping one of the Germans, I kicked them with my American boots, which were pretty heavy. One's forehead opened up and blood was all over the sidewalk. The other ran away screaming, "Help! A man is dying, hit by a Jew."

Hundreds of Germans came to the rescue. Leon saw what was going on, and he ran back to the camp and told the militia that I was in danger, surrounded by hundreds of Germans. I moved with my back to the wall, and Germans were screaming, "We are going to kill you! We are going to kill you!" I pulled my bayonet and told them, "Whoever is going to kill me is going to have to die with me."

None of them made a move to get closer, standing with my bayonet in my raised arm. The camp militia immediately called the MP, and the militia and the MP in a jeep arrived at the scene. And that was the way I got out of that trouble.

I was known in the town as the little Jew you don't mess with.

On the fifteenth of April 1948, Israel became a state and was declared a nation by the United Nations. There was a big celebration in all the DP camps in Germany. All Socialist states as a bloc voted for the establishment of a Jewish state. In spite of the U.S. behavior all the years prior to the establishment of a Jewish state, they finally voted to allow a Jewish state. Great Britain, as usual, had withdrawn its troops, and all their military hardware went to the Arabs. When the war of 1948 broke out, almost one hundred million Arabs attacked Israel from all sides. The U.S. put on an embargo to not allow them to ship any arms out of the U.S. in order for the Jewish state to defend itself. I guess oil interests made the U.S. more interested in their profits than in saving Israel from annihilation and what is right or wrong.

The Soviet bloc nations, specifically Czechoslovakia, immediately started bringing ammunition to the Jews. As we know, no Soviet satellite would dare do that without the Soviet government's permission. The Soviet government had their own reasons for helping Israel to survive, figuring that with all the help they were giving, Israel would become friendly to the Soviet Union, if not a Socialist state. Jews from Germany started to move in thousands to Israel, as Britain had no more control or quotas. Czech and also Russian officers were sent to the Jewish defense to help Israel fight off the Arabs.

My brother Shlomo and his wife and whole family were in Israel, and so was my brother Abraham. Everybody else went there during the battle, wearing Israeli uniforms. I was told by my brothers later that they used to go into battle singing Russian military songs.

The secretary of Czechoslovakia at that time was Shlonsky. He was Jewish. That was not the reason that he helped Israel. He was given the nod from Russia to send as much help to Israel as possible, as were all Socialist countries. This was when Israel was leaning towards the United States in the early 50s and voting always with the United States on almost all resolutions. Stalin realized that he did not create a friend of the Soviet Union but a friend of the U.S. Of course, Stalin made no "mistakes" so he executed the prime minister of Czechoslovakia and other Zionist agents. He arrested Jewish doctors in the Soviet Union, saying they tried to poison some of the Russian leaders. The Soviet Union had a very bad habit when severing relations with a nation. They would take it out on people of the same ancestry. As you know, in political trials in Russia, you cannot be acquitted of the charges. So the doctors, too, were executed.

An anti-Semitic wave swept through all of Russia, from end to end. In spite of the Soviet constitution's guarantee that everyone was equal under the law and that discrimination was punishable by one to ten years against any nationality, the majority of Russian Jews were assimilated and not many knew the Yiddish language. Stalin did not make much of it. You have to understand Stalin's fury. He felt that the Soviet Union would finally have a crossroad to Africa. That was the dream of the czars. To have domination of oil producing countries. The Arab world.

Israel became the only free democratic country in the Middle East. There must have been about twenty different political parties; there was even a Communist party, though very small, in Israel. The predominant party, of course, was the Labor party, under the leadership of Ben-Gurion and Golda Meir. Most of the people in our DP camp had left. The majority went to Israel, and many others went to the U.S., Canada, and Sweden.

The most humane and understandable behavior came from the Swedish government. They would accept people even if they were not one-hundred percent healthy. Canada came second, but the United States was the least understanding about what people had suffered through the war. After all that the people went through in war, the U.S. government would break up families, because one of them was not healthy to their satisfaction.

For example, my first wife's stepfather could not come to the U.S., so his wife with four children on her own, without a man, came to the U.S. and struggled to survive. She lost her father in Russia, who died of illness.

I would like to make clear that there is a distinction between the American government and the American people. The American people were compassionate and understanding, and the government could have taken lessons from them.

As the feeling of emigration was sweeping through the DP camp, I put a little more effort to be with Zbyzsek more often. Through him I mingled with a lot of Americans and started to pick up the language. As you know, that was never too difficult for me. I think English is easier than Korean, for a European anyway. And if I could master Korean, English should be a cinch. I forced myself on any American that used to hang out in bars, and we used to drink together and I got the hang of the English language.

It was approaching the end of 1948 in October. My brother Abraham had already left for Israel, and, of course, like everyone else, he wore the uniform right away. Mother, Father, and Sally were undecided if they should go to the United States or to Israel.

By that time, I had received papers to go to England signed by my relatives and a Mr. Gold. Jacob Gold had a dental office and had signed that he would employ me as one of his dental technicians. The papers my aunt sent were for Henry Goldberg, which created some problem for me as the papers I got from UNRA were for Chaim Goldberg. To correct it I had to go to the camp director, a Belgian, Mr. Petajon, and explained to him that my first name Chaim means the name of Henry in English.

I had to bring two distinguished Jews from the committee who verified that Chaim could be Henry in English and that I was the same person. He gave me a new UNRA ID under the name of Henry Goldberg. At that time I was still undecided about to where to go, England or America. I left Israel out because I do not like and cannot stand hot climates. And the Middle East is not Siberia.

What finally made me choose England over the U.S. was an incident that I witnessed in the town of Giessen. I was caught in a big storm. I finally ran under a small canopy, but the wind took the rain there anyway. I stood next to a black GI, who was also soaking wet. I said, "It's nice weather isn't it?" I always looked for a conversation in English to be able to improve.

The soldier, shaking off the rain, said, "Yes, it's beautiful. How do you like the sunshine?"

I said to him, "Well, you are being saved. There is a military bus coming."

He looked at me and said, "You are not joking, are you?"

I said to him, "What does the word joking mean?"

"You are not making fun of me, are you?"

"Joking and fun is the same?"

"Almost the same." And I learned a new word.

I said, "No, I'm not joking. There is a military bus coming to take you to the camp."

He said, "It's a white bus."

"What's wrong with you? That's a green bus." I did not realize what he meant, using the word white.

He laughed and said, "I know the bus is green. But the people inside are white."

"Are you trying to tell me they will not pick you up because you are black?"

"You got it."

That made me really think. What kind of society is this, the United States? I was thinking to myself, England, here I come. I had witnessed too much discrimination in my young life to participate in a new kind of discrimination.

It was almost a half-hour before a bus came with black soldiers and picked him up. Before Jimmy left I told him I was born in Poland, and the Polish government had a democracy similiar to that in the U.S. "They want you to die for their country even if you are Jewish. You don't enjoy the right to live as any other citizen if you are Jewish. I was too young to be drafted before the war, but I would never put on a Polish uniform and serve the country who hates me. Jimmy, you are a brave man." I could tell he was swallowing his tears, and I said, "So long Jimmy." He waved and got on the bus. Before Jimmy left I told him, "You know I would die in jail before I would put on a Polish uniform." I could have told him more, but I felt I hurt him enough. I felt bad that I said it to him, butI had to get it out of my system because I felt so strongly about it.

I thought to myself, there is a young man of African descent, born and raised in the United States, who was ready to give his life for his country, as was any other white soldier, but he did not have the same rights when the war was over. Americans call it justice for all. Jimmy had the same right to die but not the same rights to live. How could a country that claimed to fight for democracy all over the world disallow democracy in its own country? I guess, like the Soviet Union, the government does not abide by the same laws of the constitution, and they look for excuses to justify their lies. A short while ago, the Reverend Jesse Jackson told a story when he came home after the war on his way to Atlanta, Georgia. All black GIs, when they reached the South, had to give up their seats to German prisoners-of-war. Isn't this the greatest democracy in the world? Ask any American, they know it all.

14
ENGLAND

In February, 1949, our DP camp dispersed the few people left. Mother, Father, and Sally went to Wasseralfingen. I don't know just where it is located exactly. I said goodbye to my parents and sister and I left for Bremenhaven. I took a boat to England, and a train to London.

Once more our family was scattered all over the world. Father said, "We have to leave our fate to destiny. And who knows what destiny will bring?"

I said to my father, "It is one thing that no other family has. Though we are going to be separated, our whole family as a unit survived." We don't know, even today, any other family that could claim that. And if there are, you can probably count them on one hand. As you know, many people died in concentration camps and ghettos. Many of them died in Russia in labor camps. They could not take the harsh conditions. Many died of disease as we spent time in northern areas of the country in the Soviet Union, since the best doctors are usually in big cities.

The only consolation for the people who died in the Soviet Union was that they did not die because they were Jews. They died because of the hardships to most of our people, though our family was one of the lucky ones. Our people died as well as any other Soviet citizens who were uprooted and evacuated away from their homes. They had no picnic, either.

It makes you feel a little better that you suffer because of war and not because of a certain religion or race. It probably was no consolation to those who lost their loved ones, though. I guess it does not make it easier for a husband or wife to say to each other, "It's okay to die. Russians are dying, too." The truth is they did, as well as anybody else.

I felt that we were treated with kid gloves after our release from exile in Siberia.

I arrived in London. My aunt and her family did not know of my arrival so there was nobody waiting for me. But me being a half a

Yankee, I took a taxi from the railroad station and asked the driver, "Do you know where 57 Brook Road is?"

"Okay, Yankee," he said. "I know where it is."

It made me feel very good that he called me a Yankee. It meant my English was not too bad.

He asked me if I was coming from America. I only said a few words, which did not give him a chance to know that I was not an American. I kept the conversation short as I had a little problem understanding the King's English, which was a little different from the American English. I told him I was not coming from America but from Russia.

"So, you are a Russian?"

I said yes. I always say I am Russian, not Polish, since from thirteen to almost twenty years old I grew up in the Soviet Union, which I felt were my most formative years. And, besides, the taste of Poland before the war and after the war were not very pleasant memories. I tried to deny to myself that I ever lived in Poland. I choose to be a Russian. It was from my love for Russia as much as my hatred for Poland.

We arrived at the destination, and I had a small satchel with me. All it contained was one pair of shoes, two shirts, two pairs of underwear, and about three pairs of socks. I rang the bell. When my aunt opened the door, she almost fainted. She screamed with excitement to her daughter, Fay, who lived upstairs with her husband and two children. "Fay, come down. You are going to see something. It is unbelievable!"

"My God, how did you get here?"

I said, "Please pay the taxi first. The meter is running."

I had no English pounds. All I had was a five-dollar bill.

It was about twelve noon, and of course we had a question-and-answer period about my family. I told them that my parents and Sally were still undecided as to where to go and they would keep in touch. My aunt looked at my satchel and jokingly said, "My, you brought a lot of stuff with you, didn't you?"

I told her the trouble I had with customs while arriving in London, as they too were surprised that I arrived in England with almost nothing. They thought that this was a diversionary tactic, and I was searched undressed, naked. I said to the customs officer, "Is it so hard to believe that some people are poor? Or is it that you are that rich?"

He said, "No, but in my twenty years as a customs officer, you are the first one who came to our country with a 'fortune.'"

I said, "Believe me, and I promise you, I will have more as soon as I start working."

"Oh, you got a job already?"

"Yes, sir."

"Okay, lad," he said.

My aunt was surprised that they searched me because of my lack of possessions.

That evening, Lily, my aunt's youngest daughter, came home, as she lived with her mother. She was single, about eighteen or nineteen years old. My cousin's husband, Harry, who lived upstairs, came down. My other cousin Alex came that evening as well as my Uncle Sam, my mother's oldest brother. Aunt Milly, who was my mother's stepsister, could not come as she was not well. Aunt Bessie, my mother's other stepsister was there. My Uncle Barney lived in New York already and was married to a very rich woman. He spent most of his time traveling from New York to England, Europe, and back. Money was no object. For a whole week we had to go visit everyone from our family who lived in London, which took about two weeks, as we had about fifty or more relatives. My cousin Ann dropped her work to come and see me as she was only about a five-minute walk from the house. I felt very happy because of the warm, warm reception from all of the family.

As you know, Aunt Sophie was a widow. When her husband died, she was still a young woman in her thirties. She never remarried. She said it was because she promised her husband that she would never marry another man. I guess there were many times in her life that she felt sorry for that promise, but she never broke it.

My Aunt Millie had identical twins, both in show business. And beautiful girls. They were married to identical twins, two very nice Irish fellows who were full of life and jokes and so on. They used to play tricks on the bus. One pair would sit in the front and one in the back. On British buses there is a conductor who goes around and collects the money. All fares are different, according to distance. The couple in the front would pay, and when he came to the couple in the back, they would tell him, "We paid you when we were in the front." And he would say, "Oh, yes you did."

When the conductor went back to the front, he got all confused.

So he went to the middle of the bus and saw the same couple sitting at both ends of the bus, he caught on. When he finally realized that they were two sets of identical twins, he came back and said, "You know, you had me going for a moment there." Of course, they always paid up but would try the trick again for the laughs.

My grandfather, who had died years before had left a brother, Samuel. I didn't know too much about him. All I knew was that he was in London and still alive. I asked my aunt to take me to him, as I knew he was a Talmud scholar. And, as you know, I enjoy and can always learn from the wise. Stupidity I didn't need. I had my own.

We arrived Friday night, the Sabbath (Saturday) according to the Jewish religion. When my aunt and I walked in the door, my mother's uncle was studying the Talmud. He said "Studying the Talmud usually takes a lifetime." He had a big cigar in his hand and the smoke was thick. He raised his head with a smile, then embraced me. He welcomed me to London. He kissed my Aunt Sophie, his niece. After we sat down, his daughter served us tea and cookies. He looked at me, and he realized that I was a little bit amazed at him sitting studying the Talmud and smoking a cigar on the Sabbath. I had never seen that done by an Orthodox Jew. He called me Chaim.

He said, "You see, Chaim, I am a little bit different from other people who are also Orthodox. After studying the Talmud, I realize that God's wish is for people to be happy. By studying the Talmud, I make God happy. By smoking a cigar I make myself happy. This way I please God, I please myself, and there are no complaints. God is happy, and I am happy. So who is getting hurt?"

Of course, I laughed the way he explained it to me. I said, "You are reading too much Talmud. You are getting too smart."

"Knowing a lot should make you smart, but I don't know if I can consider myself smart yet. Very few Talmud scholars will ever say they are smart."

There is a Hebrew saying, "Nobody is smart, as he cannot know everything and life is too short." I told it to him, and he said, "Oh, you studied the Talmud, too."

"I wish I could. I still have a thousand miles to go to even come close to the Talmud."

"What I heard about you—you are not a dumb kid, either."

I jokingly said, "You believe all the rumors you hear?"

"Not always. But sometimes they make a little sense. So I believe it."

I told him that I knew a Talmud scholar in Russia, Mr. Wulkun, who was a neighbor in my father's house. He described people comparing them to fish; most people are center pieces, some are closer to the tail, meaning they are not bright, and those that are closer to the head are a little smarter. I said to him, "Uncle Samuel, I might be a center piece, closer to the head, I hope. But smart is a relative understanding for what it really is."

We spent about two hours there, and then I promised I would come back and visit him without my aunt. He hoped I could learn London well enough to be able to come see him without an escort. He turned to my aunt, "This is not meant to hurt your feelings. You are always welcome in my home as my favorite niece. But when men talk, women should be in the kitchen."

It was a typical orthodox view of Jewish life, as to where women belonged.

My aunt was no dummy and said, "You can't keep me in the kitchen. You got the wrong girl." My Aunt Sophie was like a replica of my mother, always joking, always laughing, telling all kinds of stories, including dirty ones, at which the children used to blush. "Don't blush," she said. "You are not babies. You know what it is all about. I almost forgot, but not you. That is why I make jokes—not to forget."

After about two weeks of celebration and meeting all of the family, my Aunt Sophie took me to meet Mr. Gold, the owner of the dental laboratory. He looked like a pretty nice man. He said to me, "Well, you are Goldberg, and I am Gold. You are Jewish and I am Jewish, so I will see what I can do for you. I am the one who signed the papers for you to come here. Me and your cousin Alex wore the same military outfit in time of war, and we are still friends."

It pleased me that he had such sentiment. He told my aunt to go home. He would have me tested for about half a day, as it was already about noon. After the day was finished, he told me that all he could pay me was seven and half a pounds a week.

That was very pleasing to me, as seven and a half pounds was a pretty decent salary, more or less, for a newcomer. I came home very happy, as none of us had expected that he would start me off with that decent a salary. I agreed with my aunt that I would give her two pounds a week, and she tried to argue that I was paying her too much money. So I reminded her that she was a widow and that Lily, her younger daughter, had to carry all of the burden, though she paid no rent, as the house belonged to Fay, the second daughter who lived upstairs. They were a very close knit and devoted family. I spent a lot of time with Lily at movie theaters and picnics, really having a good time.

My sister Sally fell in love with a boy in Germany and was married around May 1949. His name was Norbert Scheinok. He and his family and his younger sister registered to go to the United States. After the marriage certificate was introduced, my sister was added to the list for emigration to the U.S. Father and Mother decided to go to Israel. Now we had two brothers and my mother and father in Israel, my sister going to the U.S., and I in England. We covered all the continents, as now Asia was already a part of our lives.

After working for about a year for Mr. Gold—it was already 1950—we received a visit from a representative of the Foreign Labor Division, a branch of the British government whose main purpose is to check on all newcomers to England. They wanted to make sure that I fulfilled the obligation under which I had entered the country.

He spoke to me and asked me if I was happy, and I said I had no complaints. I told him I had a large family here, which made it easy for me. I told him about Mr. Gold, who was satisfied with my work, as he had told the officer that he was very pleased with me and was glad I had come to work for him. I don't know what prompted the officer to mention to Mr.Gold that I had to work four years for him. If I left the job, he has to notify the Foreign Labor Division, as I had no right to take any other job until my contract with him was fulfilled. I guess this was news to Mr. Gold, but not for me. You know what greed does to people. No matter what nationality you are.

By June of 1950, or the beginning of July, now assured that I couldn't leave him, Mr. Gold started cutting my salary all the way down to two-and-a-half pounds a week. The cleaning lady used to make three pounds a week. When I asked him why he was doing this to me after one year's work, he said he didn't feel I was worth any more. He felt strongly that I couldn't leave him.

Well, the whole family was very upset. My cousin Alex spoke to him to no avail. I quit and started to look for another job. I saw an ad in the paper looking for experienced dental technicians. I went for the test, and after the first day's work, Mr. Nacham told me that I had only a year's experience, so he could not pay me more than ten pounds a week, but that he would raise it to twelve pounds a week after six months.

When I came back home and told my aunt, she cursed Mr. Gold in any way she could, as he had almost had her believe that I was not worth more than two-and-a-half pounds.

Mr. Gold immediately notified the Foreign Labor Division, and after working six weeks in my new job, I got a visit from an officer from the labor division. He served papers on me that I had one month to leave the country, that I had broken the agreement under which I had entered the United Kingdom. I was very upset, as I really felt good living with my relatives and being a part of their family.

My cousin Alex took a week off from work. He was a custom tailor and worked for himself with only six employees. He gave them the work in the morning and the whole day we ran around to see if anything could be done to reverse the order. We visited with two members of Parliament, and they listened very carefully and both showed a lot of sympathy. But the law is the law. There was not much they could do. They suggested a plea to the Queen of England. My cousin wrote immediately.

He stated that I was a survivor of the concentration camp and that I had nobody else except them, that he lost a brother in the war and he himself received a medal of bravery, and with urgency he asked that the

Queen allow me to stay. He also explained the reason why I left the job. One of the conditions in my contract was that I should not work for a lesser wage than a British worker would, so as not to take away a job from a British subject. After one year's work, Mr. Gold, knowing that I could not leave, cut my salary from seven and a half pounds to two-and-a-half, which violated my agreement with the British government that I would not work for less than a British worker.

At the new job I had now with Mr. Nacham's laboratory, my salary was ten pounds a week, which was equal to most British technicians. He was a British-born subject. I had to tell Mr. Nacham what happened. He too wrote a letter to the Queen on my behalf when I told him I could not work until this was resolved. I did not hear anything for weeks.

Trouble was nothing new to me. At least my life was not in danger. I saved up over a hundred pounds. I acquired clothes and took my cousin Lily out every night. We went to see a movie. It was a film made in Poland called "Ulica Graniczna," the name of a street in Warsaw. The basic theme of the film showed the uprising of the Warsaw ghetto. It was not easy for me to sit through the film. My handkerchief was wet with tears. At the film ending, a twelve-year-old boy, David, survives the uprising by hiding in the sewers. The film showed the Russian army liberating Warsaw, and David, who lost all his family, sat and cried. The narrator ended the film by saying, "Little David will never die."

We were sitting in the balcony. In the row below me sat two fellows who were members of General Anders's Polish army. One Pole turned to the other and said, "If there are still Jews left, they need another Hitler." Lily did not understand because they spoke Polish. I stood up and put my hands together in one fist, and with all my might I hit him in the face. Blood ran from his nose and mouth. The people sitting next to him screamed that a man had gone crazy. I was arrested.

I told the police what happened and what the men said. I also told them that Great Britain had fought against the Nazis. And I don't think that the British want there to be another Hitler. Well, I guess the police sergeant felt I had a pretty good reason for feeling this way. He said, "Listen, my lad, I am going to let you go, but you cannot take the law into your own hands, though there is nothing we could have done, as freedom of speech is a part our constitution." I did not argue with him. I was glad that no charges were brought against me.

When I came out of the police station, Lily was waiting, and we went home. She told the family what happened. All of them agreed I had done the right thing.

Those two in the movie gave me the idea that maybe I ought to try the Polish committee, which used to take care of Polish citizens, though

I was not too crazy knowing that this was the AK and knew their philosophy, how crazy they were about Jews. I told my cousin Alex I would take help from the devil if the devil was willing to give it to me. We should go to the committee and see if they could have some influence, so I could stay in the country.

On a Monday Alex and I went to the Polish committee. We took a number and had to wait, as there were many people. There was not a single Jew. I told Alex, "I really feel uneasy, but maybe by some miracle this committee might be able to do something."

After about a half-hour I burst out laughing. My cousin thought I went bananas. He could see no reason why I was laughing. He did not understand Polish. I was listening to a conversation between two Poles sitting about two rows in front of us. One turned to the other and said, "Are you crazy? Don't you know what is going on in Poland? There is no freedom, no democracy. Do you know that if you kick a Jew in the ass they can put you in jail? And you want to go home? Is that freedom, is that democracy?"

So I burst out laughing. And my cousin said, "I guess that is what they call freedom. Maybe I'm just crazy and don't understand what freedom is."

I told him it reminded me of the story that the black GIs used to tell me, that if you kill a black man in the south, it was not considered a crime. I guess the southern white man also had freedom and democracy, and if you take those rights away from them, they may feel that the government has curtailed their freedom of action.

I guess there is freedom, freedom, and freedom. Each one sees it differently. I told him, "I really wonder what freedom is. I guess all countries have a certain amount, playing by the rules. Of course, by the rule of those who govern. They are the ones who decide what freedom is."

It took a little while longer. I was called in and my cousin went with me. Before me was a Polish officer in a Polish uniform that carried the eagle with a crown on it. On the new Polish eagle, the crown was taken off. When he looked at me and saw on the application that I was named Henry Goldberg, he knew I was a Jew.

He asked, "Why did you come to us?'"

I said, "What do you mean by 'us'?"

He said, "Polacks."

Because we were speaking in Polish, I said, "What the hell do you think I am?"

"A Jew."

I said, "This is my religion, but I am from Warsaw, born and raised."

"All Jews claim to be Polack, but we see them differently. I suggest you go to a Jewish committee. And stay away from anything that says Polack," he told me.

I looked at him with a smile and said, "I hope some day you have enough brains to think for yourself and see the world in a different light. I bet you don't know the best Poles were Jews, not Poles. You do not know how many distinguished Jews served and died for Poland. Did you ever hear of Dr. Zamenhof? He received a medal from the Polish government in the early thirties for improving the Polish language. And he was also the founder of Esperanto. For your information, Esperanto is supposed to be a universal language that would enable people to be closer through a common language."

He interrupted me very politely and said, "You would not want me to tell you how many Jewish Communists there are."

"No matter how many there are, there are still more Poles."

I said goodbye and left. I did not wait for a reply. I felt I would not change his opinion, as he was brought up by a good Catholic government. My cousin wanted to know what we talked about. I told him, "I can tell it to you in a few words. I made a mistake coming here. But it was worth a try. It helped me to continue to claim to be a Russian instead of Polish."

A few weeks later I received a reply from the royal family. The letter stated that they were very sorry for what I went through. They wished they could be of assistance, but the law of the land had to be upheld by everyone, including me. I had one more week to pack my things to leave.

15
GERMANY

I said goodbye to my family, and after about twenty months in England I boarded a ship to Holland and took the train to Hamburg. In the meantime, UNRA was dissolved, and a new organization was formed by the U.S. government, IRO—International Refugee Organization. In Hamburg I found out that Hanover in Hessen was where it was headquartered. I tried to get my DP status back, as I had lost it when I had emigrated to England.

I arrived in Hanover and immediately went to the headquarters. A little luck went my way. Of all the people in the headquarters, I met the old camp director, Mr. Petajon. When he saw me, he embraced me and said, "Oh, my soccer star is back. What are you doing here?"

I told him that I desperately needed my DP card that I had given up when I left for England. After explaining to him what had happened in England, he said in his French accent, "Don't worry. You are one of the fellows who brought a lot of pride to our camp." He, of course, was referring to the winning of the championship, which he attended and gave all the players flowers.

He told me to wait. About an hour later he came out and handed me a new DP card, which read Henry Chaim Goldberg. Now I had a new name, Henry Chaim Goldberg. He told me there were not too many camps left, but he arranged for me to go to Bavaria to a camp called Feldafing. He also gave me an introductory letter to the head of the department, Miss Hochheiser. She was also Belgian. I was very grateful to him and thanked him very much. He also gave me tickets and some money, though I did not ask for it as I had over a hundred pounds.

I arrived in Munich, bummed around for a few days, with girls of course, and then finally came to Feldafing, which was only about ten miles from Munich. When I arrived, there were only four barracks, one administration building, and in less than a quarter of a mile close to a hundred villas.

I showed the letter to Miss Hochheiser, and she was very friendly. She was a pretty woman in her late thirties or early forties. We spoke English, and she was very impressed how well I handled the English language. I received a villa with only three rooms, as I told her I would rather have a villa than live in the barracks. Smiling, she said, "I prefer a villa, too," all with a heavy French accent. "No problem. We will get you a nice place. And you are going to work with me here as we need an interpreter desperately."

I told her that I knew German, Russian, Polish, Yiddish, Czech, Ukrainian, and could also communicate with Yugoslavs as their language is a mixture of other Slavic languages. She could not wait to add me to her staff. She also told me that the CIC, which was part of the American Intelligence Corp run by the Army, came once a week and interrogated people, and they would be very glad to have me help them. I received a salary of two-hundred twenty-four marks per month.

I had to pay no rent, and as a member of the administration, I received plenty of food from the IRO, same as all others in the camp. My little three-room villa, which was on a hill, had a beautiful porch surrounded by all kinds of trees. I had no trouble keeping it clean as I had plenty of girls, as usual. I have a bad habit of liking girls! One has to have some vices.

In the second week I first met a team of three investigators from the CIC, whom I sat with and asked questions for. I did not have too much trouble with that, as most of the people in the camp were Jewish. Only those who wanted to go to the U.S. were interrogated.

I made friends with an eighteen-year-old boy, Izak Platt. He was a fantastic chess player, and I had a lot of trouble trying to win a game from him. He studied in Munich in the conservatory and was a very good classical accordion player. Very often he performed for German audiences in Munich. His teacher considered him one of the best pupils, very bright and intelligent. We got along very fine, and I was a big help to him whenever he needed a room for a girl. I would give him the keys. His father and mother resented my influence on him when it came to girls. Little did they know that their little boy did not need any help from me. But I guess they were like a lot of parents; their child is the best.

I wrote a letter to Israel to my parents giving them the address where I was now. They knew from previous mail that I left England. Father wrote to me telling me that Mother was very sick in the heat of Israel, and the heat was a big factor. It was possible that they might return to Germany and try to go to the U.S. I told my father that after a year or two, I too might go to the United States. Not wholeheartedly, but now my sister was in the U.S. and since my parents were going, I might as well join this part of my family.

My two brothers remained in Israel. Father wrote to me that Abraham got married, and, you probably know, not to a girl but a widow with one child who lost her husband in the 1948 war. Father jokingly wanted to know if I knew what's wrong with single girls.

Father reminded himself of something we all almost forgot. In 1946 Mother became very ill while we were still in Central Asia, in Kyzl-Orda, and Dr. Chun Sun had said to her that the only cure he could recommended was to get out of Asia, as Mother's system could not take that type of climate. The Israeli climate was almost the same. Of course, when the doctor told her, we did not take him too seriously, though the minute we left Central Asia, Mother's health returned to normal.

Father told me that when I registered to go to the U.S., under no conditions should I tell the American authorities that during the war we lived in Russia. The reason was that somebody signed my name in 1949 and received a thousand dollars as part of the restitution for people who survived in concentration camps or ghettos or hidden in caves. Father never told me who signed my name. I don't believe my sister or my brother did it. I think I know who did. I never asked him, but it created a little dilemma for me, that I had to go before the American authorities and not tell the truth.

It was now February, 1951. My parents arrived in Feldafing from Israel. Since I worked for the IRO, I helped them to receive their DP status back. As you know, when you emigrated you lost your DP status under the rules of the International Refugee Organization. Now with my father coming to Germany, I was forced not to tell the American authorities that I had lived in Russia during the war. I did not want to jeopardize my safety or my father's. I did not continue to supply or to be interested in the German Wiedergutmachen, the part of the German government especially set aside to work for the restitution of all those who suffered during the war in concentration camps or ghettos. I wanted no part of that.

After receiving the DP status, Father and Mother got their ration cards and a three-room apartment in a villa not too far from where I was living. I did not want to share my apartment with my parents, so as not to disturb the pattern of my life.

One afternoon in March Izak Platt ran into my office, red in his face, all excited. His father had been arrested by American military police and taken to the CID in Munich. He did not know the reason. All that they gave his mother was a piece of paper which had the address of the CID headquarters in Munich. I told my boss, Miss Hochheiser, that I wouldn't be in the next morning, because my friend's father had been arrested by the CID.

The next morning when we came to the CID headquarters we had trouble finding out where his father was being held and under what charges. It was almost four in the afternoon when I finally fought my way to the chief of the CID to find out the reason and the charges that Mr. Jacob Platt faced. To my astonishment and bewilderment, the head of the CID told me that he was arrested for cheating the German government out of three thousand dollars. He had filed a claim and received three thousand dollars from the German Wiedergutmachen. (Wiedergutmachen is a German word that means restitution.) I was speechless, which was unusual for me.

Why would the American military government arrest a man for cheating the German government? On what authority did the American government arrest him? As they personally had no charges filed against Mr. Platt, I insisted on knowing on whose authority the American military government authorized the arrest. Was it the German government telling the Americans what to do?

He explained to me that the German police had no authority to enter the DP camp, as they had no authority over DPs, and had to go through the American government. He finally admitted to me that the Germans had access to all files held in the International Refugee Organization, which the American government used as a means to check if the statement refugees gave to the American authorities about being in a ghetto or concentration camp was the same as that which the German authorities had. It really annoyed me a little, though I knew about it from Father, as he had written to me about it before. I asked the chief officer of the CID why they were still holding Mr. Platt and not turning him over to the German authorities.

I was told the CID had to conduct its own investigation to see which statement was true, the one they gave the Americans or the one they gave the Germans. He would not allow me or Izak to see Mr. Jacob Platt until the investigation was over. And we would only be able to see him if he was turned over to the Germans, which would only take a few days. It was shocking to me, the action of the American military government.

On the fourth day, before I went to Munich, I called the CID from the office to find out if Mr. Jacob Platt was already in the Germans' hands. The CID officer told me that this same afternoon he would be transferred to the German police. A copy of the findings of the CID would also go to the German police. We waited for a few hours in the German police headquarters in Munich, and the MPs brought Mr. Platt, at approximately four-thirty, to be turned over to the Germans for criminal prosecution.

When the MP and Mr. Platt arrived, his son Izak started to cry and screamed, "What did they do to you?" He had a swollen face and was unable to walk on his own. I stood in silence and could not believe my eyes. Mr. Platt said, "Can't you see what they did to me, or do I have to tell you?"

After the MP brought him inside, almost carrying him in as he was unable to walk, the German investigator did not believe the shape Mr. Platt was in, all done by the CID. He showed a lot of sympathy towards Mr. Platt and said, "We will not hurt you."

I asked the investigator, "Is there anything that could be done to have Mr. Platt released?"

He told us that it was late now, and we should come back in the morning. At eight o'clock we arrived back at the German police headquarters. The investigator took me and Isak inside to the investigating room where Mr. Platt was. Son and father both cried in disbelief. The German investigator kept calming them down. "Don't worry. In a few hours you are going to go home."

I asked the investigator, "If Mr. Platt returns the money, will the charges against him be dropped or do you insist that he stand trial?"

He had no authority to make a deal, but he left us in the investigation room and went to the chief of police. It took almost an hour before he returned. [I guess the guilt of the German people got to them, though Mr. Platt and his family personally did not suffer from the Nazi atrocities. They knew very well that brothers and sisters had parents were not here to speak and give Mr. Platt some justification for what he did.] So the German investigator told us that the chief of police, after being in touch with other government authorities, was willing to make a deal and not press charges, if Mr. Platt returned the money that was taken.

He and his son were relieved. After Mr. Jacob Platt signed all the necessary papers, which Izak and I checked to make sure that the agreement was written properly, we took a taxi from Munich to Feldafing. Mr. Platt was fearful that the Americans would come back for him, so he asked me if he could stay with my parents until he recovered. Knowing my parents would not say no to him, I told Mr. Platt that I was sure there would not be any problem. We brought Mr. Platt to my parent's villa and told Mother that Mr. Platt would like to recuperate at their house because he was so fearful of the American authorities returning.

Mother took care of him for two weeks. Our camp doctor could not do much for him, except he told my mother that to reduce the swelling on his face and the bruises on his legs, she should use ice. Mother nursed him back to health.

Mrs. Platt went home only to sleep. For the first few days she cried in disbelief that the American CID was so brutal to her husband. Mr. Platt asked his wife to bring papers, as they already had a visa to go to the United States. He ripped them all up and told his wife that they were going to Israel, and that under no conditions would they go to the U.S. after what the authorities had done to him.

If I had any doubt about telling the Americans that I was not in a Warsaw ghetto but in Russia, this incident made me positively do what my father asked, to say that we did not live in Russia but in the Warsaw ghetto.

I don't know if the Platts ever returned the money or not, but a month after this incident they left for Israel.

Our camp was getting smaller and smaller. So the IRO combined two camps, Feldafing and Forenwald, which was ten miles on the other side of Munich. All displaced persons camps were segregated. The Jews had their own; they were never together with Christians in the same camp. Miss Hochheiser asked if my parents would go to Forenwald or stay here with me in Feldafing. She did not want me to leave, as the new people coming were mostly Russians, Ukrainians, Poles, Lithuanians, Czechs, Yugoslavs, and some others. My ability to speak most of those languages would make it easier for her and the CIC, which came every week. Instead of using three or four people as interpreters, I could do it on my own. After discussing this matter with my parents, we decided that I would stay and my parents would go to Forenwald. I would come visit them on weekends.

16
HALINA

It was about mid-April of 1951 when all the Jews were transported to Forenwald. A few days later about a thousand new DPs arrived, a variety of all European nationalities. The Poles were in the majority. I was the busiest person in Feldafing. Though a few of the newcomers were hired, I had to be all over as if I owned the camp, to help in the translations into English, so when the CIC came, they would be able to read the history of each refugee. It would also help them in the process of screening people for emigration to the United States.

After a week or two, a young lady with a baby in her arms arrived. Her name was Halina Kowalska. Something about that woman made me follow her outside and watch until she disappeared into her home. The reason she came was that her husband worked for the American military authorities as a guard. They wore black uniforms and were employed as security guards. I guess the Americans did not want to stay on duty so they used a variety of nationalities as guards.

When Mrs. Kowalska came back a few days later, I went over to talk to her. I told her that I noticed she was from Warsaw, as I had looked at her file. I asked her if by any chance she ever had a teacher by the name of Bublewicz. She said yes. She looked at me and looked at me for awhile and then screamed out, "Heniek!" and almost dropped her baby with excitement. She was the girl that I had had a crush on. I had walked her home and carried her books when we both were about eight years old. She had been spotted by other children and was harassed as a Jew-lover. We hugged, almost in tears, as fifteen or so years later we met again. She insisted that I come for supper, and of course, I could not refuse my old flame.

She and the baby lived in a huge room that was divided by a half-wall. Her neighbor on the other side of the wall was a single fellow called Stasiek. He, of course, on hearing a man's voice walked right in without knocking while we were having supper and a drink. He stood for a while and then Halina asked him, "What do you want, Stasiek?" After stuttering for a while, he asked for salt. We both knew he did not need any salt, but that he wanted to see who the man was here. He had a crush on her and had tried to get close to her, and for the last two years she had been pushing him away. She told me that she could not stand him and that he was obnoxious. He was about five-foot-eight and not bad looking.

Halina showed me letters that she received from her husband's friend who was stationed with him. The reason he didn't come home for four months, although he used to have a one-week vacation each month, was that he had a lot of German girlfriends. After about three hours and the end of a bottle of vodka, we kissed and I went home.

I was very excited that I had met her. I knew that sooner or later we were going to make love. She came every day to the office with a smile on her face, and she was happy that she had met me again. After a few weeks we became very, very close and sexual relations became natural. She was a beautiful woman, about twenty-three years old, and she had a two-year-old little boy who was very lively. I played with him as if he were mine. Her neighbor Stasiek went bananas. He was looking for any excuse to come in every time I was there, as usual without knocking. As if he wanted to catch us in the act of making love.

One evening after having dinner, we were in Halina's room killing a bottle of vodka and put a record of Polish songs on the record player. I took off my shoes and lay on the bed. Halina took her shoes off, lying next to me, also enjoying the music. The door opened up, and as usual without knocking, Stasiek walked in, as he could hear everything that was going on in the room. He walked in close to the table and looked at us lying on the bed, both clothed. Halina asked him, "What do you want? Do you want more salt? Or pepper maybe?"

He said ,"No. I have to talk to you."

She told him that if he wanted to talk that it would have to be the next night as it was already eight o'clock. I lay quietly listening to their conversation as if it didn't involve me, though knowing very well that it was me that bothered him. He pointed a finger at the cross over the bed, which was pretty large, with a statue of Jesus on it, and said, "How can you fuck with a killer of Jesus Christ? He is over your bed and watching you."

After I had a few nice drinks, he triggered the violent side of my character. He didn't have a chance to say much more. I jumped off the bed, hit him with my fist; and though he was bigger and stronger than me, my speed and evasive tactics made him miss me. I did not get hit once. After grabbing his legs and throwing him over, I started hitting him mercilessly with a chair. Blood was all over the floor. Halina fell to my feet ,begging me to stop as I might kill him. Which I probably would have. I took out on him all the frustrations that I had for those types of Poles from before the war and after the war. I saw him as if he was the AK. I finally came to my senses after Halina was in hysterics and was screaming for me to stop. I stopped.

Halina's screams brought a mob from outside. They had called the police, and when the police came in, I was lying in the bed as if nothing had happened. Stasiek was lying on the floor. His head was smashed, and blood was all over him and the floor. In about five or ten minutes, the ambulance arrived and took him away on a stretcher.

I was arrested by the local police and turned over to the German police for attempted murder. I told the German investigator what had happened. With the baby, Halina came to the police station with me. She lied a little and said that Stasiek attacked me first, as he was very jealous of her and that she would have nothing to do with him. I was immediately released, and the police report read that it was self-defense.

The whole camp could not believe that a five-foot-five, skinny little Jew could have given such a beating to a five-foot-eight-inch Polack without fear, as I was the only Jew in camp. Many came and shook my hand, and some of them hated me but made no remark.

There were many types of restaurants in the camp that served food and drink. We also had a Catholic organization, Karitas, run by a priest. As Halina was a churchgoer and attended Sunday services, the priest had a long talk with her. She told me that he said she would go to hell for committing adultery. Though still going to church, Halina ignored his statements, and we continued our friendship as if nothing had happened.

Stasiek came home a few days later. His head was all in bandages. He looked like a mummy. He was teased by a lot of his friends saying, "What that skinny little Jew did to you! Aren't you ashamed of yourself?" He immediately wrote a letter to her husband, telling him what she was doing. The priest, after seeing that Halina continued the relationship, decided to approach me. He came into the office and asked me if I would come and see him after work. He would like to talk to me. That it was very important for the welfare of Halina and her future.

I told the priest, "I will come to your place on one condition. You have to give me your word as a priest that after you finish with your lecture, you will allow me, without interruptions or throwing me out, to say what I have to say."

He agreed.

After work I went to see him. He spoke very nicely to me, explaining that Halina was going to lose her husband and that I could marry her because she was a Catholic. "You will ruin her life, and if you say you love her you have to be concerned about her welfare. And not to be concerned with just sexual pleasures." He explained to me that not only was Halina sinning by what she was doing, but that what I was doing was also a sin according to the Old Testament.

I agreed with him but told him that I would like to say a few things to him. I wanted him to understand that the responsibility for what I did to Stasiek lay with the Church. They brought up Jew-haters from the day he was born. I had carried frustration against the Catholic Church since I was five years old when the Church had tried to buy my soul for a piece of bread. I told him that in 1947 I was baptized in the Vatican three times under different names and that I received a hundred dollars each time. At least the Church had increased the value of my soul, from a piece of bread to a hundred dollars.

He sat quietly without saying a single word. The story I told him about being baptized three times was not true. But the fact that the Church paid a hundred dollars for each Jew to become a Catholic was true. My brother Abraham was baptized a few times. I heard it from many, many fellows who collected the money and went to Israel or Germany. I personally would not and could not do what others did, because my bitterness against the Church since a child ran too deep. I told the priest that the most annoying thing to me was the Church using the name of Jesus, as if they had anything to do with the teachings of Jesus Christ.

The Western world believes that the Catholic Church and many nuns in convents saved a lot of Jewish children from the Nazis. I would like to make clear that the reason they saved the Jewish children was not to turn them back to their relatives or families after the war was over. It was an easy way and a chance for the Church to get Jewish children and bring them up as Catholics. To me they were soul snatchers. After the war was over, no convent or any individual nun or priest ever told the Jewish community or its committee that they had Jewish children and would like to return them.

The incident I tell right now happened to a distant relative of mine through marriage. When the Russians sent most of our people to Siberia in 1940, they had left a two-year-old baby with the maid who was a young Catholic girl working in the household. It was in the city of Lvov in the Ukraine. After the war was over, and after a long search, they located the young girl. She took them to a convent which was about thirty miles from Warsaw. She told them that the baby had been turned over to them. She was not married and was afraid to raise a Jewish child. You know how polite nuns are. When the parents came to the convent, the nun opened the door with a smile and bowed as they usually do. She asked the parents if she could help them. The parents told the nun that their child had been given to them in 1941, and according to the girl who gave it to them, the child was still there.

Claiming that she had no knowledge of it, the nun called the Mother Superior. With a cheating smile, the Mother Superior told the parents that the young lady must have lied to them.

They went back to the young girl and informed her of what the Mother Superior had said. In tears, the girl said she was willing to go to the police station with them and sign a sworn statement as to the truth of her story. The next day she signed a sworn statement to the police. The police took the parents with the young lady's sworn statement and went to the convent again.

The Mother Superior, with her usual smile, insisted that they would never do a thing like that. She offered to bring all the children outside so the parents could view them to see if they could find their child. She reinforced her view about the young lady lying. About forty children were paraded before the parents, and the parents failed to see their own child. What the parents did not know was that five children, all of whom were Jewish, had been kept in a basement in a play room and were never shown to the parents. The Mother Superior with her phony smile told the parents that that was all the children they had there. "I hope this satisfies you."

With tears in their eyes, the parents and the police sergeant left. I guess the sergeant did not believe that all the children had come out. But no judge would issue a warrant to search a convent. He told the parents that the government policy with the Church, only a year after the war, was a delicate one; and the government would not rock the boat and infringe on the rights of the Church.

Being sympathetic to them, understanding their dilemma, and the suffering of the Jewish people under the Nazis, the police sergeant suggested to the parents that they should go with him to the Russian headquarters, that the Russians would not stand on ceremony. They would not need a search warrant. The Russians were not great lovers of the Catholic Church anyway.

After they arrived at the Russian military headquarters, a Russian major listened very carefully to the story. After the police sergeant told the major that there may be more than one Jewish child still held at the convent, he asked the major to see what he could do for the parents. The major became very mad, cursing the Church and saying, "If those bastards think they can get away with that, they have another thing coming." He made a telephone call. He ordered two tanks, one in the front and one in the rear, with their big guns pointed at the convent. He came with six soldiers and the parents.

The Mother Superior saw the parents and the Russians. She refused to open the door. What the Mother Superior did was to play for time so that they could hide the Jewish children. The major told her, "You have a few minutes to open the door, and if you don't, the tank will open it."

With her back to the wall, the Mother Superior had no choice but to open the door. The major immediately ordered his soldiers to search the premises from the basement to the roof. The Mother Superior threatened the major saying that the Vatican would never stand for intrusion. All the children were brought outside, and the Mother Superior screamed at the parents, "God will never forgive you for what you did." She was referring to the fact that they had come with Russian soldiers. "You have seen all the children. What is it you want? You are antichrist, and you brought Communists, also antichrist. God will never forgive you for this."

A little over half an hour passed, and the Russian soldiers, after breaking open one locked door in the basement open, found five children. They brought the five children outside. The parents immediately recognized their girl. The major looked at the Mother Superior and said, "When will you people learn to tell the truth? Instead, you use your God for protection. I guess your God failed you this time."

The Mother Superior looked silently at him while the Russians took the other four children, after the parents took their child. They took the four children to the Jewish committee. Today, this girl is in the United States. I did not use her name at her request.

After I finished telling the priest what I thought of the Church's behavior, I said goodbye and left. After my story, he refused to shake my hand.

Halina's husband, after receiving the letter from Stasiek, arrived in the camp a few days later. I guess after he saw Stasiek in the condition I had left him in, he ruled violence out. He came into the office. I immediately knew who he was, as I had seen his picture in the house. He came over very politely, invited me for supper, and said that he would like to talk to me in front of Halina and resolve the dilemma.

That evening I took a bottle of vodka for supper as usual. We had a long conversation. I told him that I would marry Halina and take her with the baby if he continued not to come home for months and left her alone with the child. I said I was not willing to break up their marriage if he promised to behave differently from now on. Halina showed him some of the letters she received from her husband's friend, which said that he was not coming home because he was going out with German girls. Of course, Halina withheld the name of the friend so as not to create unnecessary trouble.

We discussed Stasiek, though Halina had already told her husband why I had a fight with him. I too told him the story. And he already knew that Stasiek was after his wife since he married her. He went next door and told Stasiek that he should never come in to their house unless he was home. I promised him that I would have no more sexual relations with his wife but just be friends. He trusted me that I would not continue my relationship with her that way. Afterwards we finished the bottle of vodka, shook hands, and parted as friends.

17

ENTERING AMERICA

I went back to my old routine and back to single girls. The CIC came once or twice a week to our camp, and I was very busy interrogating prospective émigrés to the U.S. After a few weeks the tactics and the form of interrogation of the CIC changed drastically. After questioning "What's the name? Place of birth? When did they get married? How many children?" then came, "Why don't you want to go home to your own country?" Their answer was that they did not want to go back to a Communist country.

Previously two of the questions were, "Where were you during the war?" and "What did you do during the war?" Those questions were no longer asked, as sixty-five percent of those now in camp wore German uniforms and had fought with the German army against the Allies. Previously this would have been a reason not to allow them to go the U.S., as many of them fought against the Americans and British.

I asked those questions on my own as the CIC investigators did not know what I was asking. After receiving answers from the people, I told the CIC that most of them were Volks Deutsche. A Volks Deutsche was a person who voluntarily pledged allegiance to Hitler's Germany and was willing to give his life for his newly adopted nationality. The CIC officer told me that those questions were omitted, that this policy came from the top, and that they must do what they were told. They did not make American policy, they just carried it out. I told them that those people might live right next door to American families who lost their husband or sons in the war and might even have been killed by them as they were Nazi soldiers. One of the CIC officers said, "I can't agree with you more. You are right. But my hands are tied, and we have to do what we are told."

After a day's work, I sat and analyzed why the U.S. government chose this new policy. The reason became clear to me. They wanted to show the world that people do not want to live under Communism and that they chose freedom instead. But in my eyes those people were traitors no matter what kind of a government was back home, as they were soldiers and collaborators with the enemy. I was very much upset with the turn of events. I realized that with a political victory, in the eyes of the world anything goes.

I spent a lot of time in Munich mingling and drinking with American GIs in the bars. It gave me an opportunity to learn more Americans and about America. The camp was getting smaller and smaller, and the time came for me to decide where to go. My sister was in the U.S., and my parents were processing their papers to go there. I finally made up my mind to go to the United States.

One afternoon when we had a break with the CIC work, I talked to one of the superior officers of the group. I told him that I was in Russia during the war, but that I stated on my papers that I had been in the Warsaw ghetto. I asked for his advice. This was an off-the-record conversation. He told me to leave the thing alone and not to be bothered with a little technicality. "It is not of big importance," he said. "Russia, ghetto, what is the difference?"

So, in October of 1951, all my papers were ready for me to go to the United States. I changed my birth date from February 1926 to September 1, 1924. The Korean War was in full blast, and I was not ready to die before I had a chance to live, as up until now my life was up and down for as long as I could remember.

The CIC officer remarked, "I don't blame you." He meant for not wanting to go fight in Korea immediately after arriving in the United States. Many friends of mine were shipped to Korea after a few weeks in the U.S. And from all the people in the world, I felt closest to the Koreans. Under no conditions would I go to war with them at this stage of my life. Though it was called "the United Nation's war," thousands and thousands of Americans died, and I did not want to be one of them, before having a chance to be an American.

Around the 22nd of October, we boarded a military vessel at Bremenhaven under the name of *General Leroy Eldritch*. I sent a telegram to my sister before I boarded, telling her that according to the schedule I would be arriving in New York on October 29 at ten A.M.

I was used on the ship as an interpreter, working with American doctors announcing the change of time in four or five different languages. Of course, I was not getting paid for that, but it gave me something to do instead of being bored like the rest of the passengers. I had my meals in the dining room with the American crew, all sailors on military duty.

After a day or two, there was a discussion about baseball. Although I knew nothing about baseball or how the game was played, I took part in the discussion as if I knew what I was talking about. I learned a lot about baseball, but never understood the game because I never saw it played. AFN was the American Forces Network in Europe, which I very often listened to on the radio. I didn't know what a home run was or a strike out but I knew about it. After I took part with the sailors, they became very suspicious listening to my accent, which was not English but American, and my taking part in baseball conversations. They were positive that I had been in the U.S. before. Their suspicions were relayed to the immigration authorities in New York.

On the 29th of October a boat with about four immigration officers came on board. Though we were more than an hour away from the port of New York, I was the first one they issued a landing permit to; that is, permission to land on American soil until Washington sends you an alien registration card or green card. I sat with the four immigration officers and helped them to interrogate the new émigrés, to make sure to check their names, how many children and their ages. After that, they received landing permits.

After about two hours of working with them, we arrived in midtown Manhattan, I don't recall what pier. While working with the officers, happy and thrilled that I finally made it, I felt as if I was being watched. I felt as if eyes were on me. When I raised my head and looked over to my left, there were three men all dressed the same, brown hats with a black band, white shirts, black ties, pale gray raincoats. Somehow I had a feeling that they were looking at me. What they were really doing was listening to my English translation. It was my American language that bothered them. I guess it was because of the captain's call that they had received. After listening to me for about a half-hour, one of those three came over to me and asked me if I had a landing permit. I said yes, I had the first one issued. He said that I should surrender it to him. I said, "No. Why?"

He said, "If you don't give it to me, you can't leave the ship anyway. We have to talk before you can go."

I had no choice but to give him my permit. I continued working with the immigration authorities for about a half-hour more. Then I stood up and said to one of them, "You better get another interpreter because I don't want to work anymore. My landing permit was taken away, and I have no reason to continue."

And I walked away from the table. They had to bring three people to do my job. It took more than two hours before the new interpreters arrived, and everything was interrupted. Most people did not know what had happened. I went to sit down, and one of the three men told me I should come with them as they wanted to talk to me.

They took me to the dining room. They identified themselves as FBI agents. We sat down at a table, and I felt almost like I did the day my death sentence was announced. Shaky and worried. It worried me that I was going to be accused; no matter what I was accused of, it is hard to defend something you didn't do.

The first question was, "Is Henry Chaim Goldberg your name? Is this your real date of birth?"

I told them that was as close as I could come to my real age.

"Have you ever been in the United States before?"

I said, "No, but if I ever had been, why would I leave and come back as a refugee?"

The FBI would not take no for an answer. Their reasoning was that no other country in Europe played baseball, and I knew who the Yankee Clipper was, Joe DiMaggio, and Babe Ruth. I said to them that if I fell over Joe DiMaggio I wouldn't know who he was or any other baseball star. The reason I knew their names was from the American Forces Network and from spending time with Americans. Since the World Series was played in the U.S., everyone was glued to their radio to listen to the outcome.

It took me about ten to fifteen minutes to calm down, as I almost stuttered in answering the questions, from nerves. After two hours with the same questions being asked over and over, and since I did not have an English accent but a New York accent, they would not accept the story I was telling them: that I had never been in the U.S. and the American slang I used was from the American Forces and GIs. The funniest part was that the man from HIAS was sent for, and he came after I had met with the FBI agent. I don't know what gave the FBI the idea to send for an HIAS person from the Jewish welfare agency. He said something quietly to the agent, and they nodded as if to agree with what he said. He took me into the next room and started speaking Yiddish to me, as if in Yiddish my story would change or be different.

"You think if I speak Yiddish my story will sound different?" I asked him.

He started to tell me that he would help me if I told him the truth; that if I told him the truth, I did not have to tell it to the F.B.I.

I looked at him. "Are you the smartest one the Jewish organization had to send, or could they have gotten someone smarter?" If I was a spy, or whatever they thought I was, why would I tell anything to someone who speaks Yiddish?

I insisted on repeating my story, even in Yiddish, that it was the truth. If I wanted to make up a story to please them, I wouldn't even know what kind of story to make up. I didn't know what they wanted from me.

About five hours later, we were still sitting, hashing over the same baloney. Under no conditions would they accept the story I was telling them. One remark from one agent was, "What are you, a genius, that you could accomplish all those things in a few months?"

I said, "No, I'm not a genius, but my capability in speaking any language is as easy as eating a piece of chocolate. There is nothing I can do to change that. People with talent make rockets and guns and invent new things. I can't do those things, and I do not claim that I have the ability to do any of them. But when it comes to languages, I could stand next to anybody with my ability."

After so many hours I became brave. I said to the chief, the one who seemed to be above the others, "I'll make a deal with you." I could see they all suddenly felt very, very good, and thought that I had broken down at last. "It's about time," he said. "We've been here almost six hours."

As I never understood what they were after, in spite of being drilled for almost six hours, I said, "I will tell you the truth under one condition. You have to give me your word that I will not be sent to Ellis Island, no matter what. If that happens, I would prefer to go back to Germany. Or you will give me my landing permit, and I will go see my sister in Brooklyn."

He said, "I give you my word you will not be sent to Ellis Island. It will be the United States or Germany."

"Okay, let's hear it," one of them said.

I told them, "I don't know how you are going to take this, so brace yourself. Now listen carefully. I'm a Russian spy who works directly with Joseph Stalin. I refuse to work with any other agents and I get a check directly from Stalin every month."

I don't know how to describe the faces of the agents. They did not expect a bombshell like that. They were looking at one another, speechless.

I realized they had a problem. Was what I was telling them now the truth or what I had been telling them before? They told me to wait outside, and they talked together very quietly. I could not hear what they were saying. I know one of the agents was on the phone, to New York, Washington, I don't know. I guess he needed instructions or advice about what to do now from someone higher up.

After about a half-hour of calling back and forth and discussing, one said, "Mr. Goldberg, I promised you would not go to Ellis Island. I will keep my promise."

I sat motionless, as I really didn't care anymore. I had never been so much harassed with stupidity, even by the SS. Though I wanted very much to settle in the United States, and I knew my sister was waiting for me outside, I said nothing to them and waited for their verdict.

"Mr. Goldberg, we decided to give back your landing permit, and you can go to your sister's."

I gave a sigh of relief that finally this mess was over.

"But we would like to advise you that we are going to watch you."

I told them, "Watch as much as you want." That bothered me very little. I couldn't be worried, since I was no Russian spy or any other kind of spy. I said thank you and took the few things I had with me in a small valise and came out. It was past eight o'clock. Of course, my sister did not wait for me that long. She had left when she saw the crew of the ship leaving. They told her there was nobody left. All refugees were gone. "Your brother probably did not make it. He will probably be on the next ship." It was very hard for her to understand, as I had sent her a telegram the day I had left and gave her the name of the ship and the day of arrival. But she accepted what the sailor told her.

New York did not scare me. I was born in Warsaw, lived for almost two years in London, was in Moscow, Prague, Vienna, and Paris, so New York to me was just another big city. After a few inquiries of passersby, I took the F train and got off in Brooklyn at the Church Avenue station. It was only about four blocks to my sister's house. When I rang the bell she could not believe her eyes that I was there. "I was at the ship and they told me nobody was left. Did you come by the same ship your telegram said?"

I said, "Yes."

She couldn't understand how come I came so late after eight o'clock when the ship was empty at three. I told my sister and brother-in-law that it was a long story and that I was too tired then to tell it. I would tell her what happened tomorrow.

My sister had a little girl who was about three-years-old, Edith. She looked exactly like my sister when she was that age, blonde and blue-eyed and smart on top of it. She jumped on my lap, screaming, "My uncle from Germany is here!" as if she wanted the whole neighborhood to know.

18

IN WHICH I SELL MYSELF

I had supper as I hadn't eaten since ten in the morning. After a good night's rest, I felt a little better than the day before. After resting for a few days, I went to the Jewish organization called the New Americans, which was a part of the HIAS. I registered with them, and they promised to get me a job, as it wouldn't be too hard since I knew the language; that would make it very easy. I should call them every day and they would let me know over the phone, should any chance for employment arise.

About two weeks later I was told to visit a Miss Smith in Personnel at the Freed Transformer Company, which was also located in Brooklyn. I went for the interview. Miss Smith was very much impressed with my English and surprised that I was able to travel about, being in the country only a little over two weeks. She said she would hire me as a laminator. I had no idea what that was. She also told me that I was the first non-citizen that she was going to hire. Their basic business was in military defense contracts. It made me wonder why I was sent there, as this was defense contractors and I was the first non-citizen to be hired. Miss Smith took a liking to me, and after the interview was over I received a button and was able to pass the gate. She took me out to lunch. She wanted to talk to me about the job, and I wanted to talk to her about her. She was a nice looking lady in her late twenties. I had a little suspicion that our conversation might wind up in the hands of the FBI. But I didn't let that bother me, as I had nothing to hide, so I had no fear.

When I came home, my brother-in-law went bananas. He worked at a transformer factory that only employed about ten or twenty people. He said, "Four times I applied for a job at Freed Transformers as an experienced laminator and was told that I had to be a citizen to work in that plant." It was a mystery to him that I, with no experience, was hired. I told him Miss Smith took a liking to me and I guessed that was the reason I was hired. I never told him the suspicion I had of the real reason behind it.

He begged me to talk to Miss Smith and tell her about him and see if he could be hired, too. My salary was forty dollars and he worked for thirty-five. I told him that I couldn't do it right away, but after a week or two I would talk to Miss Smith and hope that she would do it for me. My brother-in-law was very excited and could not wait for me to talk to Miss Smith. I took Miss Smith out twice on Saturday evenings. On the second date I told her about my brother-in-law. "It would mean a lot to me if you could find room for him."

She made an appointment for my brother-in-law at twelve noon on Monday. That whole Sunday Norbert talked about it in excitement.

He could not wait till Monday noon.

After the interview Miss Smith called me in on the intercom and told me that my brother-in-law was hired and would start working on Tuesday. He was very happy because, first of all, he would make five dollars more than his old job, and second, he felt that in a huge place he would have a chance to advance. I worked there for six weeks and I quit.

I could not take the monotony of the job. All I was doing was soldering, putting wires together. The other thing that bothered me a lot was when the foreman told me if I went to the bathroom too often, he would fire me. I explained to him that it was only a short time since I had come from Europe; and, in Europe the main meal is eaten at one or two o'clock, and besides my system was adjusting and a sandwich gives me the runs, but it shouldn't take more than a month or so until my system would get used to the idea of having the main meal at night. Of course, all he was interested in was production. "I heard those stories before. They sound nice but I don't buy 'em."

His remark helped me decide to quit. After receiving my check on Friday, I went over to Miss Smith and told her that I was not coming back. She was surprised. She told me I had a huge future, that I was bright and I learned easily. I told her I was sorry. It wasn't what I really wanted to do. I thanked her for being nice to me and I left. I was looking for a job where you are not cooped up for eight hours doing the same thing, day in and day out. Of course my sister and brother-in-law felt that I had made a mistake to quit. Only the future would tell if what I did was right or wrong.

Also very disturbing to me was when I talked to other employees and found that after working four or five years, they were only making fifty-five dollars a week. I felt I could do better.

I started to look in the *New York Times* for jobs. One particular job caught my fancy: "Drivers and chauffeurs wanted. Starting salary, fifty-five dollars. Plus tips." It was seven o'clock when I arrived at the agency, although the office opened at eight. I wanted to be the first one there. It was exactly at eight o'clock that a Mr. Cooper, who was the owner of the agency, and his secretary came.

After I filled out an application, Mr. Cooper took me into his office. He saw on my application that I had only been in the U.S. a few months, and I could give no references except Freed Transformers. He told me the job he had in the paper was taken. "But how could it be taken? I am the first one here." I realized that those ads are to bring you into the office and put you into any other job that is to be had. "Henry, I have a job for you that will also pay fifty-five dollars. It is in a plastic factory. You have to fix the machine should any problem arise. Sometimes you may just do nothing for days, but it is an easy job. You should be able to do it with no problem."

I told him I would take the job under one condition. When a chauffeur opening comes, he will switch me. He agreed to it. "No problem, Henry," he said. And he gave me a slip to give the employer.

The next morning at eight o'clock, I arrived at my new job. The boss was very pleased, and he showed me all the machines that have other mechanics, and said that I should watch them for a day or two. When Thursday came, I told the boss that I would stop working after Friday. When he asked why, I told him he has three mechanics and that not one of them had all their fingers. You had to fix the machine while it was in motion; any minor error and your fingers were not safe. He begged me to work on Saturday half a day and I agreed to do it. After taxes, I came home with about fifty-three dollars for the week.

I called Mr. Cooper on Monday morning and told him that I had quit the job, and if he could get me a driver's job I'd take it. He told me that I'd have to pay him fifty-five dollars for this work, as I worked more than five days. This was the law if you worked more than five days, sent by an agency. The first week's salary, which was fifty-five dollars, went to the agency.

I started to scream over the phone. "You are trying to tell me that after working five and a half days I have lost all fifty-three, and have to take two dollars from my pocket and pay you? I will not do things like that! I will send you fifty percent of what I earned."

"Don't worry. It's tax deductible."

I said I didn't care what it was. "Under no conditions would I work five and a half days and give you more money than I earned. I want nothing to do with you. You are dishonest, and I will have no part of it."

"I'll sue you," he shouted on the phone. "I'll sue."

"Well, if you have to sue me, sue me. I will not give you that kind of money under any conditions."

I avoided agencies and looked for other jobs in the papers. One of my friends suggested that I should try the state employment agency. They did not require payment for finding you a job. I visited a few, and at one of the state employment agencies I only waited about fifteen minutes when my name was called. A young fellow in his late twenties said to me, "Do you know why I picked your application? My name is Murray Goldberg. You could be one of my lost relatives. My parents came from Europe in the twenties. I would like to help you."

I said, "Thank you very much. I could use help."

He was impressed with my knowledge of English. I told him jokingly, "I don't know if it is an asset or a curse."

"Why? You should be glad."

I said, "It is a long story. Maybe someday I will tell it to you."

He said, "I saw on your application that you speak many languages, and German is one of them. Would you like to be a truck driver?"

I said, "Between you and me, put it in the file. I never drove anything but a bicycle or a motorcycle in my life. I never even drove a car."

"You are asking for a driver's job and you don't know how to drive?"

I told him, "Well, don't speak too loud. You should give me the address and tell me where it is. I will go. You will not be in trouble for my asking for a driving job."

He was a little taken aback after I told him I never drove. I said to Murray, "This conversation never took place. It is between you and me."

With a little hesitation he said, "I hope you are right."

After he gave me the slip where to go, he told me the owner was an Austrian and to be careful how I talked to him. I shook his hand and thanked him and promised to let him know how it worked out.

I arrived at the new job. The S & K Drug Company were wholesale distributors who supplied local drugstores in the city of New York. When I came in I greeted the man in German. I asked him if he was Mr. Sobelsen, the owner. He said yes. Our conversation was in German. He had no doubt that I was German, because, as you know, languages are easy for me. All he asked me was what part of Germany I was from. I told him Munich and Bavaria. He was very pleased. "So, you are my neighbor. Don't you know that Bavaria is right next to Austria?"

I told him yes and that I had traveled many times to Austria by train. He asked me how old I was. I told him twenty-six. How long had I been driving? I told him about seven years. He did not ask me what, and I didn't tell him that I drove a bicycle and a motorcycle. He said,

"Heinrich, you might have a little problem delivering, as you are only here in the U.S. for a few months."

"Don't worry, Mr. Sobelsen. We will work it out."

"The first day I will go with you so you can become acquainted with the route," he said. He told me the truck driver he had was leaving in two weeks. He was six-feet tall, a black guy who could pick up the truck with all the merchandise and carry it. Mr. Sobelsen was hesitant in his decision. He kept asking me, "A nice Jewish boy like you, weighing only about 145 pounds, can handle such a job?" I told him not to worry. In my life I have had harder jobs.

I had two weeks now to get a license and learn how to drive.

One friend of mine had a 1949 Chevy. After a little party at my sister's house, my friend Milton, who was a neighbor from Wetzlar in Germany, and I met Harry at a dance. The dances were organized by a group of newcomers. Milton and Harry were dead drunk, but I had only one drink. Since I was sober, I decided to take Harry's car while he slept off his drinks. I took Harry's keys and his car and drove from three until eight o'clock in the morning, all by myself. After a while, I got the hang of it and drove like a pro. I parked the car in the same spot where I had taken it from and went to sleep.

It was Sunday, about noontime, when we all woke up. My sister made breakfast for us all, and I asked Harry if he would give me permission to drive his car. "Do you know how to drive?" he asked.

"If I didn't know how to drive, I wouldn't ask you. Of course, I know how to drive," I replied.

So, from about 2 P.M. until about six, we drove around in Brooklyn.

Monday I went to the motor vehicle bureau, took a permit, and made an appointment for a test. It was scheduled for the next Tuesday. I passed my driving test with flying colors. I failed my written test, as in my excitement that I knew all the answers, I marked them on the wrong side. I was called in for another written test, and the motor vehicle officer smilingly said, "You know all the ten answers, but you marked them wrong. Now be calm and do it again." I did it, and before the end of the week I received my license as a chauffeur.

I was thrilled since I had to start my new job the following Tuesday. I had Sundays and Mondays off, but I had to work on Saturday as Monday's orders were taken and delivered the next day, Tuesday. On the first day, Mr. Sobelsen and I loaded the truck. The truck was about six months old. It was a three-and-a-half ton Dodge, a huge monster. We took off around ten o'clock with twenty-eight deliveries to make.

Under the guidance of Mr. Sobelsen, we hit the road. Every time I switched the gears in the truck, the truck would make a grinding noise.

I did not know the reason, but Mr. Sobelsen assured me that it was my nervousness, as I had never driven in New York City before. He kept on saying, "You are doing all right. Don't worry. After a while everything will be okay."

On our fourth stop, we saw another truck driver, who also made deliveries to the drugstore. While Mr. Sobelsen was sitting in the truck, I walked over to the other driver and asked him why every time I switched gears I got a grinding noise. He asked me, "Do you double-clutch?"

I looked at him, realizing that trucks have to be double-clutched. I said, "Thanks a lot."

I double-clutched, and the grinding disappeared. Mr. Sobelsen said, "You see, I told you. You are calm and everything is okay." We made all twenty-eight deliveries with no more problems. And Mr. Sobelsen said smilingly after we returned, "I am happy to have you work with us."

After working one week, he gave me full pay of fifty-five dollars and said that he would pay the taxes because he was very happy with me, and I could be trusted. I was very pleased with the job, as I could stop, have a cup of coffee, or just take a break. All I had to do was make my deliveries. I made an oral agreement with Mr. Sobelsen that I would make thirty-two deliveries a day instead of twenty-eight, and he wouldn't have to pay me overtime. All I wanted in return was to be able to take the truck home with me after work, and would return with the truck in the morning to do my deliveries.

It worked out very good for me, as after about two months I used to get home about four or four-thirty P.M. I was allowed to take home, with no charge, shampoo for my sister, toothpaste, and other things that we could use in the house. I established a very good rapport with the druggists. Mr. Sobelsen increased my salary after two months to seventy-five dollars a week, and he still paid the taxes without taking any out of my wages. I never asked for a raise, but many druggists would call in and talk to Mr. Sobelsen, praising me as being very nice, saying that I would always wait until the customers left before having them sign the delivery papers, contrary to other truck drivers, who threw the packages down, many times breaking certain contents in them, then shoving the paper in front of the druggist, no matter who was there, for him to sign.

On my day off, Monday, I had nothing to do as most other people worked. I went into the place and started to help pick out the orders. Mr. Sobelsen said, "If I give you a raise, it does not mean you have to work six days a week. I have enough people here. You should go home and relax."

"Mr. Sobelsen, you see, I don't think I want to spend the rest of my life being a truck driver. I would like to learn more about the items I deliver."

"Henry, there are about a thousand items," he said. "And to know the prices of all the items and to pick them by just coming one Monday a week, would take you more than two years to learn."

"For most people it might take two years. But I'm different," I said.

"What do you mean, you are different? You are not different."

"To show you that I am different, I am going to tell you something. But you must promise that you will not get mad at me or fire me."

He said, "I will never fire you. You are doing the best job."

I told him the whole story of how I got my license, and that I never drove anything before in my life except a bicycle or a motorcycle. Mr. Sobelsen looked at me in disbelief. He kept on saying, "It's not true, is it?"

"It happens to be true," I told him. "If I had told you the truth when I came here, would you have hired me?"

"No, I wouldn't have. I couldn't let a truck with merchandise be given to a man who can't drive. You think I'm crazy?"

"But you see, Mr. Sobelsen," I continued, "it worked out for both of us. You are happy with me, I am happy with you, and nobody got hurt."

Still not believing the story, he showed up that night at my sister's house to verify my story. When my sister told him that it was true, he said, "You told me you drove for seven years."

I told him, "Mr. Sobelsen, I drove for more than twenty years, but, I drove a bicycle and for a few years, a motorcycle. You never asked me if I drove a truck. You asked me if I drove. And I told you the truth."

"You had the chutzpah to do a thing like that to me?" He was so shocked.

"I did not do any damage. No accidents. I don't think you should complain now. It's too late."

Before he left, I said, "Mr. Sobelsen, do I come to work tomorrow or am I fired?"

"Now you talk of firing yourself? You are experienced. I am not going to fire you."

I never told my parents, who were still in Germany, that I was driving a truck in New York. It would make them very nervous. I also told Sally not to mention anything about it to them. I saved a lot of money in six months, as my sister only took ten dollars a week from me for room and board after. After I got a raise, I gave my sister fifteen, plus beauty supplies for her and my brother-in-law. I kept on going every Monday to the place, helping to take orders.

One day I came home about four-thirty, and there were two FBI agents in the house. While my sister was in the kitchen, they spoke to my three-and-a-half-year-old niece. When I came in they were in the middle of interrogating my niece with many questions. Do many Russian friends come? Does she know the names of my friends? Do we drink a lot?

I was outraged when I walked in. I was outraged that they would interrogate a three-year-old child. I asked them, "What the hell do you think you are doing?"

They tried to identify themselves. "I know who you are. You don't have to tell me." Since they all dress alike, you can spot them a mile away. They talked to me for about fifteen minutes. Stupid questions. I told them, "I don't mind you watching me, but I don't want to be harassed. And from interrogating my neighbor, they will think I am a criminal. Don't you know a subtle way of doing things, or don't you care?"

"Sorry, Mr. Goldberg, for the inconvenience. But we have to do our job."

I smiled and said, "You mean, a butcher's job."

After working for Mr. Sobelsen for nine months, I came to him and asked for a salesman's kit. I told him I would like to go out to the drugstores and do sales. He looked at me in bewilderment. "I don't think you know how. You are crazy. You think this is child's play? You know I have a college graduate. I pay him one-hundred-twenty-five dollars a week and twenty-five dollars a week expenses to get new accounts. He is five-foot-nine, and you want to take his place?"

I said, "Mr. Sobelsen, by now you know I am not German but Russian, as I always used to say instead of Polish, and when I came here you believed I was German. Don't you give me credit for my capabilities?"

"Yes! Yes!" he screamed. "But selling is a different bag."

I said, "Mr. Sobelsen, sit down. Let me explain what I want to do. I don't want to replace Arnold the college graduate, or take anybody else's job. I will go to the neighborhoods that Arnold cannot get into. You tell me the area that you cannot penetrate because bigger companies are there for years, and let me see what I can do. I am not asking you for any money. I am doing it on my time, which is Monday. I am buying a car and I cannot see why you would object, as I will only increase your business with additional customers."

He finally said, "Okay, you want to do it, do it."

"I'll tell you what," he continued, "you are so confident that you can do it that I will give you twenty dollars for every new customer you bring me."

I said, "Mr. Sobelsen, if I take twenty dollars from you for every new customer I bring, I will break you in a few months."

He laughed and said, "Go ahead. It will be my pleasure."

I told him, "Let's figure how much you will really give me for each customer, and let's get going."

"The toughest neighborhood for the trade is downtown Manhattan," he told me, and gave in to my request.

It was eleven o'clock. I took my car and went to downtown Manhattan. Before I entered any drugstore, I looked at the name. If the name was Polish, I came in and greeted the owner in Polish. If it was Russian, I greeted him in Russian. If it was Czech, I spoke Czech or Ukrainian. It was a piece of cake.

I went into ten stores and each one gave me an order. They all told me the same thing. "We know you are a pharmacist from Europe and you can't get a job here, so you must be working for a salary." I never said yes or no. My answer used to be "If life doesn't go the way you want it, you do the best you can." If I had told any of them the truth, they would not have believed it. Who would believe I was only in the country less than a year and behaved the way I did? The FBI didn't believe it, why should they?

When I came back, Mr. Sobelsen almost fell off his chair. "You made yourself two hundred dollars. You made yourself two hundred dollars," he kept repeating.

I told him that I didn't want two hundred dollars. I didn't even want a hundred dollars. "But I promised you," he said.

I said, "I know what you promised. And I know you would keep your word. I will take fifty dollars, not a nickel more."

"But your order is over one thousand dollars."

The druggists had let me go through the shelves and see what items were low in supply, and they told me to fill in the orders myself. Mr. Sobelsen was still a little bit confused. "Well, let's see what you can do next Monday. Maybe it was just luck."

"Mr. Sobelsen, everything is possible, but I don't think luck played any part in it."

But we would check it out the next Monday and see who was right, Mr. Sobelsen or me. I left from my house the next Monday at nine o'clock, went back to downtown Manhattan, and after I had ten orders it was only 2 P.M. I went back to Mr. Sobelsen. He couldn't believe his eyes. He wanted to know how I could do those things, and why the pharmacist treated me so well. They did not even want to deal with the other salesmen

"Mr. Sobelsen, do you remember the first time I came for the interview? I spoke only German to you, and you were wondering if I knew any English. You accepted me as a German without reservations. You have to realize that I speak five languages and two others not so well. Most of the pharmacists reacted to me the way you did when I came the first time. Help me out, if you can, with no harm done to yourself."

"You mean you speak Russian, Polish, and all those other languages?"

"Sure. To prove it to you, let Arnold go and try to get an order from the twenty new customers I brought in."

He did send Arnold to the new customers I had acquired, and the whole week he visited all twenty of them and did not bring back a single order. It convinced him that my ability to speak those languages played a big part. The day I was waiting for finally came.

"Why don't we get a new truck driver and you become a salesman?" he said to me.

"I thought you'd never ask," I exclaimed. "I was asking my sister, 'When will Mr. Sobelsen realize my capability as a salesman?' I told my sister that one day you would wake up. And here you are, fully awake, and offering me a job as a salesman."

It took a few weeks before we got a new driver. I became a full-time salesman with a salary of one-hundred-twenty-five dollars a week, plus twenty-five dollars in car expenses. And Mr. Sobelsen still did not deduct for taxes, but paid that as well.

The place had six American order pickers which created problems. I had to join the Teamsters' Union while I was a truck driver. I continued to be a member of the union, though salesmen were not required to join. The American employees who had worked there between five and ten years developed a hatred for me and were saying, "That damn Russian just came to this country and in less than eight months is a salesman, and we are still order pickers.'" They started calling me names: Russian salami, Commie, but I ignored them all and smiled.

But one day I brought one of the packages back that one of the order pickers had not packed properly. I went over to Marvin who was about six-feet tall and was the employee with the most years in the place. Not only did he pick orders, but he distributed work for the rest of the employees. When I brought back the package, broken and damaged, I told Marvin, "Keep an eye on those fellows. You see what happened.

The whole package is damaged. About sixty dollars worth of merchandise."

He raised his voice, "Why don't you go tell the boss about it?"

I told him, "Never in my life did I ever go tell the boss that somebody made a mistake accidentally or willfully." I told him that when I was a child in school and was attacked as a Jew, I fought back, but never went to the teacher or principal to tell who attacked me. "And I don't think I am ready now to go and tell Mr. Sobelsen about this accident. I am talking to you and I don't think Mr. Sobelsen should be involved in this. The mistake was done, has to be corrected, and that is the end of it."

"Listen, you Commie bastard. You became a big shot, and now you are telling me what to do? You are not my boss, you know."

I calmly said to him, "Marvin, don't be a fool. Don't get outraged and don't ever raise your hand to me. I might be small, but I know how to fight my battles."

"You think I am afraid of you? Because you are Russian?"

"I don't want you to be afraid of me. We are all workers here, and we have to work together. And I am not afraid of you, either."

He raised his hand and hit me. I grabbed him by the legs and threw him over my shoulder. His back was hurt. Mr. Sobelsen, hearing the commotion, came running in from his office. "What the hell is going on here? What's all this fighting?"

"It's all over, Mr. Sobelsen," I said. "I just showed Marvin how easy it is to drop a big man to the floor."

"Why? What happened?"

I wouldn't tell him, but the other workers told him. Marvin was bawled out by Mr. Sobelsen as being an ignorant bully. He told Marvin, "Once and for all, I don't want you to harass Henry. He was a truck driver. Now he is a salesman. He didn't take any job from you fellows, and being jealous because somebody is more capable than you will not get you anywhere."

Marvin said, "You never gave me a chance to become a salesman."

Mr. Sobelsen said, "You think you could be a good salesman?"

"Yes. I've been here ten years. I know all the items."

"Well, if you are so sure of yourself, I will give you a kit tomorrow. Let's see what you can do."

After three days he took his old job back as order picker. He became my best friend. We went out together, and drank together.

Since I had become a salesman, business increased about thirty percent, as I was bringing in very large orders. I used the tactic of making up my own specials, which the big companies used to do once a year. Never give the druggist who already has a special more than one. Only one to a customer. Whenever you tell someone they can't have more than one, they always ask for three or four. I used to tell the druggist, "If I have any customers who don't take one, I will give you another one." But I used to send them four. When I came the next time, they used to thank me for giving them the extra four, when in truth I could've given them a dozen.

Whenever you ask the druggist how many he wants, he would say one was enough. It was not a super market. But when I made it clear he could not have more than one, he suddenly wanted six.

I was sorry he lost his job. Arnold was gone, as we didn't need him anymore. I felt sorry that I was the cause, but I did a better job ten times over. I used to get extra bonuses every week from Mr. Sobelsen, twenty or thirty dollars.

19
LAWSUIT

A few months later I faced a judge in court because of Mr. Cooper. It was my first encounter with the legal system in this country. It was not in small claims court, but regular day court. The lawsuit was for fifty-five dollars. As I could not afford a lawyer, everyone recommended that I go to the Legal Aid Society. I called them and they gave me an appointment. After wasting almost a day, they explained to me very politely that the Legal Aid Society could not represent me. It was not at that time government-financed, but run by business donations. They could not represent me as they could not "bite the hand that feeds them." The lawyer very calmly explained to me that there was nothing he could do and told me to explain to the judge what I had told him. "Let's hope for the best."

The court was very crowded. Thousands of people were going in and out all day. Finally my case was called: Cooper Agency v. Goldberg. Mr. Cooper had a lawyer, of course, one of those lawyers who ran around from case to case. He probably heard about fifty cases a day. After being sworn in, the lawyer representing Mr. Cooper told the judge that according to the statute of the State of New York—then he rattled off about six numbers—Mr. Goldberg refuses to pay as required by law. The judge turned to me and said, "Did you work more than five days?"

I said, "Your Honor, may I explain something?"

"No. I want a yes or no answer only."

I said, "Yes."

He hit his gavel, said, "Guilty. Next case, please."

I was outraged. I didn't mind losing the case as I was tricked into working on the Saturday, but I felt I had a right to explain my side of the problem. I thought that then the judge would at least have the agency investigated for its practices. I felt that justice would be served, even if I had to pay. It would stop that agency from doing to other people what had been done to me.

Right after the judge pronounced me guilty, the bailiff immediately dragged me off the stand. "Come on, you're guilty. Let's go." He took me over to a desk and told me I had to pay fifty-five dollars. I told him I did not have fifty-five dollars. He said, "Then you will have to pay at least five dollars a week to Mr. Cooper." Still outraged, I said, "I want to appeal."

The bailiff laughed and said, "You know how much money that will cost? A few hundred dollars! If you can't pay fifty-five, where are you going to get money for an appeal?"

He went on, "You need a lawyer, and that will cost more money. And if you have no money, just sign up that you will pay five dollars a week and shut up. I have other cases."

I sent Mr. Cooper five dollars a week for seven weeks, which was thirty-five dollars, and I kept the stubs of the money orders. I felt I paid more than he deserved and didn't pay anymore. About three weeks later I got a letter from the marshal saying that I owed Mr. Cooper fifty-five dollars plus fifteen dollars for the marshal's fee, which brought it up to seventy dollars. I was already working for Mr. Sobelsen. I showed him the letter and he cried, "This guy is trying to collect twice! I don't think this is legal, what he did."

"Well," I said, "I showed this to you because I felt what he did was not legal."

I called Mr. Cooper and told his secretary who I was. She said that Mr. Cooper was busy and I should call back later. I told her, "Let me give you my number and tell him he doesn't have to call me. I will have him served with papers for extortion." And I hung up.

It did not even take five minutes for Mr. Cooper to call back. He spoke very nicely to me. I said, "Look, Mr. Cooper, I don't want to hear a word out of you. You have ten days to notify the marshal that you illegally tried to collect money from me twice, and the marshal should withdraw the threats I received. And I would like the check for thirty-five dollars returned."

He tried to explain to me that it was an oversight on his part. He tried to tell me that I didn't have to pay anymore, and that I would get a letter from the marshal to that effect. And let us forget about the whole thing.

I told him, "I made a mistake in working more than five days, so that instead of a ten percent fee you were entitled to, you asked for a hundred percent. Now you made the same mistake, and you have to pay."

He tried to "Mr. Goldberg" me. I told him, "I said what I have to say, and if I don't get my check and the letter from the marshal within ten days, I will bring charges against you." And I hung up.

Two days later, a check for thirty-five dollars arrived, accompanied by a letter that stated that the marshal was notified and the nonpayment charges were withdrawn. A week or so later I received a letter to that effect.

20
LOOKING FOR WORK

I had problems with big companies because of the questions on applications. Some of them asked about my religious belief or was I a member of the Communist Party? Some asked, "Are you a fellow traveler," and some asked, "Do you agree with the Communist philosophy?" On the question of sex—male or female—I would answer with "I liked it." I never answered as to religious belief, and the only one I answered was that I was not a member of the Communist Party. As to my religious belief or political beliefs, I would not answer as I felt it was none of their business. So when I was interviewed, I was asked why I didn't answer or finish the application as was required. I would tell them that neither my religious beliefs, nor my political philosophy, was any of their business. Of course I was not hired. I had a few minor jobs, most of them as a shipping clerk with small companies, as they did not require one to fill out applications.

I went to TWA and asked for a job, and I answered all the questions on the application, as I really wanted a job. The job I wanted was on the International Arrival Information desk, as I was able to speak so many languages and would be an asset to TWA, by giving information to new arrivals in their own language. The country was gripped by the McCarthy era, and I was told they would gladly hire me if I brought a security clearance. And me, like a dummy, traveled to Washington, D.C. to the State Department to get it.

When I arrived and went to the reception desk and told the lady what I needed, she called over another worker and they went hysterical. They said to me, "You expected somebody to sign a security clearance for you? First of all, you are not a citizen. Second, you are only a little over six months in this country, coming from behind the Iron Curtain. And you want a security clearance!" The two of them broke up again, laughing.

"What brain sent you for a security clearance?" she asked me.

I told her, "You won't believe it. It is myself. That shows you how smart I am. You know, there are some things I don't understand. To begin with, why would a person working in an airport at the information desk need security clearance to begin with? And second of all, I lived in Russia for seven years and openly defied the Soviet government, and refused to cooperate with them in any way whatsoever. But I held high position jobs and never needed a security clearance." I calmly added, "The freedoms you offer here are limited, which surprises me very much."

She looked at me and said, "I'm just a clerk. I just do what I am told. I am sorry, Mr. Goldberg, to disappoint you, but there is nothing that can be done."

I was so mad that I went to the Soviet embassy and told them I wanted to go home. I lied on the application and put my place of birth as Brest Litvosk, instead of Warsaw. I guess this was a big mistake on my part, going to the Soviet embassy, as pictures were taken by the FBI of everyone who entered or left the embassy. I didn't realize this and forgot all about what had happened on the day of my arrival. After I left the embassy, I wouldn't have gone back even if they had granted me permission to do so, as my father and mother were supposed to come to the U.S., and my sister was here. I would not have left them to go back behind the Iron Curtain.

After returning from Washington, D.C., I decided to visit a girl I knew who lived near Allentown, Pennsylvania. This was the girl I spent some time with the last few months I was in Germany. Her mother, being in her sixties, wanted her daughter to get married. So she was very happy that I came and hoped that Olga and I would get married. Although I was Jewish and they were Greek Orthodox Russians, it didn't matter. Back home in the Soviet Union, most of the marriages were not of the same nationality. Of course, in the Soviet Union, religion was very seldom practiced and with over 120 different nationalities, marriages between different nationalities were common.

There were about ten Russian families in Allentown. There was a Greek Orthodox priest, who in Russian was referred to as "Pope." He invited me and Olga and her mother for supper. After a long conversation, he said, "Genadie, when you marry Olga you are going to have to take her to New York. It will be difficult for people of the Jewish faith to get a job here. Most Jews who live in Pennsylvania are Americans, and half of them have changed their names, so as not to be detected by their names that they are really Jewish. They give it a fancy name, "Americanization," but the truth is they are hiding their Jewishness. In big cities like New York, there are too many Jews, and many run their own enterprises, so it is not easy to discriminate against them. But in little towns, though you change your name, you struggle for survival."

I had no intention of changing my name, as this is something which is carried from generation to generation. To prove what he meant, the priest pointed out companies that would not hire Jews. He said, "Show me a Jew who works, even in New York, in a bank, insurance company, or even the A & P. I could go on and on, but you understand what I am saying." He continued, "I know this may not be easy for you to understand, as you lived in the Soviet Union. You know I am not sympathetic to the Communists, but you have to give the devil his due. Those practices are illegal there."

I was not shocked by what he said, as only a few days back, three other Russians and I went to apply for a job at Bethlehem Steel, which is close to Allentown. We put in our applications, and I had to fill out the ones for the others, as they knew very little English. When the first Russian was called over by the personnel officer, he had problems as he spoke so little English. I volunteered as an interpreter. All four applications were filled out approximately the same way, as to our experience as mechanic steelworkers. Though my application was the second from the top, the personnel officer put it on the bottom. He knew that Henry Goldberg was a Jewish name. Of course, he did not know that I was the one doing the interpreting. All three Russians were hired. He was very embarrassed when he told me to tell Henry Goldberg that all positions were filled, and that they would get in touch with him when an opening came up. I looked at him and I said, "You know, I am Henry Goldberg."

He became red in the face and almost stuttered, "How come you speak so good English?"

I said, "Does it matter? Is it enough I am Jewish?"

He said, "I'm sorry, Mr. Goldberg."

"I know. Most Nazis are sorry now and so are you." And I walked away.

So the story that the Russian priest told me was not really news to me. I guess he gave me the little speech, being close to the Russian community in Allentown. He knew what happened there and that was why he gave me the speech, to let me know that that was how life was in the U.S. in small towns, so I could avoid any more disappointments. After visiting with Olga, I returned to New York.

One morning I received a telephone call from Germany. It was the chief surgeon in the Munich hospital. He told me that Father had to have a gall bladder operation, and he was very depressed from being alone with only Mother and all the children away. The doctor suggested that it would be very helpful for the recovery of my father if I could come and be with him for a few months. Since I was the only unmarried child, it should not be too hard for me to take the trip. It was already March, 1953, and I was very upset with the news I had received.

After finishing the next day's work, I walked into a bar, something I had never done before, and asked the bartender if he had vodka. He looked at me. "Vodka? It must be here somewhere. Let me look." He finally brought a bottle, covered with dust. He started to give me a shot. I said, "No. Leave the bottle here and give me a beer glass."

I told him I wanted no ice, and I put a full glass of vodka down.

"Young man, what do you want for a chaser?"

"Give me a glass of beer."

There were only about six or seven people in the bar. I did not realize that they were all looking at me, as my mind was on my father in Germany. I drank the glass of vodka in one sweep and drank the glass of beer, and the bartender said it was a dollar. I left a dollar and a quarter and walked out of the bar.

When I got into my car, I saw in the mirror that all seven people and the bartender were outside watching me, as if something should happen to me after drinking a full glass of vodka. I only then realized that what I had done was unusual in the U.S., but not in Russia. I waved to them and took off for home.

It seems like everything worked out as if planned. Mr. Sobelsen had a heart attack, and I was told by his doctor that after he recovered he would go to California. When I went to visit him, he told me it was a mild heart attack and that he was going to sell his business to his nephew. He wanted me to come with him to California and said that he would open a new business in the same line. "I know you are going to visit your father, but when you come back, I want you to come to California." He would make sure that I made a good living.

I explained to him that my parents were coming to New York, that my sister lived here, and I had friends in New York. These were things money could not replace. I told him that after I came back from Germany, after my father's operation, I would think about it. I said to him, "As of this moment I am not ready to go to California."

I had saved up a few thousand dollars, and I had all my papers from the immigration authorities. I took the ship, *Liberte*, a French liner, and four days later arrived in France. I spent a week in Paris, and though my French was not so good, I got along very well, especially with girls.

I took the train from Paris to Munich, and from there it was only ten miles to Forenwald where my parents were. By bus I arrived in

Forenwald, to the joy of my mother and father. Just seeing the happiness in my parents' eyes made the trip worth it. I spoke to the doctor, and he said it was a smart thing, that it would help Father recuperate much faster this way, as mental health is a big factor in physical recuperation.

I stayed with my parents in the DP camp, which had only about a thousand people now. After staying a month with my parents, when Father was back to his normal health, I would often go to Munich. Very seldom did I stay away overnight. I enjoyed very much Wirtschaft houses. There are none in the U.S. They are like a bar, but large, and whole families used to come. The most enjoyable thing was to be able to sit with young people, arms around each other, singing German folksongs together.

I blended in very well, as if I were a born German, which reminded me that when I lived in the Soviet Union, the Russians also would get together after a few drinks and sing folksongs. Somebody played the guitar or the bayan, which is like an accordion, but both sides have buttons instead of keys. I sang with the Koreans as if I were a Korean, I sang with the Komi, I sang with the Ukrainians, I sang with the Irish in England; so this experience was not new to me, except we sang in German.

I was very surprised when Stalin died. Hundreds of people cried in the DP camp, even though Stalin was not considered the kindest man. I liked the explanation one Jewish woman gave me as she was weeping. She was Russian, her husband was a Polish Jew, and that gave her the right to leave the Soviet Union with her husband. Many Russian Jews who married Polish girls were also allowed to leave the Soviet Union. The Soviet Union is the only country in the world where if a couple gets married, you could choose either name, the woman's or the man's, as a family name; and if the wife is foreign, you could leave with her. I don't know about the new Socialist countries, what their law is. In most countries of the world, the wife must take the husband's name, and you cannot choose the other way.

Most Russian Jews explained to me that Stalin did many things they may not approve of, but he did it to everyone, no matter who they were or what their nationality. I could not understand how it would be an asset if you execute people indiscriminately, or jail them only because they were anti-communist. I didn't want to argue with them, but that was the weirdest explanation I had ever heard for Stalin's ways.

I spent nine months with my parents. When I returned home to Brooklyn, I had to start all over in search of employment. I guess my trip to Europe rekindled the suspicions of the FBI as I left the country, and in their minds I could have gone to East Germany as I had visited Berlin twice. In Berlin you could take the subway and go to the East undetected. You could go back and forth.

I took jobs as a grocery clerk, shipping clerk, truck driver. I left all those jobs after I was visited by the FBI when my boss was questioned about me. It seems that it is a free country, but everybody is afraid of the FBI, even if they did not do anything wrong. My bosses would tell me, "Look, Henry, I don't know what you did, but I don't want those guys to come here." It amazes me how Americans are afraid of the government like in any other country. (Unless you are very rich.)

I decided to go to my old place of employment, S and K Drug Company, and see if the new manager was as nice as Mr. Sobelsen. Leon Sperling was Mr. Sobelsen's nephew. I was hired back as a part-time salesman and part-time order picker. I got along very well with Leon, who was the sole owner of the company now.

I worked there for a little over a year. Mr. Sperling decided to expand his business, and he got a new partner. The new partner, Mr. Palmer, had sons and sons-in-law and he decided to bring them into the business. He could not fire me, as I was a union man, and Mr. Sperling came to my defense most of the time. But he too realized that my days were numbered. He knew that I would not take abuse. Even if I have to eat a dry piece of bread, I would not let them abuse me. I also felt that the new partner, with his sons and sons-in-law, could not be blamed for wanting them in the business, as he had invested probably a few thousand dollars.

I finally went over to Mr. Palmer and told him that I realized in a few months his relatives would do anything to undermine me. I felt the whole thing was unnecessary. "Let's part in a friendly way instead of being enemies," I told him. I left the place with two weeks' severance pay, and he smilingly said to me, "You did the right thing, Henry. As you know, sooner or later I would find a reason to fire you. And you know the union could be paid off very easily." I knew very well what he had told me was true, because when the union representative came, instead of talking to the workers, he used to go out with the bosses.

I felt very confident that after working for more than three years in the drug business, I could get a job very easily. Only then did I realize the hang-up American businessmen have about how tall their salesmen are. After interviewing with other drug companies, everyone would tell me, "If you were at least five-foot-eight, you would have gotten the job." In spite of telling them about my achievements in sales and with a very favorable letter from S and K Drug as to the reason I was laid off, all in one voice said, "Five-foot-eight."

I was very depressed as to the stupidity and the thinking of American companies. In spite of it, I used to tell some of them that I would work for minimum wage to prove to them how good I was at sales work. To no avail. I was too short for the job.

It made me feel inferior, and I was also very sensitive when people talked about my height. I would sometimes even leave my date if the girl would ask me how tall I was. She may not have meant anything by it, but I became paranoid about it. When a girl would ask me over the phone how tall I was when I called for a date, I would hang up. It took me months to overcome my paranoia, and start thinking positive about myself. If anybody would not go out with me because I was only five-foot-five, I would turn and tell my sister that a brainless girl lost a good date. Before, I used to feel sorry for myself, but now I made them the fools instead of me.

I saw an ad in the *New York Times* from Drug Guild. It was a company created by a few hundred druggists in the New York area to have their own distributor. I went to apply for the job. I was hired as an order picker on a temporary basis. I would become a salesman at the first opening. I told them I would accept the job only on that condition. I told them I have no intention of being an order picker the rest of my life. I can't stand to do the same job every day, being cooped up inside. They assured me that with the knowledge I had, it would be no problem for me to advance. A manager was called in, a Mr. Anzes, a man about my size, wearing a yamulka. He was an Orthodox Jew with the long side curls. I was introduced to him and was told I would work with him, as he runs the whole place.

I was very glad that I got a job in the line of work that I was familiar with. After about three months, I was a lot of help to the workers, as I remembered most of the prices without looking them up. I very often unintentionally embarrassed our manager, because although he knew a lot, he had to check the prices on a sheet every once in a while. I would say, "Mr. Anzes, it is $3.98 a dozen," and when he said, "Thank you. You saved me a trip to the office," he made me feel really good. He would come over and pay me compliments. "It's amazing, a little over three years, and you know more than I know in ten years." He made me feel very good.

One day I noticed in the *Sunday Times* that the Drug Guild was looking for salesmen. I could not wait until Monday to ask Mr. Anzes why I was not given the job as promised. He said he told the Board of Directors that he needs me here and he didn't want me out in the sales office. I was very upset. I went to the main office and asked why the agreement we made was broken. I had told them that I did not intend to be an order picker the rest of my life, in spite of the salary. They told me they were going to look into it, and they would let me know. I never heard from them. Mr. Anzes became less friendly. I guess he was upset about my going above his head to the main office.

The place had about forty order pickers. A fellow working next to me always used to say, "Oh, Jesus Christ!" I jokingly turned to him and said, "If you want help, you better call Moses. Jesus Christ has enough problems with Christians. And I don't think Jesus is ready to take on the burden of the Jews, too." I don't know how Mr. Anzes heard about those remarks. He came over the next day and told me that a union representative would come and I would be suspended until a hearing. I looked at him and said, "What hearing? What did I do? What are the charges?"

He said, "The union man will tell you when he gets here."

At lunchtime the union representative arrived in his Cadillac. He called me aside and told me I was being suspended because I had made anti-Christian remarks to co-workers. I looked surprised and asked, "What did I do? What did I say?"

"You will have the hearing next week, and you will have your say. Don't worry. You will be paid for the week you are suspended."

I couldn't wait to hear what I did or what I said. The next week the hearing came. I, as the accused, sat on the right side. The young fellow who worked next to me and Mr. Anzes in his Orthodox attire sat together. The charges were that I made anti-Christian remarks, which was contrary to the rules of the union regulations. The young fellow who worked next to me was Mike. He repeated what I had said about Moses and Jesus, but the funniest thing was that my manager, in his Orthodox attire, stood up and said, "You know I am Jewish, but nobody in my place will disgrace the name of Jesus."

I couldn't believe what I was hearing, as most Orthodox Jews never use the name of Jesus. They act as if he were not or ever had been in existence.

I looked like a comedy played out on the stage. When the representative asked me what I had to say, all I said was, "The remark I made is not anti-Christian or anti anything."

"Anything else?" he asked me.

I said, "No."

It didn't take them five minutes to find me guilty of anti-Christian remarks, and it was the right of the management to fire me if they chose to do so. To add to the comedy, he stood up and said, "We do not want Christian-haters in our place. Mr. Goldberg's employment is terminated as of this moment." I was in shock. It looked like a farce. I was wondering, is this a stage and are we acting, or is it reality? I was told I would get severance pay and that I could go to the office and pick up my check.

I came to the office about fifteen minutes later, and as I was walking outside, I was bewildered as to what really happened, an Orthodox Jew defending the name of Jesus Christ. I was wondering if he belonged to the Jews for Jesus. I could not think of any other explanations. But I had not insulted Jesus. What could be his reason? It did not take me too long to find out. When I came into the office to pick up my check, Mr. Anzes was waiting. He came over to me and said, "Mr. Goldberg, I don't want you to be mad at me. I want you to forgive me. What I did has never been done before by an Orthodox Jew."

I stood silently and listened to him, and then he said, "Don't you want to know why I did it?" When I didn't answer, he said, "I am going to tell you anyway. I don't want my conscience to bother me. I have a wife and six children. This job means everything to me, and I felt that sooner or later you would take over my job. You know too much about the business to stay as an order picker." He knew I had been promised advancement. "You are a young fellow. You can get another job."

I silently walked away. He wanted me to shake his hand to show that I had forgiven him. After I picked up my check, I went over and shook his hand. I figured it was too late now to change anything. I was hurt by the whole incident. That an Orthodox Jew had to use religion, and the Christian religion at that, in order to get rid of me, to hurt me as he did.

I realized that the chances of getting a job as a salesman were slim, though I tried many companies again. My height was a big problem to them. I could not go back to factory work, so I decided to become a driving instructor.

I got a manual from the Motor Vehicle Department with all the laws pertaining to traffic and driving. You have to know the laws as well as a policeman, maybe even better, so you can tell your students the right move to make under any circumstances. After about two weeks, I went for a test. The hardest part was the written test, as the driving part was no problem for me at all. Two weeks later I received a driving instructor's license with my picture attached to it, similar to a taxi driver's license.

I went back to search the *New York Times* for a job as a driving instructor. I had a problem now, as most wanted experienced instructors. But after a week or so, I got a job for a dollar an hour in Brooklyn. My boss was a woman. I was bothered by the drop in my salary. While working for a dollar an hour, I didn't stop looking for the same kind of work with a higher salary.

After about two months, the *New York Times* ran an ad: experienced driving instructors wanted. This time I had experience. I took one Monday off and went down for an interview. The driving school had four locations. The owner, Nick, was very bright, an Italian guy. Of course, having a job already as a driving instructor made me feel a bit more confident. He did not give me a written application. It would have probably gotten me into trouble. I was glad he did not have one.

I told him I had been working a year and a half, and that I was earning $2.95 an hour, which wasn't true, but I said it anyway. I told him I wanted $4.50 an hour. He looked at me and said, "We have people here for years that don't get that kind of money. The highest I pay is $4 an hour."

I said to him, "If others get $4, I deserve $6."

He said, "We are only charging $7.50 an hour and you want $6?"

"I'm worth $6, because what I have none of your other instructors have."

"Well, explain to me why you think you are worth that much."

"I speak a minimum of five languages, and we have a lot of people from the embassies. Knowing foreign languages would be an asset when you advertise. That would make it easier for the students to receive instruction in their own language, if their English is not too good."

He said, "I like what you got. I like what you said about increasing my business tremendously. Other schools couldn't say that in an ad. And if diplomats want a license, they could get if from me—a New York State license. The others are only good for a year."

He agreed to pay me $4 an hour by check, which would be equal to the other drivers, and he would give me 75 cents extra, in cash, as he didn't want even his accountant to know that I was making more than the other drivers.

I would have taken the $4, but I held out until he agreed to give me $4.75. It was a big jump from a dollar an hour. He asked me why I was leaving the Brooklyn company after a year and a half. I told him the woman who owned the company was not business-minded, and would not advertise about instructions in different languages to help the business. I felt he was a smarter business type who could see the advantages. Besides, I did not get along with the woman, as she was very domineering.

I was hired, and I had to work six days a week, which made me a little unhappy, but I wasn't about to refuse. The money was good. I told

Nick that I had to give notice at my other job, that it was unfair to walk off without giving notice, so she would have time to get a replacement. I told him I would start the next Monday. That pleased him. "You are a gentleman," he said. He knew from that that I wouldn't walk out on him without notice, too.

He also did what he promised. He advertised the next day. He sent letters to the United Nations. My first pupil was from the German embassy. Mr. Singh, who was a U.N. representative and later became the defense minister in India, was a pupil. After I had worked about three or four months, my boss was very pleased, as the number of pupils had increased by about fifty percent.

The school I was assigned to was at 59th Street and Lexington Avenue. The school received a letter from the Soviet Union Mission, located at 68th and Park Avenue, inquiring about sending a student. The mission was about three blocks from the school. I knew that this might get me into more trouble with the FBI. I could not tell this to my boss; it might scare him if I told him the FBI was watching me. I tried to talk him out of giving the new student to me, instead of to somebody else. But the letter said they were glad there was an instructor who spoke Russian. There was no way I could get out of it. On a specified day I went to the Soviet Mission and picked up a Mr. Fomin, one of the permanent representatives to the United Nations.

I knew this assignment was going to get me into trouble, as the Soviet Mission was being watched daily and anybody entering or leaving it was photographed. But I had no choice. Mr. Fomin took ten lessons, which took about ten weeks, one lesson a week. About four weeks after we had finished with the Soviet Mission, my boss received a visit from the FBI. He was shown a picture of me shaking hands with Mr. Fomin. The FBI wanted to know if I requested the job or had it been assigned. My boss explained, showing the letter he had received from the U.N. He told them I had tried to talk him out of taking the pupil, but there was no one else to speak Russian, so I had to take him.

After I finished my day's work, he told me about the visit he had from the FBI. I did not tell him that they had visited at other jobs I had. I explained to him that since I had come from behind the Iron Curtain and for ten weeks had been going to the Soviet Mission, they had to check and find out the reason I was there. There was nothing to worry about, I told him.

He said, "I hope they don't come back. I don't like them snooping around."

21

MARRIAGE, REAL ESTATE, AND CITIZENSHIP

My parents had arrived in 1956. I don't recall the month. My sister owned a four-family house in Brooklyn and, because of difficulties, had to dispossess a tenant. She gave my parents that apartment. I lived with my parents after they came. As I was thirty years old, as most parents would, they thought I should get married. I was going out with a Russian girl, Glasha. My parents tried to impress on me that in the Soviet Union it was normal for Jews to marry Russians or other nationalities. Religion played no part in it. But in the U.S., life is different and they would prefer that I marry a Jewish girl.

I did not have too many Jewish friends but many, many Russian ones. I chose my friends not according to religion or nationality but according to the person himself. Very often my Russian friends would come to our house with a guitar or an accordion, and we would party till early in the morning. Glasha came, too. Listening to my parents' advice, I introduced Glasha to one of my Russian friends, Tolia. Most of the Russian groups I was close with were entertainers back in Russia. So song and music was a part of our parties. Two months later Glasha and Tolia got married, and I was the best man at their wedding, which took place in a Greek Orthodox church. The wedding lasted for three days, Friday, Saturday, and Sunday.

My father introduced me to a twenty-year-old Jewish girl, and I started dating her. After urging by my parents to get married, I proposed to her. Her name was Dora. She accepted me without hesitation. The wedding was set for March 3, but after getting to know her family better and better, six weeks before the wedding I told my parents that I would like to back out. I explained to them that I didn't think the marriage would work. Her background and her environment weren't something I was too excited about.

Dora had lost her father in Russia to a disease, and her stepfather was not allowed to come to the U.S. because he was not a hundred percent healthy. She came from one of those families that broke up because of the health of some family member. Her mother was illiterate and very religious, but none of the children—two brothers and a sister— were not religious at all. My parents explained to me that she was only twenty years old, and she could go to night school and pull herself up to my expectations.

On March 3, we got married. Her mother rented a big hall and there were about one-hundred-fifty people from both sides. Of course, all my Russian friends came. I went to Niagara Falls on my honeymoon. On December 17, 1957, Dora gave birth to our son, Nathan, named after her deceased father. It is a Jewish tradition to name after close relatives who have died.

Though I was making a good salary and big tips, I was trying to change jobs. As a driving instructor, I had a limited income. At the same time, the FBI visited my boss again. That shook him up very badly. He told me he didn't want those guys to come all the time, and he gave me two weeks' notice.

I decided to go into real estate, to become a real estate salesman. I felt real estate was the only job where I could earn as much as my ability would allow. I saw an ad in the paper stating that the biggest real estate office in Brooklyn was looking for experienced salesmen. I went for an interview. The man liked my aggressiveness, as I told him a few facts about what I had done while in the U.S. The most impressive thing to him was my first job as a truck driver.

I asked him what he thought I could earn a year. There were twenty salesmen, and he showed me the records of ten of them. Their earnings were from ten to twelve thousand dollars a year. If they could do it, he said, he thought I could do it, too. He guaranteed it according to the ability of each salesman. He told me to spend a day with other salesmen and talk to them, and then to come back to him with my decision, as there was no salary involved, only commissions.

After I spent a day with some of the salesmen, Mr. Eisberg, one of the owners, called me in and said, "You think they are smarter than you?"

I replied, "I don't think so. If they can make it, I think I can, too."

I got a temporary license that was good for six months. The test for a permanent license had to be taken within six months.

My wife and I had bought a house in a newly developed area, Canarsie, for $23,500, a two-family, four-rooms-over-four-rooms, with a full basement and a one-car garage in the rear. I was not working in real estate yet when we bought the house in August of 1957. I had saved some money, and my wife had some money from working as an operator in a sweat shop. She worked until a month before the birth of our son, Nathan.

My first encounter with how banks work came at the time of closing. We had to put down fifteen hundred dollars, and we received a mortgage from the bank. While I was still a driving instructor, my boss put down that my earnings, including tips, were two-hundred-fifty dollars a week. Plus, the four-room rental from the house made me eligible for the mortgage. Since the closing was in August, and in New York the houses are assessed for tax purposes every April, that meant that from August until April, I would pay no tax.

At the closing, the bank's attorney told me I had to put a thousand dollars into escrow for tax purposes. My attorney said that this was standard practice. I was very much annoyed by it. I wanted to know on what grounds they wanted a thousand dollars, plus already collecting eighty dollars a month for taxes and that I wouldn't even pay until April of the next year. I told the bank's attorney that I didn't have a thousand dollars to give him and that I felt a thousand dollars was unnecessary because the bank is going to collect from August until April, eight months, eighty dollars a month, and that would be the escrow. That money would be there before they had to pay, and at that time taxes were paid back. It meant that the next July they would have to pay for three months. That would give the bank almost two thousand dollars before they had to pay out only about two-hundred-fifty dollars.

I told the bank's attorney that I would gladly give him a thousand dollars if he wanted, provided he would give me interest on it. He explained that the bank did not pay interest in escrow. I told him, "When I take money from you I am paying five-and-a-half percent interest, but you want to take my two thousand dollars and not give me a penny in return? I am not about to do it."

My attorney called me aside and tried to convince me that every bank does that, that if he had known I was going to make a scene, he would not have handled my case. I told him he could leave if he wanted to, that I did not really need him. Of course, he did not leave, because he might not get paid then. I told the attorney to not interfere with my handling of the bank, no matter how unhappy it might make him. When we came back to the table, the bank's attorney asked, "Is everything okay now?"

I said, "No. Under no conditions will I give the bank money without receiving the normal interest that the bank pays on deposits." I raised my voice a little bit and exclaimed, "This is highway robbery."

Other closings were going on at the same time, and as we were in little cubicles alongside each other, others could hear me. "Mr. Goldberg, you don't have to raise your voice," the bank's attorney said. I knew he didn't want others to hear what was going on. He closed his folder and said, "There will be no closing."

"If there is no closing," I said, "I will sue the bank for reneging on their commitment. There is nothing in the statement about a thousand dollars escrow."

My attorney explained to me, "It is not necessary to put it in writing, as it is common practice."

I told him it might be common practice with giving loans but not with me. And if he wants to leave, he can leave, and I will take appropriate actions.

The builder who was selling the houses took the bank's attorney aside. They whispered together for about ten minutes. My attorney kept saying to me, "Why do you have to create trouble? You are the only one in the whole bank who wants to be treated differently."

I told him, "Counselor, you are better off being quiet. I feel that I am right. I know I am right. And when I am right, I insist on right. There are about two hundred homes being built in Canarsie. The bank will get two hundred thousand dollars, and they don't have to pay a penny to anyone. If you want to tell me this is right, then I can promise you, if I ever buy something else, you will not be my attorney."

I continued, "Counselor, if you have a chance to be quiet, then just be quiet and leave this fight to me."

The bank's attorney and the builder came back and cut the escrow to five hundred dollars. "If you don't accept that, there will be no closing."

"I am going to give you a hundred dollars. Take it or leave it. If you want a hundred and one, you won't get it. This is it," I said.

I guess the attorney could not take the responsibility to agree to it. He left the table to talk it over with someone who was allowed to make a decision. He came back about a half hour later and he cut it to two-hundred-fifty dollars.

I said, "I told you a hundred. Not a hundred and one."

He finally said okay and we closed.

My mother-in-law and her two sons had bought a house at the same time as we did, two doors away from us, and they had paid a thousand dollars into escrow. When we came back from the bank, I asked my brother-in-law if he had paid a thousand, and he said yes. I told him I had only paid a hundred. He couldn't understand. I explained to him why I had not paid a thousand, and he still could not understand very well. The whole family was half illiterate.

I started to work in real estate in October, as I was fired from the driving instructor's job because of the FBI's visits to them. It was the first time I applied for unemployment.

I told the man at the unemployment office that I was now doing training to become a real estate salesman. He was very nice to me and gave me a new application. He told me not to mention that I was now working in real estate. As a trainee, I would not be entitled to unemployment. The fifty-six dollars a week I received from unemployment was my main income, because even if I had sold anything in real estate, it would take months to see any money, since it is only received after the deal closes.

I worked seven days a week. I had to make a go of it. I liked the real estate business since you could work your own hours. This gave me a certain amount of freedom. I worked from nine in the morning, came home for supper at five, and by seven was back in the office until nine or ten at night. The first six weeks I had twelve deposits, but none of them went to contract. I was very depressed and could not understand why from twelve deposits I did not have a single sale. Even my boss could not understand it. There were eighteen people employed, and I was the only newcomer in the office.

I took more deposits than any other salesman in the same period, but could not consummate any of the deals. Mr. Eisberg suggested that when I got messages from my customers, to tell the receptionist not to put them in the message book but on a separate slip of paper so the other salesmen would not know on what deal I was working. He said he had a suspicion that some of the guys were probably jealous of my success, and they might be calling my customers and killing the deal for me.

I looked at Mr. Eisberg and said, "Why?"

"This is a dog-eat-dog business. Most of the newcomers who come into this office have problems, and the people who have been here for years don't want the office to get bigger, so they may play all kinds of tricks on you. So be very careful."

One day, an Italian woman walked into the office and walked right over to the man sitting next to me, Maury Stern. He was one of those flag-waving Americans. In a heavy Italian accent she said to him, "You son of a bitch! You calla me and tell me not to buy the house this man has sold me," and she pointed to me. "You say house is full of termites. I could have gotten house for twenty-four thousand dollars. My friend bought this house from another real estate and pay twenty-six and no termites. You are a liar. My husband come and kill you for this."

I sat very calmly and quietly. I really did not know what to do. I went and told Mr. Eisberg in his private office what Mrs. Caruso just said to Maury Stern. I knew that Mr. Eisberg was not going to fire Maury as he had been there six years and was a good salesman. Since I was new, he was not going to stick up for me and lose an established salesman to take a chance with me, not knowing how I was going to work out.

He said, "I told you of my suspicions and that you should continue to keep your messages out of the message book so nobody will be able to get in touch with your customers."

I went back to my desk and was encouraged by the salesmen to beat Maury up for what he did. I decided against it. I knew if I caused a scandal by fighting, I would be the one to be fired. Maury told the lady that she was mistaken, that he had never called her. The lady insisted that she knew his voice and the way he talked.

For about a week Maury would come into the office and say good morning to me, but I wouldn't answer. He tried to talk to me, but still I would not answer. I just refused to have anything to do with him. He could not take the silent treatment; it bothered him. One day he sat at my desk and said, "I have to talk to you, Henry. I want you to know that I did not do it by myself. Others helped me."

I didn't answer him. "I know you hate me," he went on. "I want to make it up to you."

I said to him, "Maury, I don't hate you. I just feel sorry for you."

"You feel sorry for me? I didn't hurt myself. I hurt you."

I told him, "You are only a flag-waving American. My wife is about to give birth to a baby, I live on unemployment, and you denied me the right to earn a living. I feel sorry for you as you have a sick mind. Is that what America is all about?"

He sat silently for a few minutes. He didn't know what to say. I said to him, "I don't hate anybody. I've been hated too long, and hate is a harsh word. It is extreme. People who hate resort to inhumane tactics."

He all but begged me to become his friend. He said he wanted to make up for what he did in any way he could. He stretched out his hand, "Please forgive me. You will see. From now on it will be different."

I told him, "I forgave people who did worse things to me in my lifetime. It's not too hard to forgive you, too."

He became my best friend. Every Wednesday we played pinochle, me and Maury and Marty Wagner. If I needed any favor, Maury was the first to volunteer. His wife called me to tell me that I did the right thing, that for two weeks he could not sleep because of what he did to me, in denying me a right to a livelihood. I told her thank you for her call, and I didn't think he would do it again. She said she could not understand why he did it because he told her he liked me and had said what a nice guy I was.

My son was born on December 17. Right before Christmas I decided to go down to the Motor Vehicle Bureau to see if I had any outstanding tickets. I had a written agreement with my employer at the driving school that all violations, except traffic violations, would be paid by the school. If there were any traffic violations, I would have to pay them myself. I took off one day from work, went to the M.V. Bureau, walked over to the window, gave my license number, and told them I had outstanding tickets, and asked them to tell me how much I owed. The man pulled out about thirteen tickets, which amounted to about eighty-five dollars. I showed him the written agreement I had from the school. There were twelve tickets for stopping and parking in restricted areas. Only one was a traffic violation, for making a right turn on a red light. Though it was done by a pupil, I was responsible for it. The clerk suggested that I go before the judge and show him the letter of agreement. He thought the judge might cut down the fine.

As I was not a habitual law violator, it seemed like a good idea. I went before the judge. After I sat a few hours, the bailiff called my name. The presiding judge was La Picollo. The bailiff read out the tickets and then gave them to the judge. The judge marked on each ticket what the fine was supposed to be. "Your Honor, may I explain please?" "Go ahead," the judge said. "I did not pay those tickets because I had an agreement with my boss that he would pay all tickets that were not driving violations." He paid no attention what I was saying but kept on writing and mumbling, "I see, I see." After he was all through, the judge said, "You have to pay the cashier on the other side."

The bailiff said, "Come with me." He gave all the tickets to the cashier. I had shown the letter to the judge. He told me that the agreement was not valid, as it was contrary to the law of the state. But I still felt that he should not have done what he did.

When the clerk told me that the fines totaled two hundred and twenty-five dollars, I counted my money. I was thirteen dollars short. I wanted to give a check for the thirteen dollars, but the cashier said they did not accept checks. So I said to the bailiff that I could go outside to a check-cashing place and cash a check and come back and pay the thirteen dollars.

He went back to the judge and said he had no permission to let me go without the judge's okay. The bailiff talked to the judge, explained the situation to him, and told him what I wanted to do. The judge turned to him and said, "Lock him up."

I almost got hysterical. "Your honor," I said, "There was no warrant for my arrest. I came voluntarily. The cashier has two hundred and thirty-seven dollars. You think I will run away for thirteen dollars?"

The judge turned to the bailiff, "I told you to lock him up."

I took out the hospital release of my wife and newborn son and showed the judge. I told him that my wife had just come home from the hospital with my baby and said, "If you lock me up, she will be all alone with a newborn baby, and nobody to help her. Please, have some understanding. I was not brought in by a sheriff. I came in voluntarily. Please let me go get the thirteen dollars."

The judge turned to the bailiff and said, "For the third time, I told you, lock him up." The bailiff put the handcuffs on me as if I were a big criminal.

The jail was only a few blocks away. About ten other people were also taken to jail. I was fingerprinted, photographed, and thrown into a cell. There were about thirty people in there, when the cell was supposed to have only about fifteen. I have been in a few Russian jails, but what I saw here was indescribable. A toilet at the side of the cell was overflowing, and there was feces and urine all over the floor. Drunks and bums peeing on the wall—what's the difference? It was still going to go on the floor. I was allowed a phone call. I did not call my wife, but my father. I told him he should come down and bail me out, as I was short thirteen dollars. He wanted to know what had happened, what did I do? I told my father I didn't do anything. I came to pay a fine and was short thirteen dollars. So my father and brother-in-law came as soon as possible.

In the whole cell of thirty people, I noticed one gentleman dressed in a suit and wearing a tie. When he saw me, he came over and asked if I was here for the same reason he was.

"I was short fifty dollars. It was not even my ticket but the truck driver who works for me," he told me. He asked me how much I was short, and I told him thirteen dollars.

He said, "Here is twenty dollars." They hadn't taken any of his money at all. "Go pay your fine. I am the owner of the Golden Dragon in Chinatown, just a few blocks from the jail." He wrote down in Chinese a note to give to any employee in the restaurant.

I went to the front of the cell, by the bars, and called one of the policemen and told him I had the money to pay my fine now. He said, "It's too late, Mac."

"Too late for what?" I asked him.

"Your money is no good now."

I couldn't understand his reasoning. He couldn't explain to me why. "Forget about it. Don't ask questions."

I figured that now even if my father came with the thirteen dollars, I couldn't get out either. What the hell were they going to do to me? The Chinese guy could not understand either. "What is going on?"

"I think justice is being given to us, American-style."

If something like this were to happen to an American while in another country, the papers would be full of reports on how their justice system works.

When my father and brother-in-law came to pay the rest of the fine, it was almost eleven o'clock. As the court system is a mess, nobody knew where to go to pay the thirteen dollars. My father finally found the place. It was past twelve o'clock. The officer told him that I didn't have to pay anymore. It was after twelve o'clock and that meant that I had sat a day in jail, which was the value of fifteen dollars. I would be released soon. It was almost one o'clock in the morning when I was released. I told my father that I had to take the note from the Chinese man to the Golden Dragon.

When I gave the note to the man at the restaurant, he ran with the note to the manager, all in excitement. They were speaking loud in Chinese as if they were angry. He asked me if I had eaten. I said no, not since morning. He served us dinner on the house, as he was so pleased that I had brought the note.

I got home after 3 A.M. and, of course, my wife did not know what had happened to me. She could not understand, either, why it was done to me. I told her, "Don't ask questions that I cannot answer. Or anybody else can about this particular deal."

I wanted to do something, but I did not know what. I felt the judge's behavior was cruel and unusual. I wrote a letter to the *New York Post* describing what the traffic court was doing to people, how they were treating them as if they were big criminals. The *New York Post* did not print the letter, as I had not signed it; but they did send down an investigating reporter. After two years, the law was changed so that a fine could be paid by personal check. The *New York Post* had an article hailing their investigative reporter as a kind of hero for his big achievement. I guess that satisfied me a little bit, though the experience in the cell will be with me forever.

I worked very hard in real estate, seven days a week, and about ten to twelve hours a day except for Saturdays and Sundays, when I only worked about eight hours. By the time my unemployment ran out, I had about eight sales to my credit. My boss gave me advances, as I told him

I needed the money. He felt I was doing well, and he could take a chance.

I became a broker in 1962 after a six-hour test. I was averaging about fifteen thousand dollars a year. I was taking a draw against my commissions of about a hundred dollars a week. By the end of the year I would get a lump sum of money.

On January 1, 1959, my wife gave birth to a girl we named Brenda. That was the name of my grandmother on my mother's side. My wife had worked up to the time of the birth of my son, Nathan; and although I earned a decent salary, my home life was not a happy one. My wife refused to go to night school and bring up the level of her education, which contributed to the unhappiness at home.

Our biggest disagreement arose from the fact that I had grown up in a home that liked people and company. No matter how poor we were, we always had company and shared whatever we had. In contrast, my wife and I had very few people come to our house. Even when my parents came, she would go upstairs to her bedroom and not take part in conversations or anything else.

My Russian friends stopped coming, as they are usually friendly and liked company. On Wednesdays, the fellows from the office used to play pinochle, and we used to alternate houses. We played one week at one place and another at my house. I would call my wife on Wednesday afternoon and tell her the phone number where we were playing in case of any emergency. Every Wednesday we had the same discussion. "Henry, I want to go to the movies tonight."

I told her the same thing every week. "There are seven days in the week. And Wednesday I play pinochle after a hard day's work." I finally stopped arguing with her. I just gave her the phone number and hung up.

In every house where we played, the wife would prepare us coffee and cookies or little sandwiches before she went to bed, as we usually took a break at one o'clock. We played till about 3 A.M. My house was the only one where the wife would go to bed without saying goodnight and wouldn't prepare anything. Dora would do it every time, and the fellows would ask, "Is she mad?"

"No. She's not mad. That is just the way she is."

It was about the worst thing anyone could do to me. To ignore and not be nice to company and welcome them.

Once a week, on Saturday, Sunday, or Friday night, I would go visit my parents. Dora very seldom came along. I would take the children and go by myself. She tried to explain why she didn't want to visit my parents. She said that my parents loved my sister more than me and that was the reason she didn't want to go. I told her, "If you think for one moment that you can put a wedge between my parents and me, don't even try. It is true, maybe they love my sister more, but it is normal. She was the youngest and the only girl."

The only people that she made friends with were my friend Milton and his wife, Esther. If we went to a party, New Year's Eve or any other, she would sit in a corner, not talking to anyone, and I would go and mingle with the people and have a ball. She would throw it in my face that I was having a good time and ignoring her. I told her, "You know the people as well as I do. You could mingle and have a good time, too. If you want to sit in the corner and be miserable, that is your business."

In 1960, we went to the Catskill Mountains for the summer along with Milton, my sister, and my parents. I would come out on Thursday nights and leave Monday mornings. Dora always found something to say against my parents. She said my parents liked my sister's children better than mine. I was very annoyed and told her that I didn't want to hear anything else from her about my parents or my sister, as I had heard enough. I told her, "One of these days I am going to leave you if you continue this way and try to make me hate my own family."

In 1956 the immigration authorities from Washington, D.C. sent me a letter stating that I should apply for citizenship. I was really surprised, because everyone else I spoke to and asked if they ever received a similar letter, they would say no. I decided to file an application for citizenship together with my wife. She received her citizenship a few months later, but when I was interviewed, the INS was not satisfied with my answers. An investigator asked me how come I read (in their opinion) left-wing liberal newspapers and magazines.

When I asked him how come he was not upset and never mentioned that I read the *National Review*, which is a right-wing, conservative magazine, he answered, "That magazine is okay." He asked me what I thought about Castro and was not too pleased with my answer. I told him, "There is a man who belongs to one of the richest families in Cuba, who took all his wealth and gave it to his state. I am not interested in his political views or how he runs his government, but any man who gives up his wealth for the good of a nation cannot be all bad."

The investigator did not say I was rejected, just, "You will be notified."

I really did not care what he thought or what he was going to do. As I jokingly said to him, "When I become a citizen, will I pay less taxes?"

"No. But you will have the right to vote."

"For Macy's or Gimbel's?" I asked.

This remark did not sit well with him.

The next year I got another letter from the immigration people in New York for another interview. Almost exactly the same questions were asked, and I gave the same answers. But when I was called in 1962, which was after ten years of being in the country, and my cousin and her husband from England were here, I told her to prepare herself, that tonight we were going to celebrate that I was going to be a citizen.

She looked at me in surprise. "Why do you think they are going to give it to you now?" I told her that a few months ago I had acquired a thirty-eight-family apartment house that cost two-hundred-forty-thousand dollars, and I also had stock worth approximately twenty thousand dollars. When I went there and gave it to the investigator, he would be very pleased that I finally made it.

When I came in to the investigator, he said, "How are you, Mr. Goldberg?"

I said, "Fine, very fine." I did not give him a chance to ask any questions, as I would have given the same answers as before. Instead, I threw on his desk the deed to the apartment house and a bunch of stocks. He looked them over very carefully. He asked no questions. He just stood up, shook my hand, and said, "Mr. Goldberg, congratulations. You will be called next week to be sworn in as an American citizen."

Most people, especially Americans, feel that if you have money, the hell with everything else. You belong to the upper class. I smiled and said thank you. And that night, we celebrated my citizenship.

What he said to me without saying a word was, now you are one of us. And there is no reason why I should not give you your papers. I felt how ignorant people could be, as they feel that everybody changes just because they have money. It is true that most people do think this, but I was always different from everyone else and remained different from everyone else.

22

A PAIN IN THE TUCHAS
AND DIVORCE

I was bleeding from the rectum very bad. I went to the doctor. After giving me tests, one after the other, he said that I had cancer of the colon. He wanted me to go immediately to the hospital. I told Dr. Gardstein that I didn't want anybody to know what he had just told me. I was going to go home and tell my wife and my family that I had a bleeding hemorrhoid, and that I was going to go for an operation. He should make the reservations at the hospital, and I would be there in the morning.

Dr. Gardstein and another doctor, a specialist on colon cancer, made one more test. The results were the same. It was cancer, and I would have to be operated on immediately. What he told me was not very pleasing. They would cut off some of my colon, and I would have to wear a bag for the rest of my life. They said the sooner they operated, the better; the cancer would not move any further and I already had three growths. He also remarked that all the tests given to me were between ninety and ninety-five percent correct. I told him I wanted the five percent chance test, as it might show a wrong diagnosis, which he doubted very much.

While I was on the operating table, they took a biopsy, and the doctor ran to the laboratory to check if it was benign or malignant. He came back while I was still on the table, with a smile on his face. He kissed me on the forehead and said, "You bastard. You have more luck than brains. All the tests were wrong. It is not malignant."

It was the best news I had received since my death sentence was commuted. It took a stone out of my heart. They cut out all three growths and I spent two weeks in the hospital. It was only after the operation that I told my family, but Father got upset that I had not at least told him. "Why?" I asked. "Do you think if you cried it would be any help to me? Cry for a hemorrhoid operation?"

Maury and Marty came to visit me as our pinochle game had been interrupted for two weeks. Dr. Gardstein ordered me to stay another week and I was very bored and told him I would like to go home. He said, "You can go home under one condition. You must take a vacation for at least three weeks or a month."

I promised that I would. My brother-in-law had just sold a grocery store, so it was an opportune time for my sister and her husband and me and my wife and two children to go to Florida for a month.

I had trouble with my wife, of course. She said that we didn't have too much money in the bank and couldn't afford it. I tried to explain to her that we were talking about my health, and to recuperate was an important factor, as I had lost a lot of blood. I had received a blood transfusion, and I had to regain my health. My sister and brother-in-law were going, and we could share expenses. My wife insisted that she was not going. I told her that if she did not come along, I would go myself. I packed all my things in a valise, realizing that I was going without her. In the middle of the night, she packed her things too. Monday morning my family and I, Sally and Norbert took our car and left for Florida.

We experienced a lot of discrimination on the road from New York to Florida, as many places refused to serve Jews. This was in 1962. When I saw the sign in the window that stated: "This state gives us the right to serve whoever we wish," I told my brother-in-law that we should not go in. He could not believe it. I told him, "It means that we won't be served."

He was laughing at me as he had never left New York and did not realize that when you pass Hickstown, discrimination is a part of life. My brother-in-law looked Spanish, dark skin and dark hair, which was no asset either. In one restaurant we sat for almost an hour after we ordered four steaks. All we got was four glasses of water and two sodas for the children. We stood up and pretended to walk out, to see if we would be called back to be told the steaks were almost ready, but they did not even ask for money for the sodas. They let us go. They never had any intention of serving us. I tried to explain to Norbert that New York City was only a part of the United States, not the whole of it. After about twenty more miles we went into a Howard Johnson's where we were served.

We arrived in Florida on the third day, as we had stayed in Howard Johnson's motels for two nights. We would not take a chance on any other motel, though Howard Johnson's was the most expensive on the road. We took sandwiches with us the next morning, so as not to have to stop at small restaurants anymore and be embarrassed by not being served. We felt that being denied food three times was enough.

After a few hours in Miami Beach, prices being outrageously high, we decided to stay in North Miami, which is only about five miles from

Miami itself. The prices were less than half there. We spent three weeks in Florida, and we came back home about a month later.

I had a lot of problems in the real estate office where I worked. When a black customer called, the salesmen would say, "Oh, there's a jungle bunny on the phone. Who wants him?" The names *nigger*, *monkey*, *spiks*, and *jungle bunny* among other names, were used to describe non-white customers. I was the only one who accepted black customers. They called me a nigger-lover. One day at an office meeting, I stood up and said "I've had enough from you." "Now look," I told them all, "I'm tired of the way you talk about black people and this name-calling. It is against the laws of the state. If you continue, I am going to report you, and you will lose your licenses. I mean it. I don't want to start using those words, and I don't need to hear them around me. I mean it."

And they knew by now that I did mean what I said.

I could not react to the name-calling in the beginning, as my boss didn't give a damn what went on in the office, so long as the sales came in. Now, with me being the top salesman, I had more courage to stand up and say what I felt. I did not fear that I would be fired. Money was the most important thing to my boss, and I was making money for him.

My boss used devisive tactics to instigate arguments and fights in the office. The reason was to make us hate each other so we would never get together and open our own office. I used to get along very well with Mr. Eisberg and Mr. Lunz. I was always friendly with them and if anything bothered me, I told them about it.

About a month after we came back from Florida, Maury Stern wanted us to work as a team. He used to come in at three o'clock and work till about nine at night, and I would come in at nine in the morning, and we could take care of each other's customers as partners and share all commissions on a fifty-fifty basis. I told him I would do it under one condition. I told him, "I know you are a flag-waving American, but if you want to work with me, you cannot discriminate. You have to treat all customers on an equal basis. If you are willing to give up your prejudices and work that way with me, I will gladly work with you."

He tried to convince me that blacks are different, and he pointed out all the wrong things about blacks. He reminded me of something I had told him when I decided to work—that I had been held up by three black youths while working in Harlem. I told him I will not hold all blacks responsible for what three thugs did to me. I said to him, "The Catholic Church holds all Jews responsible for the killing of Christ over two thousand years ago." I asked him, "Do you feel any guilt for killing Christ?"

He looked at me in amazement. "What are you talking about?"

"Yes," I said, "You are held responsible. How do you feel about that?"

He said, "If you like black people so much, how come you don't have any black friends?"

I told him, "If you think I am going to stand on the corner and force myself on the first black fellow I see to be my friend, you are wrong. The difference between us is you hate blacks, period. I don't love them and I don't hate them. I behave towards them on an individual basis. If he's nice, I'm nice. If he is a bastard, I am a bastard. But he doesn't have to be nice or a bastard just because he is black. I choose my friends, not according to nationality or religion or race, but by having something in common with them. And if I ever meet a black person that I would like to be friends with and he feels the same about me, there will be a black friend, too."

Then I said, "Maury, you know I am Jewish, and most of my friends are not Jewish. I only have two Jewish friends, and it doesn't bother me a bit."

He kept on saying, "I don't understand you. You are going to learn about blacks. You think all Americans are crazy?"

"No. Just prejudiced."

He agreed to my conditions anyway, and we worked as a team. Any time he saw anything in the newspaper, he would bring it in for me to read. He still tried to prove to me that blacks were inferior to whites, and that jails were full of black people.

I told him, "The reason there are many black people in jail is because they are poor and cannot afford a good attorney. If you think that whites are a better race and don't commit crimes, you should check into Europe where only whites live. The jails are still full."

The New York State Department of Real Estate controlled our licenses, and they were all confused. They did not know how to handle complaints of discrimination by black people. If you took a black customer out to an integrated area, you could be accused of steering. If you took him to an all-white area, you could be accused of blockbusting. So whatever you did, they could get you for discrimination or blockbusting if you tried to put blacks into white neighborhoods. Though it is true that many brokers did blockbust. After selling a house to one or two black persons in a white neighborhood, they would go around to the neighbors and scare them into believing that the neighborhood was changing and that they better sell. Brokers used to buy properties from the white owners way below market value and resell to blacks above market value.

I was only called once before the Human Rights Commission and accused of discrimination. A young black fellow had no money down, as he was a GI and did not need money down, but he earned only seventy-five hundred dollars a year, which would not qualify him to receive a mortgage. I refused to show him the house, as the price was thirty-two-thousand dollars, and there was no way he could qualify. Seven months later, he filed a complaint with the Human Rights Commission. As I stood before the all-white commission with an attorney, they asked me why I had refused to show him the house.

I told them the only reason I had refused was that he did not qualify. I said, "I do not show houses to anybody, black, white, green, or blue, unless they qualify. I don't get paid for showing houses, only for selling. When there is no chance of making a sale, I refuse to take a customer out. It has nothing to do with his race or religion."

The head of the Human Rights Commission made a statement that made me almost burst out laughing. He said, "When a black customer comes in, you have to bend over backwards to please him. Even if he can't afford the house."

I became annoyed. "I am not a born American, and I carry no guilt as the white man does for mistreating blacks in this country. And I will continue treating them on an equal basis with any other customer. I don't bend backwards for anybody."

The thing that saved me from their suspension, or whatever they might have done, was my attorney pointing out to them that it had happened more than seven months ago, and the statute of limitations for filing a complaint of this kind was six months. On those grounds, the case was dismissed. Though the hearing was over, the head of the committee said, "Mr. Goldberg, I would like to give you friendly advice. This is off the record. If a black customer comes in, show him the damn house. Whether he can afford it or not is not important."

I looked at him with a smile and said, "You know, if you had one black on this committee, he would agree with me, not with you. All black customers demand equal treatment under the law, and they do not want to be lied to. It is a waste of their time and mine."

"Mr. Goldberg, if you understand the real estate business, you better change your attitude."

My attorney, Mr. Holstein, said, "Let's get out of here. You know who is going to win."

On the way out, I told the lawyer, "You are an attorney for our office. You know that I integrated the Brooklyn College area, which is an expensive and beautiful area. It is basically all professionals. And the black people I took there were also professionals." The area is still integrated today. It did not go all-black.

"Henry, I know all that. I know when you sold the first house in that area you didn't work for almost a month, as a lot of whites came looking for you."

But they could not find my address in the telephone book, as my name in the office was Mr. Henry, not Goldberg. The reason I used my first name was only because there were two other Goldbergs in the office already. When a message came in for Mr. Goldberg, it created problems as to whom the customer belonged to. Using Mr. Henry eliminated more problems.

Maury Stern, my partner, was questioning me about Russia one day. I always gave him honest answers. "Can you buy the *New York Times* there?" he asked, for instance.

"I don't believe so. If it were available it would probably be in Moscow or Leningrad. But I don't believe the Russians would let the *New York Times* in."

He said to me, "You see, in this country you can read any paper you want. Nobody will bother you."

"You really mean that?" I asked.

"Sure. It's a free country."

"Maury, you know what? I would like to subscribe to the *Daily Worker,* which is a Communist paper here."

He said, "No problem. You could do it."

I said, "You aren't serious, are you? It's a Communist paper."

"So what? You can read whatever you want."

I made a suggestion to him. "Maury, you know, when you come from Russia you are not free to do things the government might consider anti-establishment. But being a free American and not afraid of anything, I am going to subscribe to the *Daily Worker* under your name and your address, and you can bring it to me every day."

Of course, I had no intention of reading the *Daily Worker* or subscribing to it. I did not think it would have any news I would be interested in. He jumped up and screamed, "Are you crazy? You want the *Daily Worker* to be sent to my house? Don't you know I have a security clearance and would lose it for that?"

"Maury, are you telling me the government would punish you for reading a paper published in the United States?"

He went berserk. "You don't understand. I have a security clearance."

I said, "You see, in Russia you know what things are not allowed, and you would not dare to do them, as you know the punishment under a dictatorial government. If you are smart, you stay out of trouble. But what you are telling me is that in this country you are allowed to publish a Communist paper, but you are afraid to read it." I told him I had no intention of reading the *Daily Worker*, but I just wanted to see his reaction, to see how free he really was.

"You mean you tricked me?"

"Yes, I did."

In 1964 Mr. Eisberg called me in and told me that he had heard rumors from the other salesmen that I was going to open my own office. I told him, "If I wanted to open my own office, you would be the first one to know. As you know, I am always honest with you. If I wanted to open an office, I am not committing any crime, and I never left a place of employment where my boss was angry at me."

In 1966 I went into Mr. Eisberg and told him that I would like to open an office with a partner which was going to be less than one mile from his office. The real estate law states that if you want to open your own office, it has to be at least one mile from your previous employer. I told him the office I wanted to open will be only two blocks from him. I asked if he would have any objections. If so, I would have to wait six months after leaving to be able to have my own office anywhere I wanted.

He said, "Henry, you have been here almost ten years, and as long as you worked here, you have always been honest and straightforward with us. I will have no objections if you open in the next block."

He asked me when I intended to do it. I told him sometime in the next two months. I was the only person that he allowed to work until the last day, as he felt I would not do anything dishonest and I would not take anything with me that I was not allowed.

I opened the office with a partner, Sol Hizme, about eight months later. Unable to get along with him, I sold my interest to him. He was not very pleased, as I knew much more about the business than he did, but he had no choice as he would not sell his share to me. I did not go back to Eisberg Real Estate, but went to Best Realty, located at Avenue J and Nostrand.

We had already sold our two-family house in Canarsie and bought a single-family house on East 47th and Avenue J, which was only about fifteen blocks from my business. My third child, Allen, was born on Christmas, 1965, and the two-bedroom house with three children was too small and uncomfortable.

My new bosses were Marty Melser and Richard Jasmine. Richard was Syrian, but born in the U.S. Richard and I developed a beautiful relationship. We talked about politics, religion, and we would go often to the opera together. He used to give the guy at the gate twenty dollars, and he would let us in without tickets. He told me he had been going to the opera for years this way. Best Realty was not too prejudiced against blacks. Mr. Jasmine would not stand for it.

Back in 1964 while in the Catskill Mountains, I had met a Russian woman, Tania, who was married to a Jewish fellow and had three children. It was a mutual attraction, and it developed into an affair. I told my parents about it. She said she would divorce her husband and marry me.

My parents had a long talk with Tania. They told her I could not leave my wife Dora with our six and seven-year-old children. My parents could not stand Dora because of her behavior towards them and because of how she made my life miserable. But my parents told Tania it was unfair to leave her with the two minor children. Tania's husband was going berserk, as Tania was a beautiful woman in her early thirties. I guess my parents made a lot of sense. They persuaded Tania and me not to go through with our plans, and after a year, we broke it off.

I had many fights with Dora about mistreating her mother. It is true that her mother was old-fashioned and religious, but many times Dora threw her mother out of our house for minor things. Her mother would complain that she was mixing dairy and meat, which was against Jewish ritual law. I would scream at Dora when I came home and found out what had happened, especially when it had happened in front of the children. I made her call her mother and apologize.

I tried to lecture her by telling her that this was her mother, and no matter what your mother says, you never throw her out of the house. "And I mean never," I repeated. "This is your mother, and you do not try to change her. It is too late and you can't get another mother, so you have to learn to live with her."

She always cried. "I don't know what you want from me. She is my mother. I can treat her the way I want."

I told her, "In this house you have to respect your parents. I know it's difficult for you, but you do not want to teach your children to disrespect their parents. With your actions, you teach the children to disrespect your parents. You would not want them to treat you the way you treat your mother." After crying for awhile, she would call her mother and apologize. In Yiddish, her mother would tell her that she knew I made her do it, as Dora never apologized before in her life.

In July of 1970, I met a black woman. She was from British Guiana and her name was Tabitha Stewart. She was one of the brightest and most intelligent persons I had ever met in my life. She came into the office looking for a house. She was the head nurse at Brookdale Hospital and was separated from her husband. Though he lived in the same house, he had his own rooms. We started dating. Sometimes we talked on the phone for hours. We always found subjects to talk about. She had a daughter attending Boston College who was about eighteen years old. Her name was Hazel. She also had a daughter, Suzzette, who was fourteen years old, and a son, Paul, who was seven.

My son Nathan was now thirteen years old, my daughter Brenda was twelve, and my youngest son, Allen, whom I called Jesus Goldberg because he was born on Christmas Day, was five.

Of course, like a good son, I told my parents that I was going to divorce Dora. Fourteen years was enough. I could not continue any longer, as I had such a miserable home life. Usually parents try to talk you out of divorce. My sister Sally was the only one who wanted me to stay with Dora for the sake of the children. Everyone else felt I was doing the right thing this time. My brother Abraham and his wife and three daughters were already in the U.S. from Israel.

My father said, "Dora will never give you a divorce."

I told him, "That's not a problem. All I have to say to her is that I don't want a divorce, and she will do just the opposite." Ever since we were married, she would always do the opposite of what I asked her to do. My mother cried, feeling guilty that she was the one who had brought about the marriage in the first place. I told her not to cry and that everything would work out okay. "I will take care of the children and come once a week to visit them."

In 1971 we had a separation agreement. I moved out of the house. I had no lawyer. Her lawyer drew up the papers and I told him under no conditions would I pay alimony, only child support of seventy-five dollars a week. The house was in both of our names. I let her stay in the house and told her she could rent out the basement, which would almost cover the mortgage payments. She tried for alimony, but I said, "She is eleven years younger than I. She can go back to work and would have no financial problems. Plus the seventy-five dollars a week would help a lot." She finally agreed to the settlement. Every Saturday, I came and picked up the children and spent the whole day with them. I also bought them clothes for school and toys.

Dora and I were still on speaking terms. I told her I wanted one year of separation, and then I would decide what I was going to do. Under no conditions did I want a divorce. And as I had figured, the next day she called her lawyer and filed for divorce. I received a letter from her attorney stating that she was filing on the grounds of adultery. The first procedures were filed in the supreme court in Brooklyn. It said I should have my lawyer contact her lawyer, but I told him, "I have no lawyer, I don't need a lawyer. I will take care of this myself."

Her attorney was surprised, as she had told him I did not want a divorce, and here I was, not doing anything to try to stop it. When I came the next Saturday to pick up the children, I gave her an argument, asking her what was her hurry in running to a lawyer for a divorce. I jokingly said, "What? You got a boyfriend? You want to get married again?"

She said, "You are going out with a nigger, and I can't have a boyfriend?"

I told her that I would fight the divorce. Of course, I had no intention of doing so. I did not even appear at the trial. Three months later the divorce was granted on grounds of adultery. I paid the lawyer three-hundred-fifty dollars. Her attorney asked me, "Henry, I want to know one thing. You told your wife you were going to fight it. You didn't hire a lawyer, and you didn't even show up at the trial. I don't understand how you meant to fight it."

I told him that I wanted the divorce, and the only way to get it was to convince my wife that I didn't want it. He said, "Oh, that was a pretty smart move. You wanted the divorce all along!"

"That's right."

Earlier, to prove to her that I did not want a divorce, we had gone to marriage counseling. One counselor was from a Jewish organization, one from the state, and one from a Catholic charity. She was always called in first; and, before I was called in, she left them with a picture of me as being brutal and unconcerned for the children. She told them she was a good wife and mother, and she gave me the best years of her life. When I was called in, all the counselors were shocked. After they talked to me, they seemed to be siding with me against her. All of them said, "You two don't belong together." They did not believe that if we ever got back together it would work out, as our backgrounds were as far apart as the North and South Poles, even though we were both Jewish.

The first few months after the divorce, I guess she felt victorious and happy that she got the divorce in spite of my objections. She allowed the children to go out with me every Saturday, and the children could visit their grandparents. My son Nathan was six months older than Sally's son, Allen. They were very close, as we spent summers together, and Nathan spent many weekends at my sister's house. Before the divorce, when my nephew Allen came to our house he would always wait until I came home on Fridays and would ask me for permission to stay the weekend. When he asked Dora, she would always say no, which made him cry. When he asked me if he could stay, I always said yes. He and my son were like brothers.

My son and daughter attended Hebrew school. Though I am not religious and never had a kosher home, I wanted my children to know of their heritage. If they decided to become religious later, it was up to them to make the choice. When I asked my wife why she did not want Allen on the weekends, she came out with the dumbest excuse. "Do you know that they giggle until two and three in the morning?"

"Well, if they giggle tonight, I am going to shoot them," I said. "Don't worry about it."

What she failed to understand was that my parents and my family would not disown me because I divorced her and was going out with a black woman. She was outraged when I would visit my parents and sister and brother. She felt that they should all side with her. She didn't realize that they could not stand her, since she always tried to make me hate my own family.

Then she refused to let the children be in touch with anybody from my family. When I came on Saturday, she had taken the children to her mother. I put the check for the children in the mail slot, realizing that I would not be able to take the children out anymore. Even for the holidays, if any of my relatives called, she would hang up on them, and not allow them to talk to the children.

I went to family court complaining of breach of agreement in not being able to see my children. The judge was blind, so he could not see Dora. He took her into his chambers and had a long talk with her. The judge then asked me if he could hold her in contempt of court and lock her up and put the children in a foster home. I said definitely not. I would not want my children in a foster home. The judge said there was nothing else he could do but order her again to allow me one visitation day a week, on Saturday or Sunday. The judge called me into his chambers and said, "You know I am blind. I can't see you or your ex-wife. But I want you to know that you are dealing with a viper."

I laughingly said, "That is her nickname."

He suggested that I not go to the house, as she would create an incident and have me arrested. I don't think she realized the harm she did to the children, but I guess she was happy that she was hurting everyone else. She kept poisoning the minds of the children, not just against me but against my whole family. The children, being so young, took her word as true.

I used to pay her by check every week, throwing it in the mail slot. One time I noticed in my bank statement that the last three checks were not cashed. A week later I received a summons from the court to appear and show cause why I had stopped the payments. When I appeared before the blind judge again, I showed him my checkbook and he told the court clerk to look at it. There were three checks made out to Dora Goldberg. I told him of all her actions against my family, not only me, and said that as the court knew that I could not visit my own children, she purposely did not deposit the checks so she could put me in jail for non-payment.

The judge, having talked with her before and having described her as a viper, did not take her word for it. He believed that I did make the payments and that she had not deposited them on purpose so I would be held in contempt of court and jailed. The judge turned to my ex-wife and said, "Mrs. Goldberg, I believe your husband did pay you, and you maliciously withheld the checks from deposit. I don't believe that your husband, in spite of the fact that he cannot see his children, would deny them support. I guess you have had it too good until now. From now on, your husband will mail the checks to us, and it will take four to eight weeks for you to get them. But that way, you cannot complain that you did not receive them. The payments will come from family court."

She was very upset with this turn of events, as she was sure that she had a good case against me. She came home and told the children that I had bribed the judge to side with me. My children told me that later on.

After about a year, when Nathan was about fifteen, I received a phone call from my ex-wife. She was crying on the phone saying that Nathan beats her and that he carries on like a maniac in the house and that everybody was afraid of him and that he had dropped out of high school. She wanted me to come and talk to Nathan, as she could not handle him. I told her, "You have to understand what you have done to the children. You hurt them more than anyone else, but I will come and talk to him."

The next day after work, I met with Nathan and my daughter Brenda and my little boy Allen. We went out to eat, and I had a long conversation with Nathan. Nathan cried, stating that he had nobody. "I have no father, no grandfather, no grandmother, no uncles or aunts or cousins." Though Dora had a brother and a sister with two children, my son could not stand them. All they talked about was money.

All of the children said that they would like to meet with me once a week. They would not tell their mother. They would meet me around the corner, as she never knew where they were anyway most of the time.

Nathan was even arrested when he was fifteen for being involved in drugs. He felt very bad and apologized for having once attacked me with a bat when I left Tabitha's house. I guess the hatred Dora had tried to instill in them was so great that he would not have hesitated in killing me.

He struck me with the bat. Two policemen passing by came to stop it. They wanted to arrest Nathan for assault, but I told them no, that he was my son and I would press no charges. I told them to leave. I told them, "I do not hold it against him. Anyone could be poisoned. His action was out of frustration, so forget about it."

After meeting secretly with my children for the next few months, I persuaded Nathan to get an equivalent high school diploma so he could try to go to college. I told him I would help him financially.

In the second half of 1974, no more mortgage monies were available. The real estate business came almost to a standstill. I took a job as a taxi driver in New York and worked from six at night until three in the morning. At nine or nine-thirty, I went to the office. When my ex-wife found out, she sued for more money. Instead of seventy-five dollars a week, she wanted a hundred, as I had two jobs. I brought all my real estate transaction records and the stubs from my checks from the taxi company. I said I would leave it up to the court to decide if I was able to pay a hundred dollars a week.

To Dora's shock, the judge said that she should only receive fifty dollars a week until the real estate business picked up again. Of course, right away she told the children how mean and cruel I was; that I had cut her down, not that she had tried to get more money. And, as usual, she told them I had the judge in my pocket.

I sent fifty dollars to the court and gave twenty-five dollars in cash to the children to give to their mother because of an earlier incident where she had lied to them about me not giving her any money. It had happened about two years after the divorce. I sold our apartment house, took a big loss, and wound up with only six thousand dollars. Of course, my wife told the children that I did not give her one nickel. I explained to them what I did with the money. The apartment house had a second mortgage of twenty-one thousand dollars. The bond was signed by me and my ex-wife, which made her personally responsible for the money we owed. The property I sold in a hurry and sold it to the wrong people. His intension was to collect a few (3-6) months rent that would give the new owner about $20,000 or more. If he did not pay any mortgage or any other bills, the property would be taken by the city. Because a second mortgage was also not paid, me and my ex-wife are responsible and the man that held our second mortgage was ready to take away our private house where my ex-wife and the children live.

I did not tell my children that I went to the man who owned the second mortgage with a gun. I told him that if he took away the property and my children were put on the streets, I would put the gun to his head and he would not live long enough to enjoy the money. I said to him, "After I kill you I won't even run away. So you better think about what you are doing." He knew I was serious. I received a letter from his lawyer, and I went to my lawyer. I told him to try to negotiate a settlement. He was willing to settle for about half, ten-thousand five-hundred. I told my lawyer that all I had was six thousand and that was all I could give him. The attorneys finally settled for seven-thousand, five-hundred dollars.

I went to my father, and he gave me fifteen hundred dollars. That was the way I saved the house for my children. I would not use the tactics many people suggested, to let her lose the house since I was not living there. I told them, "I cannot hurt her, because my children would suffer, too. I must do what my conscience dictates and make sure my children have a home."

I realized what the man I sold the building to was trying to do. He was going to collect the rent for a few months, pay no bills to anybody, and let the bank foreclose on him; he would have about twenty-five thousand dollars and the bank could keep the building. I realized what he was doing and immediately went to the bank and spoke to the mortgage officer in charge. I told him what was going on.

The bank immediately put a receiver on the building, which was collecting rents, and denied the new owner any more access to the money. Of course, in a few months he had already taken out about eight thousand dollars in rents. He came to my office with his brother, who was over six-foot and weighed three hundred pounds. I saw them coming and called the police.

They threatened me, as what I did was illegal and I could be sued for a lot of money. A few minutes later the police arrived. I told the police to remove them from the office as I had been threatened with bodily harm. They had already pushed me a few times, and I was lucky the police arrived in time.

I went to my father and my brother Abraham and told them that I could work out a deal for them to take over the building. All they had to do was to pay the back taxes and legal fees, which would be no more than three to five thousand dollars. They would own the property with only one mortgage to the bank. I had a third mortgage on the property that I did not want any money for. I told them I could recommend a lawyer, but my brother found a different lawyer who was a rabbi.

The lawyer said that he would take care of everything, and he wanted us to sign some papers. I told him I would go with him and check what kind of papers they were. When I looked over the papers, I told my father and brother that they should not sign the papers. It would only create trouble for them. After they gave the lawyer the money, he might end up owning the building, not them. As usual, my family did not listen, even when their lawyer told them if I came back, he washed his hands of the whole deal and wanted no part of it. My father called me and told me he didn't want me there. I told my father the lawyer was crooked, and if they signed the papers that he prepared for them, they would never own the building.

Father told me they had signed the papers last night. I told him he had made the biggest mistake ever. My father said, "Come on, Henry. He is a rabbi. We trust him."

"I don't care what he is, but he is a thief for sure."

A few months later the building was signed over to my brother, my father, another friend of mine, and the lawyer. Now the lawyer was an equal partner. Not only did he become a partner, but on the mortgage for fifteen thousand dollars that I had relinquished, he put his son as second mortgagee on my money. After a few months he collected the rents, and there was a second mortgage made out to his son.

As always, when my family was in trouble, they came to me. All three partners, not the lawyer, invested about five thousand each. [And it was only necessary to do it for six or seven thousand dollars.] That meant he had already skimmed about seven to eight thousand in his pocket. My father and brother were all upset, only now realizing that I had told them the truth. The rabbi was a thief.

My father, brother, and the partner went to the rabbi's house with me. I asked him what he had done with the extra money he had left over. He said that was part of his fee. When I asked him how come the second mortgage was in his son's name, as I had signed the mortgage satisfaction papers, he became very fresh. "There is nothing you can do about it. My son's name is on it, and that is the way it is going to be." He was a skinny man weighing about a hundred pounds. When he became arrogant, I grabbed him by the throat, threw him on the couch, and almost choked him to death.

If my father and brother and friend had not stopped me, he would have been dead in a few minutes. When I was pulled off, I smashed his face with my fist a few times. The screams were loud enough to bring his wife and son to the room to see what had happened. He cried, "Call the police! Call the police!"

Before they arrived, I told the rabbi's wife and son that it was made clear that if he didn't straighten out this mess, return the property to the rightful owners, and liquidate the second mortgage in his son's name, she would be a widow and her son an orphan. I told her I had lived through both the Hitler and Stalin eras, and a skinny rabbi was not going to get away with anything. "You better put it straight in your minds that what I told you is true, before the police arrive."

Of course we were all arrested. My friend was immediately released, as the rabbi said he had not taken part. He pressed charges against me, my father, and my brother. I told the sergeant what this man did, that was the reason for what happened and my becoming violent. I told him that my father and brother had been swindled. The policeman smilingly said, "But he is a rabbi."

I said, "Sergeant, if this man does not do what he is supposed to, he will not live long enough to enjoy the fruits of his action."

The sergeant looked at my father and said, "You don't look like a murderer." He was joking, of course. As my father was about 120 pounds and not much bigger than the rabbi, the sergeant said jokingly, "You know, you two look okay. Only your father looks vicious." We were all smiling, and the sergeant knew exactly what had happened.

Charges were filed against us. The rabbi told the sergeant to keep me in jail until the trial, that he was in fear of his life if I were free. I told the rabbi in front of the sergeant, "You got the message, didn't you?"

The sergeant said he could not hold us until trial, and he had to release us. The rabbi begged him not to let me go until he got home and locked the doors. I told the rabbi, "You better not leave home because I am going to wait for you."

After I had almost choked him to death, he knew I wasn't kidding. He was released about fifteen minutes before us so he could get home and bolt the door. Then we left. We had been told we would be notified when the trial would be held. But the next morning, the rabbi called my friend Ben and told him we could all talk to a lawyer and see what could be done to straighten it out. Only now did we go to the lawyer I had recommended. His name was Cornfeld. He was very mad and did not want to handle the case. "How stupid can you people be? I don't want to deal with you."

I finally persuaded him to do it for me as a personal favor. He said, "You are all lucky that I like Henry, because the mess you created won't be easy to resolve."

The first thing Mr. Cornfeld found out was that the rabbi had been disbarred four years before, and he had no right to practice law. After a few weeks of negotiations between Mr. Cornfeld and the rabbi, the rabbi wanted to settle, give up the second mortgage which his son had, and take his name off the deed as partner. For this, he wanted five thousand dollars. He finally settled for three thousand dollars. But he would only go through with it on one condition, that I would not be present at the signing of the agreement, as I was too violent. He wanted to take no chances should any arguments develop. I knew I could depend on Mr. Cornfeld so I did not attend. A few months later, after all the aggravation, Ben, the third partner, wanted out, and my father and brother paid him off.

The tenants were very happy that Father and my brother now owned the building. When I owned it, I was very lenient with them. For example, many tenants wanted to postpone the January rent and would pay it out in three payments, as they wanted to have a nice Christmas. Of course, I could not tell my wife, as she would never agree to a thing like that. Most of the people in the building were working people and it meant a lot to them to give them a break at Christmas.

When I owned the building we had a tenant in his seventies who was ninety percent blind, a Mr. Gorelick. He used to go several times a week to the veteran's hospital for treatment. After I owned the building for six months, instead of paying seventy-six dollars, he only sent fifty. When I asked him how come he left twenty-six dollars off the monthly rent, he said he couldn't afford it or he would be without food. He asked me, "Mr. Goldberg, are you going to throw me out?"

I told him I could not do that even if he paid no rent at all. I told him that twenty-six dollars less a month income did not mean that much to me and it meant a lot to him.

It is true that the building did not give me too much profit, but I didn't care. My main income was from real estate sales and the building was a good tax write-off.

When my wife found out about Mr. Gorelick, she was upset. She wanted me to evict him right away. I told her if she wanted that, she could go to court. Under no circumstances would I say in court that I wanted him put out into the street. "You're good to everybody else, but not to me," was her answer to that. But she did not pursue it.

23

LORRAINE

I kept my friendship with Tabitha for four years. It was her friendship and encouragement that helped me make it through the times after the divorce when I was unable to see my children. She was very understanding and sometimes abused by me, unjustifiably so.

After having a little bit of Asian culture, European culture, and American culture, I now got a taste of West Indian culture for four years. Parties with the West Indians began at twelve o'clock midnight. Once Tabitha told me she would come and pick me up for a party. I waited until after ten in the evening, decided the party was off, and went to bed. About midnight she arrived and wondered why I wasn't ready! When I explained, she laughed. "Oh, I forgot to tell you. Our parties start at midnight. Sometimes even after twelve."

The company I kept with her circle of friends were mostly professionals—doctors, lawyers, diplomats, and other professions. Back home in Guyana she came from a wealthy family, and, having a college education, mixed with that kind of society. But she was not snobbish. She found all kinds of people interesting and was curious about them.

I learned a few things from her. One was not to answer when you are angry, as you usually say things that you don't mean and though you apologize afterwards, you can never erase what you said from the mind of the person you said it to. Which is very true. She was a good listener, and that was something I learned was a good trait. The other important thing was not to retaliate when someone did something wrong to you. That in time, destiny will pay it back, and the person will get what he deserves.

It was not easy for me to adapt to her way of thinking and behaving, but I worked very hard on it, as my nature was boisterous and I had problems controlling my anger. It did not take me long to become a Jewish West Indian. My accent and West Indian dancing used to amaze all at the parties, and they could not believe it. "If your skin wasn't white, we would all think you were West Indian," everyone told me.

I would have married Tabitha, but there was a clash of character. She was very strong and I did not know how to handle it. We parted as friends and even today I can call her up and ask for a favor I need from her or vice versa.

I never had too much faith in the medical profession in any part of the world, but the stories Tabitha used to tell me were hair-raising. To make the medical bill higher, the hospital where she worked would give unnecessary blood transfusions, operations, and do other minor procedures. I could not believe it but knew she was telling the truth about it. Many people pay with their lives for doctors' mistakes and cover-ups.

On October 14, 1974, Columbus Day, while driving the taxi, I picked up a passenger at the Plaza Hotel. The parade was passing on 5th Avenue and many cars were stopped waiting for a break in the parade. Then the police would let them pass. While sitting waiting for a break, I got hit from behind by another taxi, at about sixty miles an hour. I don't know what happened to the passenger, but I bet she was hurt. I crashed through the windshield with my head. I was unconscious for a few minutes. When I opened my eyes, I was in the Plaza Hotel being attended to by a nurse they had on the premises. I was taken to King's County Hospital, but Tabitha had me transferred to Brookdale Hospital. She made sure I got the best doctors, which as the chief nurse she knew who to pick. I was in the hospital for six weeks, and I was not allowed to drive after that for at least a year. They feared that I might have blackouts.

Now being unable to work in real estate or as a taxi driver, I spent most of my time at Tabitha's house and played a lot of cards in the club I belonged to. No-fault insurance paid the medical bills, and it was explained to me by an attorney that the maximum I could receive from the insurance was ten thousand dollars. There are ways that big taxi companies can get out of paying any more. Though they had a fleet of fifty cabs, each two cabs were in a different corporation. So whenever an accident happened, they would dissolve the corporation of those two cabs and form a new one. Five years later I received a check for six thousand, three hundred dollars, after the lawyer deducted his fee. I did not get my loss of wages, not to mention the pain and suffering I had for at least six months.

In 1975 I became the manager of Shick Realty in Queens. When I came to work there, there was only one person employed. In one year, it became the most aggressive and busiest realty in the Woodhaven area.

Mr. Shick, who was Hungarian, came to the U.S. after the Hungarian uprising, and by the time I came to work for him had opened another office in midtown Manhattan. I ran the office without interference as if I was the owner. I got a hundred and seventy-five dollars a week and also a two-room apartment above the office, rent and utility free.

I had many girlfriends. But I had no intentions of ever getting married again.

We had seven salespeople employed. I was the only one who handled commercial properties, as I felt that it would be unfair for me to compete with the salespeople. I did not want them to worry that I might finagle and take some deals away from them. I trained the employees myself to do business only one way. They must tell the customer the truth, and if the truth might hurt them, they could avoid an answer but never lie. Mr. Shick put a lot of trust in me and allowed me to sign checks for the office, as he would have to come from New York, where the main office was located. I had full control. I did very well income-wise.

Two of my salespeople, a young lady and a young man, had come recently from Russia. After working awhile in the office, the fellow, Michael, tried to influence me to make deals and avoid paying the office the forty percent. I made it clear to him that I never took a nickel that belonged to Mr. Shick, and I had no intention of starting now at his suggestion. After a year and a half, I had to let him go. I had liked him very much. He was very sharp. But I caught him a few times using dishonest practices.

I was very good to my sales staff. I had the office pay for Christmas parties, Chamber of Commerce parties, et cetera, for the employees. They were twenty-five dollars a ticket. Mr. Shick complained many times about it, but I explained to him that I wanted to keep a good sales force that would not leave, because without them there would be no office. They must be treated better than in any other office. When your sales personnel are happy, they produce more. I did not consider the money a loss but as a part of the expense of running a good office. He could not argue with me, as he realized no manager before had ever produced as much as my office did.

In March of 1978, one of my sales ladies sold a house for a Mr. and Mrs. John Lutz. Since I did all the negotiations in order to give the sales personnel more free time, I negotiated with Mr. and Mrs. Lutz myself. The first time they came into the office was on a Saturday. Mr. and Mrs. Lutz told me, as I always asked, why they were selling their property and what their intentions were after they sold. Mr. Lutz told me that he worked for the New York Telephone Company. He had been transferred to Denver, Colorado. He already lived in Denver now. He left power of attorney with his wife, and he was leaving the next day for Colorado, as he had to be back at work on Monday.

The offer that we had for their house was about three thousand dollars short. I told them I would have to get in touch with the buyer and I would get back to his wife and let her know if I was able to raise the price to what they wanted. Mrs. Lutz spoke very little.

After they left, for no reason whatsoever, I stood up and said, "I want you all to know that Mrs. Lutz is not going to Denver. And that I am going to marry her."

Of course, the whole office went hysterical with laughter.

"Let's make a small bet," I said. They wanted $20.00 each.

One of the girls asked me, "What made you say that? It's the stupidest thing you ever said. We thought you were smart."

I told them that often in my life I had said something or other which seemed ridiculous or stupid, but in time what I had predicted came to be. "This would be the first time I failed. I won't," I said.

"What do you think you are—psychic?" one of them asked.

"No. Most people would brand me psycho, not psychic."

Then one of the girls said, "Let's analyze it. There is a young American woman who is approximately five-six, about twenty-nine or thirty-years-old, with an over six-foot-six husband who could be no more than ten years older than she is. He has a good-paying job and, besides, she is Catholic, which you aren't too crazy about. She is American, and you always have told us you would only marry an American if there was a miracle. She is chubby, you prefer slim types."

I replied, "You know, all the things you said happen to be right. And under normal conditions, I should stand no chance. I am at least twenty years or more older than her, five-foot -five, and am a bald-headed Jew, which Catholics are not too crazy about."

But all my life I have accomplished the impossible, without ever making any plans for it.

It was not an easy task for me. She refused to even go out with me. The first time I had a chance to get close and to talk to her was when I called to tell her that there was a Chamber of Commerce party and the whole office was going. I told her I would love for her to join us and that I had already bought her a ticket. By that time, we had already sold her property. The closing was to be finished in about ninety days. It took a lot of talking on my part to convince her to join us at the party. I got "no" for an answer. I came to ask again two hours before the party officially started. I wanted to make sure she did not leave the house and not show up at the party. I broke down her resistance, and she got dressed. I took her to the office and held her there for about an hour to make sure she did not change her mind and disappear.

At the party I sat next to her. There was an orchestra. We danced. Food and drinks were free. After a few drinks, I gained a lot of courage. I kissed her while we danced. All I can tell you is that she did not go to Denver; she became my wife and still is today.

Of course, I got the better of the deal.

After the closing, we took an apartment together. Being Catholic, she had to wait for an annulment from the Church before we could get married. Her parents did not know we were living together, as they were devoted Catholics and would never miss Mass on Sunday.

Lorraine was a little bit bitter towards the Church. When she was a child they would not accept her at a Catholic school because her parents didn't leave enough money in the envelopes after Mass. Her mother and father went to church and explained to the priest that they gave what they could afford, but to no avail. She went to public school, and she never forgot that.

Lorraine told me that she had told her parents about us. But she did not mention to them that we lived together. It was a big disappointment to her parents that her decision was to not go to Colorado but to stay with me. She told me the only objection her parents had to her marrying me was not that I was Jewish, but my age. I was only a year or two younger than her father. I promised Lorraine to give me three months and her parents would come around, since most people hate me or love me as I am: always honest as to what my views are. I never tried to butter people up to like me. I always spoke my mind, though many times it got me into trouble.

It took me six months instead of three, but they did at last begin to like me as a person, in spite of the fact that I used to speak out against the Catholic Church. The things I told them about my experiences with the Catholic Church were not very good or favorable to the Church. I do not know if they believed me that from the age of five until the seventh grade I attended Catholic school, nor of the many arguments I had with the priest.

On October 9, 1981, we were married in the Church. It cost a few thousand dollars to pay the Church for the annulment. We married in the Church, which meant a lot to her parents. I explained to them why I would not mind getting married in the Catholic Church, though I dislike it with a passion. I told them the Church in the U.S. does not have the power it does in Europe. The behavior of the Church here, for whatever reason, keeps a low profile. They are not the dominant religion in the U.S. Let us hope they never get the power they use in other countries.

We were called in to talk to a priest before the marriage. It is normal procedure in the Church. They want to make sure that if there are children, they will be brought up as Catholic. Father Tunney turned to me and said, "You know, Henry, I know you are Jewish and would want to be married by a rabbi. If you do, feel free to do so."

I said, "Thank you, Father Tunney. But I would like to ask you a question. If I bring in a rabbi, which God would he represent?"

"What do you mean? There is only one God."

I asked him, "You both represent the same God then?"

He said, "Yes."

I asked him if he thought it would be smart on my part to pay two commissions to different brokers to reach the same God. Of course, he started to laugh and said, "Well, I can't answer that. You may be right."

My son Nathan and my brother's family attended the services. We had a beautiful reception with music. My sister-in-law, Golda, waited in the house until the reception as her memory of the behavior of the Church in Poland made her never want to enter a Catholic Church ever.

The apartment that I had above the office I gave to Nathan, as he did not want to live with his mother anymore. He felt his life was empty. My mother and father and sister had moved to San Diego, California, so they did not attend the wedding, as my father had a fear of flying. They had already met Lorraine when we had visited the San Diego area, and they fell in love with her, as most people who know her do. She is unusually kind and well mannered.

The most important asset in this marriage was that Lorraine liked people and her parents are the same. Her parents treated my children as if they were a part of their family. My nephew, who was studying medicine in Santo Domingo, came to my in-laws house with friends once in the middle of the night. Lorraine's mother got out of bed, fed them, and made sure they had a place to sleep. Lorraine's parents considered anyone from my family as a part of theirs.

At least once a week we visited her parents. We always had the greatest of times. I called them mom and dad, though there was only a few years difference in our ages. Not only did I get a wife that is the most loving and caring of persons, I also inherited another mother and another father. Lorraine takes after her father. He is very soft-spoken and as good-natured as she is. If she saw a hungry dog on the street, she would run into the store and buy some food and feed it. Sometimes I get mad at Lorraine for being so good to other people and they take advantage of her. But I start thinking about what I would want to change in her, and I always come to the same conclusion: she better stay as she is.

Lorraine had a big, black tomcat. The day we moved in together, I was attacked by that cat and bitten many times. My arm was black and blue from the bites. My legs were bitten also. If I lay relaxed, he would jump on me and bite me. If I told anybody why my arm was black and blue, they said I should get rid of the cat. Lorraine, of course, felt very bad.

One evening we talked about Blackie. We both decided to put him to sleep. I could not sleep the whole night, thinking and remembering the things Lorraine told me about when she found a little kitten two or three weeks old, how she fed him with a pacifier, and how she was so attached to him. When we got up in the morning, I told her, "Darling, Blackie is not going to be put to sleep. John, your ex-husband, will take him. Or else I will just have to learn to live with him. I will not allow us to destroy anything I don't like or have problems with. Under no conditions should anybody destroy anything because he is unable to get along with it or dislike it."

This made Lorraine very happy. I told her I could not take away from her something that she loved very much. After one year, Blackie and I became the best of friends. He knew when I would be coming home from work and would sit by the door and wait for me. He slept on my side of the bed. Lorraine could not believe it. I used to talk jokingly to Blackie, "I almost put you to sleep. What a stupid idea I had! I guess you forgave me. You are my best friend now."

My youngest son, Allen, being a teenager, was able to shrug off the influence of his mother. He came very often to visit us, but he never told his mother where he was going. We became very close. I will never forget the remark he once made. "Don't ever let Lorraine go. She is one in a million." I don't know if he bought his mother Mother's Day gifts, but he always made sure Lorraine got one. The only child we have not been in touch with for years is my daughter. She got married, her mother would not allow me to attend the wedding. Knowing my ex-wife, I respected her wish, though both sons tried to talk sense into her. They told her that it was already more than fifteen years after the divorce, and she should become more human and not feel bitter. It did not do any good.

When Nathan was attending college, he skipped most of the time, and we had a lot of trouble. I kept talking to him and explaining, but I guess I couldn't reach him. In 1982 he moved with a friend to Manhattan and would call me once in a blue moon. He was eventually thrown out of college. Lorraine and I talked very often about him, but we did not know what to do.

One night in 1983 the phone rang at about two o'clock in the morning. Lorraine picked up the phone. I did not know who she was speaking to. She took a pen and paper and wrote down an address. She said, "Henry, you have to get dressed." I thought something had happened to her parents. She would not tell me where we were going or why. At three A.M. we stopped the car in Manhattan at 14th Street and 2nd Avenue. There was my son standing with three suitcases, waiting for us. She said, "You see now why I didn't want to tell you where we were going?"

I might have refused to go if I had known. There were so many things I had done for him before to no avail. Without asking or saying anything, we picked up my son and took him home.

Lorraine did not go to bed again. Neither did I. We asked my son what had happened. He had a fight with his roommate and was thrown out. And Lorraine, without asking me, told him that our house was his home and he could stay with us. I told her I hoped she would not be sorry for what she was doing.

She sat up with him nights, talking and talking. I guess she finally succeeded in turning him around. He went back to college. I guess the love and devotion that he never had from his own mother convinced him that we cared. You would not recognize him today. He is now at law school and in about a year and a half he will become a lawyer. Whenever he calls, after speaking to me for fifteen or twenty minutes, he talks with Lorraine for an hour or two. He came to visit us at Christmas.

Lorraine had fifteen thousand dollars of her own money. She wanted to put it in a joint account, but I refused.

In 1982 I left Shick Realty after some problems developed. I opened my own office, which was right across from Shick Realty. We parted on friendly terms, and Mr. Shick allowed me to open an office across the street. Without his permission, I would have had to wait at least six months.

I had a clear conscience for the six years I worked for Shick Realty. I never took a nickel that did not belong to me. I used Lorraine's money for real estate investments, however. In a short two years I made a couple hundred thousand dollars. All of the money is still in Lorraine's name and everything we own is in her name.

We had many arguments and fights. She felt it was not her money, but our money. I explained to her that it was her money that made all the other money, and when I did all the buying and selling, I charged a commission to her and her parents as if they were strangers. For that reason the money is hers.

I often joke with her by telling her that if the money were in my name, too, she might poison me and wind up with all the money, and this way she has to live with me as is. If she poisons me or kills me she would not gain anything. I tell everyone why I want her to have all the money. "This way she has no reason to get rid of me." Though it is a joke, you very often read in the newspapers about how even sons kill mothers for fortunes. Or husbands kill wives and vice versa.

In 1984 we took off two weeks for a vacation. We spent one week with my parents and sister in San Diego. We spent a few days in Las Vegas. I could afford it. I had a rich wife. Then we flew to Portland, Oregon, rented a car, and took the scenic drive and came to Bend, Oregon. My wife had been there before and fell in love with Bend when her husband John was transferred there by the telephone company ten years before. She had lived there for six months. Her husband had a lot of trouble with the people at his job, as he was a New Yorker. Even the manager was none too kind to him and after six months he came back to New York. But Lorraine's dream was to someday return and live in Bend.

In 1984, when we came to Bend, I too fell in love with it. I told her if she wanted to stay here that we should look around and see if we could get some kind of business. We wound up buying Van Duyn Chocolate Shop in Wagner Mall.

We went back home and started to liquidate most of the real estate, and in September of 1984, Lorraine, two dogs, and her mother drove across the country to Bend. A few weeks later she took over the chocolate shop. I came at Thanksgiving, as I had stayed to liquidate other real estate possessions. I sold the office and came to Bend to join her.

The hardest thing for us to live with for almost two years was that we had no close friends. We missed that a lot. In New York we must've spent ten thousand dollars a year on barbecues! When my wife told me, "This time it will be a small barbecue," that meant between fifty and twenty people. We always invited our neighbors so they would not complain that we were up till two or three in the morning. The music and dancing and drinking made the parties loud.

The chocolate shop didn't bring in an income even close to that in New York. Lorraine used to work for the Metropolitan Museum of Art, which was only about five minutes from the house. She worked in the computer room and was very good. She had previously worked for more than ten years for American Airlines until they liquidated the New York office and moved to Tulsa, Oklahoma. American Airlines wanted her to come with them and offered a raise in salary, but after we visited Tulsa, neither of us was excited about the town.

I think more important was that we were going to be away from my children. She was very close to my two sons. And Nathan especially needed us.

The FBI did not forget me. I received a few calls from them in Bend, to find out what I was doing and how I was doing.

After about four years, we came back to New York. The main reason we returned was because of my in-laws. We all missed each other terribly. We bought a house in the same neighborhood we had lived in before, Woodhaven. We had three dogs so we had to make sure that we got a place big enough for them to have room to run and play. My wife made sure that my son Nathan got the financial and moral help that he needed until he graduated and passed the bar for Missouri and Illinois.

My parents kept getting older, as we all do, and my darling wife made sure that we visited them in San Diego at least once a year. There are very few people who would be willing to sacrifice every vacation to see their in-laws. What wife is willing to work a whole year and when vacation time comes, to make sure that hotel and air reservations are taken care of so we could spend it with two old people, my dear parents? Lorraine did this for seventeen years, year after year, and my mother lived to the age of ninety-six and Father to the age of ninety-eight. Father passed away in August, 1995, and Mother in 1993.

Mother's last year of life was not as good as Father's, as she lost her voice. But Father, up until the last minutes of his life, had his mind and his humor, which were both as good as ever. There are very few people who have the wisdom Father did. The Talmud is a powerful tool. I'm very lucky to have had my parents for almost one hundred years.

My wife loved Father and Mother very much, and my parents in return, were crazy about her. Father kept saying that she was so good and nice and kept telling me that Lorraine was a blessing, not just for me, but for the whole family, and who could argue with Father.

I spoke to Father and Mother at least once a week, and it wasn't short conversations. One conversation that I always remember was my father's views of a God or something like it. Most people, as they get older, start believing in God, but not my father. He was as always, unmovable. I guess World War II helped him to see what he wanted to see.

In 1988-89 a couple moved to San Diego from Los Angeles, and they were introduced to Father and Mother. They were about fifteen years younger than my parents. The wife's name was Miriam and her husband's name was Berel. They became very close to my parents.

Miriam was born in Warsaw and Berel came from Wilno. They took my parents anywhere they wanted to go: shopping, to the theater, the park, you name it. They would drive them all over San Diego.

When I spoke to Father he was telling me how happy he was, as my sister Sally worked all week and could only take them on the weekends. I tried to be smart and said to my father, "You see, Dad. You say there is no God. Then what or who did this for you?" Father was listening very carefully to what I was telling him. "God sent you Miriam and Berel to take care of you."

Father's answer was, "The way you put it all together, it makes a lot of sense. In other words, God took care of all of his other problems; no wars, no hunger, no children are dying of sickness and starvation, and now let's see what I can do for Mr. and Mrs. Goldberg. They are really nice people. They deserve more than anybody on earth."

There was no argument or answer to what Father's understanding of God is.

Lorraine worked for Estee Lauder for all those years after we came back from Bend, Oregon. I worked as a mortgage broker, a property manager, and now, in 1999, I'm freelancing, which is not too much.

To finish it all, I must say that in spite of all the trouble I lived through and all that I suffered, I still believe that I am a very lucky person. I could find reasons to complain, and there were many reasons, too many. But looking on the positive side, not only did I survive the Holocaust, but my whole family did. Though there were very few families who did, my parents made sure that our family stayed in touch.

We used to be a family of close to a hundred people, uncles, aunts, and cousins. Only one of the hundred survived, Uncle Peter, who lives in London, England. Uncle Yosel, who we knew as Mother's younger brother, is now about ninety years old.

My second wife, Lorraine, and my in-laws are the best and finest people on Earth, and I have been around and met many people. My son Allen is worth his weight in gold. My other son Nathan is good too. Unfortunately, he was hurt by his mother. We have an on-and-off relationship. I have not seen my daughter Brenda in more than twenty years. She too is the product of my first wife. Destiny will pay her what she deserves.

But in spite of anything that is going on in my life, and the hundreds of teachers through all my life, I'm very happy to report that none of them could make me hate. I'm very glad that my mind could not absorb the reason why I should. I feel sorry for people who do know how to hate. They have a miserable life.

I must include a little true story that happened while we were in Bend, Oregon. One day in our little gift shop, a middle-aged man came over to me and asked me, "Henry, I heard that you are Jewish. Is it true?"

I jokingly said, "Today is Tuesday. On Tuesday's I'm Jewish. Wednesday's I'm Russian. Thursdays I'm Polish."

He interrupted me and said, "I love Jews very much."

I looked at him and said, "It's a good thing you don't hate Jews."

He interrupted again and said, "No, no, Henry. Let me tell you why. When I was in Korea, a young Jewish man named Abraham saved my life by risking his own."

"And that's why you love Jews, right?" I asked him.

"Henry, isn't that a good reason? What is wrong with you?"

I told him, "There is nothing wrong with me. I just feel sorry for you. Yes, for you. Let's understand what happened. A man saved your life and was a Jew, and I'm getting the benefits for what this young man did."

"What's wrong with that, Henry?" he wanted to know.

"Mr. Collins," I asked, "have you ever been to New York City? No? Well, there are three million Jews in the city. Let's say you and your wife went for a vacation to New York, and one evening you are walking in Central Park. Let's say a young man attacks you, takes your wallet, and rapes your wife. He is arrested the next day. You go to the police station to identify him, and to your surprise he has a Star of David on a chain around his neck. That means he is a Jew. Now you come back to Bend. What is going to happen to me? Are you still going to love, because of Abraham who saved you life, or hate me for that Jew who robbed you and raped your wife? Now you know why I feel sorry for you."

There was a story told to me while I was visiting in Israel. In 1949, Levi Eshkol, a cabinet minister, came to see the prime minister, Ben-Gurion. Eshkol was very upset. He said to Ben-Gurion, "I have something to tell you, and I don't know how. I don't want to upset you, but I have to tell you."

"What is it?" Ben-Gurion screamed. "Let's hear it. I can't do anything about it unless you tell me."

"Mr. Ben-Gurion," said Eshkol, "I just came from Tel Aviv, and I saw many prostitutes and they were young Jewish girls."

Ben-Gurion very gently replied, "How do you know they were Jewish and not French? Did they speak Hebrew?"

Eshkol answered, "Yes, they did."

Ben-Gurion's answer was, "Thank the Lord. Now we're truly a nation like all other nations."

To finish my story, I'm going to share a poem that my father wrote and sent to all of his four children in 1975:

Life! Has it some meaning?

When I was young,
When I was physically strong,
I was then more concerned
With material earnings.

As my years piled up
When I see the sign "STOP,"
I am starting to realize
That I must analyze,
So things may become clear.
What am I doing here?

Is my life of any need?
Or am I just a growing seed?
And if I can in my remaining years
Work to lessen men's tears;

Help to people who suffer,
My helping hand to offer.
By helping people to smile,
Then my life was worthwhile.

Leo Goldberg

Author at fifteen years old, 1942

The author (center) with his brothers, Abraham (left) and Shlomo (right)

The author with his mother and father in 1994

The author (second from left) with (from left) his sister, wife and oldest son, Nathan in 1984

The author's father, wife and younger son, Allen